EXPERIMENTS IN SOCIAL PSYCHOLOGY

Stressing the development of research skills in experimental social psychology, this text exposes the student to a variety of research areas and problems of methodology including observer bias, brainstorming, conformity, psychological gaming, and attitude change.

Designed for use in experimentally oriented undergraduate courses in conjunction with a basic social psychology text, this volume provides stimulating experimental research projects requiring no specialized equipment. Statistical study is not a prerequisite, since the student is encouraged to plot, examine, and understand his data rather than concern himself with establishing the reliability of differences.

A comprehensive introduction precedes each project, and reprinted articles provide the theoretical background.

EXPERIMENTS IN
SOCIAL PSYCHOLOGY

SOCIAL PSYCHOLOGY

A series of monographs, treatises, and texts

Edited by

Leon Festinger and Stanley Schachter

Jack W. Brehm, A Theory of Psychological Reactance. 1966

Ralph L. Rosnow and Edward J. Robinson (Eds.), Experiments in Persuasion. 1967

Jonathan L. Freedman and Anthony N. Doob, Deviancy: The Psychology of Being Different. 1968

Paul G. Swingle, Experiments in Social Psychology. 1968

In preparation

E. Earl Baughman and W. Grant Dahlstrom; Negro and White Children: A Psychological Study in the Rural South

Anthony G. Greenwald, Timothy C. Brock, and Thomas M. Ostrom, Psychological Foundations of Attitudes

EXPERIMENTS IN
SOCIAL
PSYCHOLOGY

EDITED BY

Paul G. Swingle
McGill University

ACADEMIC PRESS   New York and London

ACADEMIC PRESS INC.
111 Fifth Avenue, New York, New York 10003

United Kingdom Edition published by
ACADEMIC PRESS INC. (LONDON) LTD.
Berkeley Square House, London W.1

LIBRARY OF CONGRESS CATALOG CARD NUMBER: 68-14649

PRINTED IN THE UNITED STATES OF AMERICA

Preface

More often than not, psychology students complete their training
with almost no experimental training in social psychology. This state
of affairs is not only unfortunate but is also somewhat paradoxical.
If we consider social behavior important and social problems such as
prejudice, aggression, and behavior disorders, as areas badly in need
of greater understanding, then efforts should be made to offer the
student first-hand experience with the problems he must overcome
when exploring complex human behaviors. In short, the methodologi-
cally talented student must be given the opportunity to expose himself to challenging social research if the able researcher is to be
attracted to social problem areas.

The experiments in this book are designed to expose the student
to a variety of areas in experimental social psychology and to provide
him with experience in human experimentation in both the laboratory
and the field. Each chapter consists of one experiment to be conducted by the students and several reprinted articles to provide
theoretical background to the problem. The articles should also
provide some understanding of the methodological problems which
must be faced when exploring social behavior.

The projects in this book are of pilot study length and require no
specialized equipment. No preparation in statistics is required as
only a few simple descriptive statistics are used. For the most part,
the student is encouraged to plot, examine, and understand his data
rather than concern himself with establishing the reliability of differences. Students with a background in statistics or those taking a
concurrent course can, of course, apply the appropriate statistical
tests.

The revisions of each section of this volume have had the benefit
of suggestions from many people. I am grateful for the constructive
criticisms of the undergraduate students who were exposed to various
forms of the manuscript and to the graduate students and colleagues
who have read and commented on the book.

PAUL G. SWINGLE

February, 1968

Contents

CONTENTS

EXPERIMENTS IN
SOCIAL PSYCHOLOGY

Experimental Social Psychology

The purpose of this book is to stimulate interest in social psychology and to acquaint the reader with experimental approaches to the study of social behavior. Before beginning an experiment, however, it is essential that the experimenter be familiar with the terminology, methods, and procedures of the particular area of research. In this section, therefore, some of the basic techniques and problems of experimental social psychological research will be reviewed.

The best definition of social psychology is the study of social behavior, but as this seems to beg the question let us try to be more precise. Social behavior refers to those behaviors of one or more persons which are influenced by the person's association with, or awareness of, another person or group of persons. Thus, international conflict, two-handed poker, lynchings, attitude change, bargaining behavior, communication, etc., are all areas in which social psychologists have interest. It should also be noted that the study of social behavior is not limited to the study of human behavior. Many psychologists have used lower forms of life, from the ant to the ape, to explore some basic social phenomena.

Now, "experimental" social psychology requires still a more specific definition. As the reader may have guessed by this time, the term "experimental" simply refers to the method of inquiry used in the study of social behavior as opposed to any basic change in the domain of the behaviors of interest. By experimental social psychology one refers to the study of social behavior under highly controlled situations in which the experimenter deliberately manipulates the independent variable(s) under investigation. In short, an experimental social psychologist is an experimental psychologist whose interests happen to be in the area of social behavior. Several examples should suffice to make the point clear.

A subject is provided with a button which delivers a very painful shock to himself and is told by the experimenter to push the button on several different occasions. For one group of subjects the experimenter represents himself as "Dr. Jones" who is studying pain tolerance, while for the other group the experimenter represents himself as an undergraduate student doing a class project on pain tolerance. In this study the investigator is manipulating a very complex set of independent variables which are intended to alter the subject's perception of the authority, status, and intentions of the person asking the subject to discomfort himself. The number of times the subject pushes the button when requested and the latency between the command and the execution of the response are both dependent measures. In this example, as is true in much social psychological research, the subject's response is fairly complex and may afford a number of different but related measures. In the above case the number of obeyed commands (button pushes) would indicate the subject's obedience to the command, whereas the latency would indicate the subject's hesitancy at following the order.

A rat is placed in a Skinner box test-chamber and required to press a lever for its food. For every 10 lever presses the rat is given one food pellet. [This schedule of reinforcement is referred to as fixed ratio 10 (FR 10).] By a suitable lighting arrangement another rat is made visible to the test rat during some periods of time but not others. The investigator is manipulating the visual presence of another organism (independent variable) and is measuring the rat's lever pressing rate (dependent variable) to determine if the visual presence of another organism affects performance.

Students of 18 years of age hear a lecture on why the driving age should be raised to 21. Of these students group one is told what the lecture topic is one hour before it is heard, group two is made aware of the topic 30 minutes before the lecture, group three is given the topic five minutes before, and group four is not forewarned. A final control group of subjects is not told the topic and does not hear the lecture. After the lecture, all the students complete a questionnaire designed to determine their attitudes toward drivers under 21. The experimenter has manipulated the independent variable of the amount of forewarning a subject has to prepare for hearing a point of view opposite to his own (i.e., length of time the subject has between the forewarning and the event). The effect of the manipulation is measured by the opinion questionnaire.

The above examples should give some idea of what is meant by experimental social psychology. The two crucial factors are manipulation of the independent variable, and objective and controlled measurement of the dependent variable. It should be pointed out again, however, that it is the manipulation of the independent variable which distinguishes experimental social psychology from other approaches to the study of social behavior.

The main class of techniques which are quite different from the manipulatory methods described above are the observational and survey techniques. There is a wide variety of such nonmanipulatory techniques including field and participant observation, questionnaire assessment, content analyses of various sorts, surveys and similar procedures in which, generally, the investigator attempts to objectively observe, measure, and classify the behavior of specific groups under specific conditions.

Much of the experimental social psychological research is conducted under laboratory conditions. The laboratory experiment might be thought of as the social psychologist's microscope. If this analogy is kept in mind, the purpose and rationale of laboratory experimentation should become clear thereby correcting several common misunderstandings.

The laboratory experiment is used by the scientist to manipulate variables under conditions of precise control and to clearly observe the behavior associated with the variables. The laboratory social situation is artificial and is created by the scientist to provide the exact conditions he needs to permit careful examination of the particular behavior he is interested in. Since the experimenter creates the situation as he sees fit, he may set up special conditions that are not readily available in nonlaboratory social situations. In short, the laboratory situation is not supposed to be a miniaturized or artificial replica of real-life situations but rather an experimental "culture" created and manipulated by the researcher to allow him to clearly observe and measure certain behaviors under precisely stated conditions.

The major advantage of laboratory experimentation lies in the control which may be obtained over the variables affecting social behavior. All three of the major classifications of variables affecting behavior lend themselves to more stringent control under laboratory conditions. First, the independent variables, those which the experimenter manipulates, may be more systematically defined and varied and, therefore, more systematically examined. Consider the question of the effects of different amounts of incentive upon a group's productivity. The incentive may be rigorously controlled by offering the group five cents per completed unit of work, or 10 cents, or five dollars, as required for the particular experiment.

Second, the dependent variables, the subject's or group's behavior under study, may be rigorously measured. If one were concerned with communication flow in groups, for example, the direction of the communication (i.e., does A speak to B or C?), the content of the messages, the transmission time, and the amount of information per unit time may be precisely and objectively measured under laboratory conditions.

Finally, extraneous variables may be controlled—those factors which are not the object of the experiment but which may contaminate and, therefore, invalidate any experiment. Extraneous variables may be almost any factor which influences subjects. The friendship or lack of it among group members, the time of year (e.g., college student subjects at mid-term examination time), the IQ, age and sex of group members, distracting stimuli, etc., are all potential contaminating factors which may be controlled under laboratory conditions. There are many well-established experimental techniques designed to enhance control of extraneous factors. Many of these procedures will be discussed and applied in the experimental exercises.

To illustrate how and why the experimental social psychologist creates controlled experimental situations, manipulates variables and measures behavior, an interesting series of experiments has been reprinted. Some of the methodological details of these experiments will be discussed to emphasize the important matters which the student should consider in his own experiments.

The series of experiments used to illustrate laboratory-based experimental social psychology was reported in an article by Stanley Milgram entitled, "Some Conditions of Obedience and Disobedience to Authority." This fascinating and well-known series of experiments illustrates remarkably well the value and need for laboratory experimentation. First of all, as the reader will soon realize, the nature of the problem is such that it would be difficult, if not impossible, to rigorously study it under field conditions. That is, the special conditions which are necessary to understand the behavior under investigation are not readily available to the researcher in real-life social situations. Second, the behavioral process being examined by Milgram is so very complex that strict control is necessary to permit independent appraisal of each factor contributing to obedience and disobedience to authority.

The study has been reprinted in its complete form so that the student may follow the scientist's attack on the problem and appreciate the value of and necessity for highly controlled laboratory situations.

Reprinted from Human Relations, 1965, Vol. 18, pp. 57–75, by permission of the author and the publisher.

Some Conditions of Obedience
and Disobedience to Authority

STANLEY MILGRAM[1]

THE SITUATION in which one agent commands another to hurt a third turns up time and again as a significant theme in human relations. It is powerfully expressed in the story of Abraham, who is commanded by God to kill his son. It is no accident that Kierkegaard, seeking to orient his thought to the central themes of human experience, chose Abraham's conflict as the springboard to his philosophy.

War too moves forward on the triad of an authority which commands a person to destroy the enemy, and perhaps all organized hostility may be viewed as a theme and variation on the three elements of authority, executant, and victim.[2] We describe an experimental program, recently concluded at Yale University, in which a particular expression of this conflict is studied by experimental means.

In its most general form the problem may be defined thus: if X tells Y to hurt Z, under what conditions will Y carry out the command of X and under what conditions will he refuse? In the more limited form possible in laboratory research, the question becomes: if an experimenter tells a subject to hurt another person, under what conditions will the subject go along with this instruction, and under what conditions will he refuse to obey. The laboratory problem is not so much a dilution of the general statement as one concrete expression of the many particular forms this question may assume.

One aim of the research was to study behavior in a strong situation of deep consequence to the participants, for the psychological forces operative in powerful and lifelike forms of the conflict may not be brought into play under diluted conditions.

This approach meant, first, that we had a special obligation to protect the welfare and dignity of the persons who took part in the study; subjects were, of necessity, placed in a difficult predicament, and steps had to be taken to ensure their

1. This research was supported by two grants from the National Science Foundation: NSF G-17916 and NSF G-24152. Exploratory studies carried out in 1960 were financed by a grant from the Higgins Funds of Yale University. I am grateful to John T. Williams, James J. McDonough, and Emil Elges for the important part they played in the project. Thanks are due also to Alan Elms, James Miller, Taketo Murata, and Stephen Stier for their aid as graduate assistants. My wife, Sasha, performed many valuable services. Finally, I owe a profound debt to the many persons in New Haven and Bridgeport who served as subjects.

2. Consider, for example, J. P. Scott's analysis of war in his monograph on aggression:

'. . . while the actions of key individuals in a war may be explained in terms of direct stimulation to aggression, vast numbers of other people are involved simply by being part of an organized society.
'. . . For example, at the beginning of World War I an Austrian archduke was assassinated in Sarajevo. A few days later soldiers from all over Europe were marching toward each other, not because they were stimulated by the archduke's misfortune, but because they had been trained to obey orders.' (Slightly rearranged from Scott (1958), *Aggression*, p. 103.)

wellbeing before they were discharged from the laboratory. Toward this end, a careful, post-experimental treatment was devised and has been carried through for subjects in all conditions.[3]

TERMINOLOGY

If Y follows the command of X we shall say that he has obeyed X; if he fails to carry out the command of X, we shall say that he has disobeyed X. The terms *to obey* and to *disobey*, as used here, refer to the subject's overt action only, and carry no implication for the motive or experiential states accompanying the action.[4]

To be sure, the everyday use of the word *obedience* is not entirely free from complexities. It refers to action within widely varying situations, and connotes diverse motives within those situations: a child's obedience differs from a soldier's obedience, or the love, honor, and *obey* of the marriage vow. However, a consistent behavioral relationship is indicated in most uses of the term: in the act of obeying, a person does what another person tells him to do. Y obeys X if he carries out the

---

3. It consisted of an extended discussion with the experimenter and, of equal importance, a friendly reconciliation with the victim. It is made clear that the victim did not receive painful electric shocks. After the completion of the experimental series, subjects were sent a detailed report of the results and full purposes of the experimental program. A formal assessment of this procedure points to its overall effectiveness. Of the subjects, 83·7 per cent indicated that they were glad to have taken part in the study; 15·1 per cent reported neutral feelings; and 1·3 per cent stated that they were sorry to have participated. A large number of subjects spontaneously requested that they be used in further experimentation. Four-fifths of the subjects felt that more experiments of this sort should be carried out, and 74 per cent indicated that they had learned something of personal importance as a result of being in the study. Furthermore, a university psychiatrist, experienced in outpatient treatment, interviewed a sample of experimental subjects with the aim of uncovering possible injurious effects resulting from participation. No such effects were in evidence. Indeed, subjects typically felt that their participation was instructive and enriching. A more detailed discussion of this question can be found in Milgram (1964).

4. *To obey* and *to disobey* are not the only terms one could use in describing the critical action of Y. One could say that Y is cooperating with X, or displays conformity with regard to X's commands. However, *cooperation* suggests that X agrees with Y's ends, and understands the relationship between his own behavior and the attainment of those ends. (But the experimental procedure, and, in particular, the experimenter's command that the subject shock the victim even in the absence of a response from the victim, preclude such understanding.) Moreover, cooperation implies status parity for the co-acting agents, and neglects the asymmetrical, dominance-subordination element prominent in the laboratory relationship between experimenter and subject. *Conformity* has been used in other contexts in social psychology, and most frequently refers to imitating the judgements or actions of others when no explicit requirement for imitation has been made. Furthermore, in the present study there are two sources of social pressure: pressure from the experimenter issuing the commands, and pressure from the victim to stop the punishment. It is the pitting of a common man (the victim) against an authority (the experimenter) that is the distinctive feature of the conflict. At a point in the experiment the victim demands that he be let free. The experimenter insists that the subject continue to administer shocks. Which act of the subject can be interpreted as conformity? The subject may conform to the wishes of his peer or to the wishes of the experimenter, and conformity in one direction means the absence of conformity in the other. Thus the word has no useful reference in this setting, for the dual and conflicting social pressures cancel out its meaning.

In the final analysis, the linguistic symbol representing the subject's action must take its meaning from the concrete context in which that action occurs; and there is probably no word in everyday language that covers the experimental situation exactly, without omissions or irrelevant connotations. It is partly for convenience, therefore, that the terms *obey* and *disobey* are used to describe the subject's actions. At the same time, our use of the words is highly congruent with dictionary meaning.

prescription for action which X has addressed to him; the term suggests, moreover, that some form of dominance-subordination, or hierarchical element, is part of the situation in which the transaction between X and Y occurs.

A subject who complies with the entire series of experimental commands will be termed an *obedient* subject; one who at any point in the command series defies the experimenter will be called a *disobedient* or *defiant* subject. As used in this report, the terms refer only to the subject's performance in the experiment, and do not necessarily imply a general personality disposition to submit to or reject authority.

SUBJECT POPULATION

The subjects used in all experimental conditions were male adults, residing in the greater New Haven and Bridgeport areas, aged 20 to 50 years, and engaged in a wide variety of occupations. Each experimental condition described in this report employed 40 fresh subjects and was carefully balanced for age and occupational types. The occupational composition for each experiment was: workers, skilled and unskilled: 40 per cent; white collar, sales, business: 40 per cent; professionals: 20 per cent. The occupations were intersected with three age categories (subjects in 20s, 30s, and 40s, assigned to each condition in the proportions of 20, 40, and 40 per cent respectively).

THE GENERAL LABORATORY PROCEDURE[5]

The focus of the study concerns the amount of electric shock a subject is willing to administer to another person when ordered by an experimenter to give the 'victim' increasingly more severe punishment. The act of administering shock is set in the context of a learning experiment, ostensibly designed to study the effect of punishment on memory. Aside from the experimenter, one naïve subject and one accomplice perform in each session. On arrival each subject is paid $4.50. After a general talk by the experimenter, telling how little scientists know about the effect of punishment on memory, subjects are informed that one member of the pair will serve as teacher and one as learner. A rigged drawing is held so that the naïve subject is always the teacher, and the accomplice becomes the learner. The learner is taken to an adjacent room and strapped into an 'electric chair'.

The naïve subject is told that it is his task to teach the learner a list of paired associates, to test him on the list, and to administer punishment whenever the learner errs in the test. Punishment takes the form of electric shock, delivered to the learner by means of a shock generator controlled by the naïve subject. The teacher is instructed to increase the intensity of electric shock one step on the generator on each error. The learner, according to plan, provides many wrong answers, so that before long the naïve subject must give him the strongest shock on the generator. Increases in shock level are met by increasingly insistent demands from the learner that the experiment be stopped because of the growing discomfort to him.

---

5. A more detailed account of the laboratory procedure can be found in Milgram (1963). A similar and independently evolved experimental procedure, employing a shock generator, victim, and learning task, was reported by Buss (1961). Buss used the technique for studying aggression, not obedience, and did not make use of the fundamental measure employed in the present study: break-off points. His investigation promises to be a useful complement to the present research.

However, in clear terms the experimenter orders the teacher to continue with the procedure in disregard of the learner's protests. *Thus, the naïve subject must resolve a conflict between two mutually incompatible demands from the social field. He may continue to follow the orders of the experimenter and shock the learner with increasing severity, or he may refuse to follow the orders of the experimenter and heed the learner's pleas. The experimenter's authority operates not in a free field, but against ever-mounting countervailing pressures from the person being punished.*

A few technical points need to be considered before the findings of the study are described. For the purpose of delivering shock, a simulated shock generator is used, with 30 clearly marked voltage levels that range from 15 to 450 volts (and each activated by one of 30 individual lever switches set in a horizontal line). The naïve subject is given a sample shock of 45 volts to convince him of the authenticity of the instrument. The generator bears verbal designations that range from 'Slight Shock' to 'Danger: Severe Shock'.

The responses of the victim are standardized on tape, and each protest is co-ordinated to a particular voltage level on the shock generator. Starting with 75 volts the learner begins to grunt and moan. At 150 volts he demands to be let out of the experiment. At 180 volts he cries out that he can no longer stand the pain. At 300 volts he refuses to provide any more answers to the memory test, insisting that he is no longer a participant in the experiment and must be freed. In response to this last tactic, the experimenter instructs the naïve subject to treat the absence of an answer as equivalent to a wrong answer, and to follow the usual shock procedure. The experimenter reinforces his demand with the statement: 'You have no other choice, you must go on!' (This imperative is used whenever the naïve subject tries to break off the experiment.) If the subject refuses to give the next higher level of shock, the experiment is considered at an end. A quantitative value is assigned to the subject's performance based on the maximum intensity shock he administered before breaking off. Thus any subject's score may range from zero (for a subject unwilling to administer the first shock level) to 30 (for a subject who proceeds to the highest voltage level on the board). For any particular subject and for any particular experimental condition the degree to which participants have followed the experimenter's orders may be specified with a numerical value, corresponding to the metric on the shock generator.

This laboratory situation gives us a framework in which to study the subject's reactions to the principal conflict of the experiment. Again, this conflict is between the experimenter's demands that he continue to administer the electric shock, and the learner's demands, which become increasingly more insistent, that the experiment be stopped. The crux of the study is to vary systematically the factors believed to alter the degree of obedience to the experimental commands, to learn under what conditions submission to authority is most probable, and under what conditions defiance is brought to the fore.

PILOT STUDIES

Pilot studies for the present research were completed in the winter of 1960; they differed from the regular experiments in a few details: for one, the victim was placed behind a silvered glass, with the light balance on the glass such that the victim could be dimly perceived by the subject (Milgram, 1961).

Though essentially qualitative in treatment, these studies pointed to several

STANLEY MILGRAM

significant features of the experimental situation. At first no vocal feedback was used from the victim. It was thought that the verbal and voltage designations on the control panel would create sufficient pressure to curtail the subject's obedience. However, this was not the case. In the absence of protests from the learner, virtually all subjects, once commanded, went blithely to the end of the board, seemingly indifferent to the verbal designations ('Extreme Shock' and 'Danger: Severe Shock'). This deprived us of an adequate basis for scaling obedient tendencies. A force had to be introduced that would strengthen the subject's resistance to the experimenter's commands, and reveal individual differences in terms of a distribution of break-off points.

This force took the form of protests from the victim. Initially, mild protests were used, but proved inadequate. Subsequently, more vehement protests were inserted into the experimental procedure. To our consternation, even the strongest protests from the victim did not prevent all subjects from administering the harshest punishment ordered by the experimenter; but the protests did lower the mean maximum shock somewhat and created some spread in the subject's performance; therefore, the victim's cries were standardized on tape and incorporated into the regular experimental procedure.

The situation did more than highlight the technical difficulties of finding a workable experimental procedure: it indicated that subjects would obey authority to a greater extent than we had supposed. It also pointed to the importance of feedback from the victim in controlling the subject's behavior.

One further aspect of the pilot study was that subjects frequently averted their eyes from the person they were shocking, often turning their heads in an awkward and conspicuous manner. One subject explained: 'I didn't want to see the consequences of what I had done.' Observers wrote:

. . . subjects showed a reluctance to look at the victim, whom they could see through the glass in front of them. When this fact was brought to their attention they indicated that it caused them discomfort to see the victim in agony. We note, however, that although the subject refuses to look at the victim, he continues to administer shocks.

This suggested that the salience of the victim may have, in some degree, regulated the subject's performance. If, in obeying the experimenter, the subject found it necessary to avoid scrutiny of the victim, would the converse be true? If the victim were rendered increasingly more salient to the subject, would obedience diminish? The first set of regular experiments was designed to answer this question.

IMMEDIACY OF THE VICTIM

This series consisted of four experimental conditions. In each condition the victim was brought 'psychologically' closer to the subject giving him shocks.

In the first condition (Remote Feedback) the victim was placed in another room and could not be heard or seen by the subject, except that, at 300 volts, he pounded on the wall in protest. After 315 volts he no longer answered or was heard from.

The second condition (Voice Feedback) was identical to the first except that voice protests were introduced. As in the first condition the victim was placed in an adjacent room, but his complaints could be heard clearly through a door left slightly ajar, and through the walls of the laboratory.[6]

The third experimental condition (Proximity) was similar to the second, except that the victim was now placed in the same room as the subject, and 1½ feet from him. Thus he was visible as well as audible, and voice cues were provided.

The fourth, and final, condition of this series (Touch-Proximity) was identical to the third, with this exception: the victim received a shock only when his hand rested on a shockplate. At the 150-volt level the victim again demanded to be let free and, in this condition, refused to place his hand on the shockplate. The experimenter ordered the naïve subject to force the victim's hand onto the plate. Thus obedience in this condition required that the subject have physical contact with the victim in order to give him punishment beyond the 150-volt level.

Forty adult subjects were studied in each condition. The data revealed that obedience was significantly reduced as the victim was rendered more immediate to the subject. The mean maximum shock for the conditions is shown in *Figure 1*.

Expressed in terms of the proportion of obedient to defiant subjects, the findings are that 34 per cent of the subjects defied the experimenter in the Remote condition, 37·5 per cent in Voice Feedback, 60 per cent in Proximity, and 70 per cent in Touch-Proximity.

How are we to account for this effect? A first conjecture might be that as the victim was brought closer the subject became more aware of the intensity of his suffering and regulated his behavior accordingly. This makes sense, but our evidence does not support the interpretation. There are no consistent differences in the

---

6. It is difficult to convey on the printed page the full tenor of the victim's responses, for we have no adequate notation for vocal intensity, timing, and general qualities of delivery. Yet these features are crucial to producing the effect of an increasingly severe reaction to mounting voltage levels. (They can be communicated fully only by sending interested parties the recorded tapes.) In general terms, however, the victim indicates no discomfort until the 75-volt shock is administered, at which time there is a light grunt in response to the punishment. Similar reactions follow the 90- and 105-volt shocks, and at 120 volts the victim shouts to the experimenter that the shocks are becoming painful. Painful groans are heard on administration of the 135-volt shock, and at 150 volts the victim cries out, 'Experimenter, get me out of here! I won't be in the experiment any more! I refuse to go on!' Cries of this type continue with generally rising intensity, so that at 180 volts the victim cries out, 'I can't stand the pain', and by 270 volts his response to the shock is definitely an agonized scream. Throughout, he insists that he be let out of the experiment. At 300 volts the victim shouts in desperation that he will no longer provide answers to the memory test; and at 315 volts, after a violent scream, he reaffirms with vehemence that he is no longer a participant. From this point on, he provides no answers, but shrieks in agony whenever a shock is administered; this continues through 450 volts. Of course, many subjects will have broken off before this point.

A revised and stronger set of protests was used in all experiments outside the Proximity series. Naturally, new baseline measures were established for all comparisons using the new set of protests.

There is overwhelming evidence that the great majority of subjects, both obedient and defiant, accepted the victims' reactions as genuine. The evidence takes the form of: (a) tension created in the subjects (see discussion of tension); (b) scores on 'estimated pain' scales filled out by subjects immediately after the experiment; (c) subjects' accounts of their feelings in post-experimental interviews; and (d) quantifiable responses to questionnaires distributed to subjects several months after their participation in the experiments. This matter will be treated fully in a forthcoming monograph.

(The procedure in all experimental conditions was to have the naïve subject announce the voltage level before administering each shock, so that – independently of the victim's responses – he was continually reminded of delivering punishment of ever-increasing severity.)

FIGURE 1   MEAN MAXIMA IN PROXIMITY SERIES

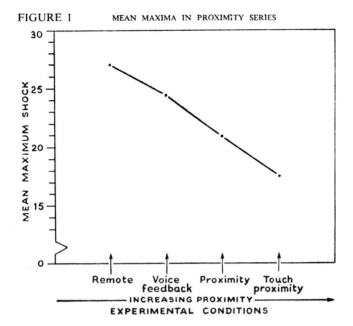

attributed level of pain across the four conditions (i.e. the amount of pain experienced by the victim as estimated by the subject and expressed on a 14-point scale). But it is easy to speculate about alternative mechanisms:

Empathic cues. In the Remote and to a lesser extent the Voice Feedback condition, the victim's suffering possesses an abstract, remote quality for the subject. He is aware, but only in a conceptual sense, that his actions cause pain to another person; the fact is apprehended, but not felt. The phenomenon is common enough. The bombardier can reasonably suppose that his weapons will inflict suffering and death, yet this knowledge is divested of affect, and does not move him to a felt, emotional response to the suffering resulting from his actions. Similar observations have been made in wartime. It is possible that the visual cues associated with the victim's suffering trigger empathic responses in the subject and provide him with a more complete grasp of the victim's experience. Or it is possible that the empathic responses are themselves unpleasant, possessing drive properties which cause the subject to terminate the arousal situation. Diminishing obedience, then, would be explained by the enrichment of empathic cues in the successive experimental conditions.

Denial and narrowing of the cognitive field. The Remote condition allows a narrowing of the cognitive field so that the victim is put out of mind. The subject no longer considers the act of depressing a lever relevant to moral judgement, for it is no longer associated with the victim's suffering. When the victim is close it is more difficult to exclude him phenomenologically. He necessarily intrudes on the subject's awareness since he is continuously visible. In the Remote conditions his existence and reactions are made known only after the shock has been administered. The auditory feedback is sporadic and discontinuous. In the Proximity conditions his inclusion in the immediate visual field renders him a continuously salient element for the subject. The mechanism of denial can no longer be brought into play. One subject in the Remote condition said: 'It's funny how you really begin to forget that there's a guy out there, even though you can hear him. For a long time I just concentrated on pressing the switches and reading the words.'

Reciprocal fields. If in the Proximity condition the subject is in an improved position to observe the victim, the reverse is also true. The actions of the subject now come under proximal scrutiny by the victim. Possibly, it is easier to harm a person when he is unable to observe our actions than when he can see what we are doing. His surveillance of the action directed against him may give rise to shame, or guilt, which may then serve to curtail the action. Many expressions of language refer to the discomfort or inhibitions that arise in face-to-face confrontation. It is often said that it is easier to criticize a man 'behind his back' than to 'attack him to his face'. If we are in the process of lying to a person it is reputedly difficult to 'stare him in the eye'. We 'turn away from others in shame' or in 'embarrassment' and this action serves to reduce our discomfort. The manifest function of allowing the victim of a firing squad to be blindfolded is to make the occasion less stressful for him, but it may also serve a latent function of reducing the stress of the executioner. In short, in the Proximity conditions, the subject may sense that he has become more salient in the victim's field of awareness. Possibly he becomes more self-conscious, embarrassed, and inhibited in his punishment of the victim.

Phenomenal unity of act. In the Remote conditions it is more difficult for the subject to gain a sense of *relatedness* between his own actions and the consequences of these actions for the victim. There is a physical and spatial separation of the act and its consequences. The subject depresses a lever in one room, and protests and cries are heard from another. The two events are in correlation, yet they lack a compelling phenomenological unity. The structure of a meaningful act—*I am hurting a man*—breaks down because of the spatial arrangements, in a manner somewhat analogous to the disappearance of phi phenomena when the blinking lights are spaced too far apart. The unity is more fully achieved in the Proximity conditions as the victim is brought closer to the action that causes him pain. It is rendered complete in Touch-Proximity.

Incipient group formation. Placing the victim in another room not only takes him further from the subject, but the subject and the experimenter are drawn relatively closer. There is incipient group formation between the experimenter and the subject, from which the victim is excluded. The wall between the victim and the others deprives him of an intimacy which the experimenter and subject feel. In the Remote condition, the victim is truly an outsider, who stands alone, physically and psychologically.

When the victim is placed close to the subject, it becomes easier to form an alliance with him against the experimenter. Subjects no longer have to face the experimenter alone. They have an ally who is close at hand and eager to collaborate in a revolt against the experimenter. Thus, the changing set of spatial relations leads to a potentially shifting set of alliances over the several experimental conditions.

Acquired behavior dispositions. It is commonly observed that laboratory mice will rarely fight with their litter mates. Scott (1958) explains this in terms of passive inhibition. He writes: 'By doing nothing under ... circumstances [the animal] learns to do nothing, and this may be spoken of as passive inhibition ... this principle has great importance in teaching an individual to be peaceful, for it means that he can learn not to fight simply by not fighting.' Similarly, we may learn not to harm others simply by not harming them in everyday life. Yet this learning occurs in a context of proximal relations with others, and may not be generalized to that situation in which the person is physically removed from us. Or possibly, in the past, aggressive actions against others who were physically close resulted in retaliatory punishment which extinguished the original form of response. In contrast, aggression against others at a distance may have only sporadically led to retaliation. Thus the organism learns that it is safer to be aggressive toward others at a distance, and precarious to be so when the parties are within arm's reach. Through a pattern of rewards and punishments, he acquires a disposition to avoid aggression at close quarters, a disposition which does not extend to harming others at a distance. And this may account for experimental findings in the remote and proximal experiments.

Proximity as a variable in psychological research has received far less attention than it deserves. If men were sessile it would be easy to understand this neglect. But we move about; our spatial relations shift from one situation to the next, and the fact that we are near or remote may have a powerful effect on the psychological processes that mediate our behavior toward others. In the present situation, as the victim is brought closer to the man ordered to give him shocks, increasing numbers of subjects break off the experiment, refusing to obey. The concrete, visible, and proximal presence of the victim acts in an important way to counteract the experimenter's power and to generate disobedience.[7]

CLOSENESS OF AUTHORITY

If the spatial relationship of the subject and victim is relevant to the degree of obedience, would not the relationship of subject to experimenter also play a part?

There are reasons to feel that, on arrival, the subject is oriented primarily to the experimenter rather than to the victim. He has come to the laboratory to fit into the structure that the experimenter—not the victim—would provide. He has come less to understand his behavior than to *reveal* that behavior to a competent scientist, and he is willing to display himself as the scientist's purposes require. Most subjects seem quite concerned about the appearance they are making before the experimenter, and one could argue that this preoccupation in a relatively new and strange setting makes the subject somewhat insensitive to the triadic nature of the social situation. In other words, the subject is so concerned about the show he is putting on for the experimenter that influences from other parts of the social field do not receive as much weight as they ordinarily would. This overdetermined orientation to the experimenter would account for the relative insensitivity of the subject to the victim, and would also lead us to believe that alterations in the relationship between subject and experimenter would have important consequences for obedience.

In a series of experiments we varied the physical closeness and degree of surveillance of the experimenter. In one condition the experimenter sat just a few feet away from the subject. In a second condition, after giving initial instructions, the experimenter left the laboratory and gave his orders by telephone; in still a third condition the experimenter was never seen, providing instructions by means of a tape recording activated when the subjects entered the laboratory.

Obedience dropped sharply as the experimenter was physically removed from the laboratory. The number of obedient subjects in the first condition (Experimenter Present) was almost three times as great as in the second, where the experimenter gave his orders by telephone. Twenty-six subjects were fully obedient in the first condition, and only 9 in the second (Chi square obedient *vs.* defiant in the two conditions, 1 d.f. $= 14 \cdot 7$; $p < \cdot 001$). Subjects seemed able to take a far stronger stand

7. Admittedly, the terms *proximity*, *immediacy*, *closeness*, and *salience-of-the-victim* are used in a loose sense, and the experiments themselves represent a very coarse treatment of the variable. Further experiments are needed to refine the notion and tease out such diverse factors as spatial distance, visibility, audibility, barrier interposition, etc.

The Proximity and Touch-Proximity experiments were the only conditions where we were unable to use taped feedback from the victim. Instead, the victim was trained to respond in these conditions as he had in Experiment 2 (which employed taped feedback). Some improvement is possible here, for it should be technically feasible to do a proximity series using taped feedback.

against the experimenter when they did not have to encounter him face to face, and the experimenter's power over the subject was severely curtailed.[8]

Moreover, when the experimenter was absent, subjects displayed an interesting form of behavior that had not occurred under his surveillance. Though continuing with the experiment, several subjects administered lower shocks than were required and never informed the experimenter of their deviation from the correct procedure. (Unknown to the subjects, shock levels were automatically recorded by an Esterline-Angus event recorder wired directly into the shock generator; the instrument provided us with an objective record of the subjects' performance.) Indeed, in telephone conversations some subjects specifically assured the experimenter that they were raising the shock level according to instruction, whereas in fact they were repeatedly using the lowest shock on the board. This form of behavior is particularly interesting: although these subjects acted in a way that clearly undermined the avowed purposes of the experiment, they found it easier to handle the conflict in this manner than to precipitate an open break with authority.

Other conditions were completed in which the experimenter was absent during the first segment of the experiment, but reappeared at the point that the subject definitely refused to give higher shocks when commanded by telephone. Although he had exhausted his power via telephone, the experimenter could frequently force further obedience when he reappeared in the laboratory.

Experiments in this series show that the physical *presence* of an authority is an important force contributing to the subject's obedience or defiance. Taken together with the first experimental series on the proximity of the victim, it would appear that something akin to fields of force, diminishing in effectiveness with increasing psychological distance from their source, have a controlling effect on the subject's performance. As the victim is brought closer, the subject finds it harder to administer shocks to him. When the victim's position is held constant relative to the subject, and the authority is made more remote, the subject finds it easier to break off the experiment. This effect is substantial in both cases, but manipulation of the experimenter's position yielded the more powerful results. Obedience to destructive commands is highly dependent on the proximal relations between authority and subject.

TENSIONS

The description of final scores does not fully convey the character of the subjects' performance, and it would be useful to interrupt our reporting of quantitative relationships to remark on the subjects' general reaction to the situation.

One might suppose that a subject would simply break off or continue as his conscience and temperament dictated. Yet this is very far from what happened. There were powerful reactions of tension and emotional strain in a substantial proportion of the participants. Persons were observed to sweat, tremble, stutter, bite their lips, and groan as they found themselves increasingly implicated in the experimental conflict. Some sense of the subjects' mood can be gotten from a transcript of their remarks at break-off point. Here are the remarks of two defiant subjects:

---

8. The third condition also led to significantly lower obedience than this first situation, in which the experimenter was present, but it contains technical difficulties that require extensive discussion.

Is he banging? . . . Is he hurt out there? Well, I don't want to be responsible for anything that happens to him. No, I can't go on with it. I don't know whether he's all right or not. I mean he may have a heart condition or something; I wouldn't feel right doing it. He's banging for help. He's evidently in trouble or he wouldn't bang . . . I don't see any sense to this—to knocking him out or something. I just can't see it.

(Subject refuses to administer shocks)   [*Subject 0108*]

The man is banging. He wants to get out . . . I'm sorry. If the man wants to get out I'd just as soon stop . . . I don't want to administer any more [extremely excited] . . . I will gladly refund the check, but I will not harm this man . . . I'm sorry, I will not give him any more if he obviously wants to get out. There is no money in the world that will make me hurt another individual. [*Subject 010X*]

And here is a transcript from an obedient subject. He began the experiment calmly, but became increasingly tense as the experiment proceeded. After administering the 150-volt shock, he began to address the experimenter in agitated tones:

150 volts delivered. You want me to keep going?
165 volts delivered. That guy is hollering in there. There's a lot of them here. He's liable to have heart condition. You want me to go?
180 volts delivered. He can't stand it! I'm not going to kill that man in there! You hear him hollering? He's hollering. He can't stand it. What if something happens to him? . . . I'm not going to get that man sick in there. He's hollering in there. You know what I mean? I mean I refuse to take responsibility. He's getting hurt in there. He's in there hollering. Too many left here. Geez, if he gets them wrong. There's too many of them left. I mean who is going to take responsibility if anything happens to that gentleman?
[*The experimenter accepts responsibility.*] All right.
195 volts delivered. You see he's hollering. Hear that. Gee, I don't know. [*The experimenter says: 'The experiment requires that you go on.'*]—I know it does, sir, but I mean—hugh—he don't know what he's in for. He's up to 195 volts.
210 volts delivered
225 volts delivered
240 volts delivered. Aw, no. You mean I've got to keep going up with the scale? No sir. I'm not going to kill that man! I'm not going to give him 450 volts! [*The experimenter says: 'The experiment requires that you go on.'*]—I know it does, but that man is hollering in there, sir . . .

Despite his numerous, agitated objections, which were constant accompaniments to his actions, the subject unfailingly obeyed the experimenter, proceeding to the highest shock level on the generator. He displayed a curious dissociation between word and action. Although at the verbal level he had resolved not to go on, his actions were fully in accord with the experimenter's commands. This subject did not want to shock the victim, and he found it an extremely disagreeable task, but he was unable to invent a response that would free him from *E*'s authority. Many subjects cannot find the specific verbal formula that would enable them to reject the role assigned to them by the experimenter. Perhaps our culture does not provide adequate models for disobedience.

One puzzling sign of tension was the regular occurrence of nervous laughing fits. In the first four conditions 71 of the 160 subjects showed definite signs of nervous laughter and smiling. The laughter seemed entirely out of place, even bizarre. Full-blown, uncontrollable seizures were observed for 15 of these subjects. On one occasion we observed a seizure so violently convulsive that it was necessary to call a halt to the experiment. In the post-experimental interviews subjects took pains to point out that they were not sadistic types and that the laughter did not mean they enjoyed shocking the victim.

In the interview following the experiment subjects were asked to indicate on a 14-point scale just how nervous or tense they felt at the point of maximum tension (*Figure 2*). The scale ranged from 'Not at all tense and nervous' to 'Extremely tense

FIGURE 2   LEVEL OF TENSION AND NERVOUSNESS

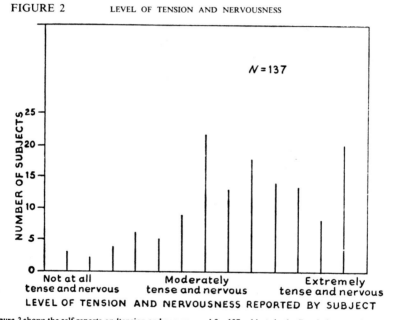

Figure 2 shows the self-reports on 'tension and nervousness' for 137 subjects in the Proximity experiments. Subjects were given a scale with 14 values ranging from 'Not at all tense and nervous' to 'Extremely tense and nervous'. They were instructed: 'Thinking back to that point in the experiment when you felt the most tense and nervous, indicate just how you felt by placing an X at the appropriate point on the scale.' The results are shown in terms of mid-point values.

and nervous'. Self-reports of this sort are of limited precision, and at best provide only a rough indication of the subject's emotional response. Still, taking the reports for what they are worth, it can be seen that the distribution of responses spans the entire range of the scale, with the majority of subjects concentrated at the center and upper extreme. A further breakdown showed that obedient subjects reported themselves as having been slightly more tense and nervous than the defiant subjects at the point of maximum tension.

How is the occurrence of tension to be interpreted? First, it points to the presence of conflict. If a tendency to comply with authority were the only psychological force operating in the situation, all subjects would have continued to the end and there would have been no tension. Tension, it is assumed, results from the simultaneous presence of two or more incompatible response tendencies (Miller,

1944). If sympathetic concern for the victim were the exclusive force, all subjects would have calmly defied the experimenter. Instead, there were both obedient and defiant outcomes, frequently accompanied by extreme tension. A conflict develops between the deeply ingrained disposition not to harm others and the equally compelling tendency to obey others who are in authority. The subject is quickly drawn into a dilemma of a deeply dynamic character, and the presence of high tension points to the considerable strength of each of the antagonistic vectors.

Moreover, tension defines the strength of the aversive state from which the subject is unable to escape through disobedience. When a person is uncomfortable, tense, or stressed, he tries to take some action that will allow him to terminate this unpleasant state. Thus tension may serve as a drive that leads to escape behavior. But in the present situation, even where tension is extreme, many subjects are unable to perform the response that will bring about relief. Therefore there must be a competing drive, tendency, or inhibition that precludes activation of the disobedient response. The strength of this inhibiting factor must be of greater magnitude than the stress experienced, else the terminating act would occur. Every evidence of extreme tension is at the same time an indication of the strength of the forces that keep the subject in the situation.

Finally, tension may be taken as evidence of the reality of the situations for the subjects. Normal subjects do not tremble and sweat unless they are implicated in a deep and genuinely felt predicament.

BACKGROUND AUTHORITY

In psychophysics, animal learning, and other branches of psychology, the fact that measures are obtained at one institution rather than another is irrelevant to the interpretation of the findings, so long as the technical facilities for measurement are adequate and the operations are carried out with competence.

But it cannot be assumed that this holds true for the present study. The effectiveness of the experimenter's commands may depend in an important way on the larger institutional context in which they are issued. The experiments described thus far were conducted at Yale University, an organization which most subjects regarded with respect and sometimes awe. In post-experimental interviews several participants remarked that the locale and sponsorship of the study gave them confidence in the integrity, competence, and benign purposes of the personnel; many indicated that they would not have shocked the learner if the experiments had been done elsewhere.

This issue of background authority seemed to us important for an interpretation of the results that had been obtained thus far; moreover it is highly relevant to any comprehensive theory of human obedience. Consider, for example, how closely our compliance with the imperatives of others is tied to particular institutions and locales in our day-to-day activities. On request, we expose our throats to a man with a razor blade in the barber shop, but would not do so in a shoe store; in the latter setting we willingly follow the clerk's request to stand in our stockinged feet, but resist the command in a bank. In the laboratory of a great university, subjects may comply with a set of commands that would be resisted if given elsewhere. *One must always question the relationship of obedience to a person's sense of the context in which he is operating.*

To explore the problem we moved our apparatus to an office building in industrial Bridgeport and replicated experimental conditions, without any visible tie to the university.

Bridgeport subjects were invited to the experiment through a mail circular similar to the one used in the Yale study, with appropriate changes in letterhead, etc. As in the earlier study, subjects were paid $4.50 for coming to the laboratory. The same age and occupational distributions used at Yale, and the identical personnel, were employed.

The purpose in relocating in Bridgeport was to assure a complete dissociation from Yale, and in this regard we were fully successful. On the surface, the study appeared to be conducted by RESEARCH ASSOCIATES OF BRIDGEPORT, an organization of unknown character (the title had been concocted exclusively for use in this study).

The experiments were conducted in a three-room office suite in a somewhat run-down commercial building located in the downtown shopping area. The laboratory was sparsely furnished, though clean, and marginally respectable in appearance. When subjects inquired about professional affiliations, they were informed only that we were a private firm conducting research for industry.

Some subjects displayed skepticism concerning the motives of the Bridgeport experimenter. One gentleman gave us a written account of the thoughts he experienced at the control board:

> . . . Should I quit this damn test? Maybe he passed out? What dopes we were not to check up on this deal. How do we know that these guys are legit? No furniture, bare walls, no telephone. We could of called the Police up or the Better Business Bureau. I learned a lesson tonight. How do I know that Mr Williams [the experimenter] is telling the truth . . . I wish I knew how many volts a person could take before lapsing into unconsciousness . . .

> [*Subject 2414*]

Another subject stated:

> I questioned on my arrival my own judgment [about coming]. I had doubts as to the legitimacy of the operation and the consequences of participation. I felt it was a heartless way to conduct memory or learning processes on human beings and certainly dangerous without the presence of a medical doctor.

> [*Subject 2440 V*]

There was no noticeable reduction in tension for the Bridgeport subjects. And the subjects' estimation of the amount of pain felt by the victim was slightly, though not significantly, higher than in the Yale study.

A failure to obtain complete obedience in Bridgeport would indicate that the extreme compliance found in New Haven subjects was tied closely to the background authority of Yale University; if a large proportion of the subjects remained fully obedient, very different conclusions would be called for.

As it turned out, the level of obedience in Bridgeport, although somewhat reduced, was not significantly lower than that obtained at Yale. A large proportion of the Bridgeport subjects were fully obedient to the experimenter's commands (48 per cent of the Bridgeport subjects delivered the maximum shock *vs.* 65 per cent in the corresponding condition at Yale).

PAUL G. SWINGLE

How are these findings to be interpreted? It is possible that if commands of a potentially harmful or destructive sort are to be perceived as legitimate they must occur within some sort of institutional structure. But it is clear from the study that it need not be a particularly reputable or distinguished institution. The Bridgeport experiments were conducted by an unimpressive firm lacking any credentials; the laboratory was set up in a respectable office building with title listed in the building directory. Beyond that, there was no evidence of benevolence or competence. It is possible that the *category* of institution, judged according to its professed function, rather than its qualitative position within that category, wins our compliance. Persons deposit money in elegant, but also in seedy-looking banks, without giving much thought to the differences in security they offer. Similarly, our subjects may consider one laboratory to be as competent as another, so long as it *is* a scientific laboratory.

It would be valuable to study the subjects' performance in other contexts which go even further than the Bridgeport study in denying institutional support to the experimenter. It is possible that, beyond a certain point, obedience disappears completely. But that point had not been reached in the Bridgeport office: almost half the subjects obeyed the experimenter fully.

FURTHER EXPERIMENTS

We may mention briefly some additional experiments undertaken in the Yale series. A considerable amount of obedience and defiance in everyday life occurs in connexion with groups. And we had reason to feel in the light of many group studies already done in psychology that group forces would have a profound effect on reactions to authority. A series of experiments was run to examine these effects. In all cases only one naïve subject was studied per hour, but he performed in the midst of actors who, unknown to him, were employed by the experimenter. In one experiment (Groups for Disobedience) two actors broke off in the middle of the experiment. When this happened 90 per cent of the subjects followed suit and defied the experimenter. In another condition the actors followed the orders obediently; this strengthened the experimenter's power only slightly. In still a third experiment the job of pushing the switch to shock the learner was given to one of the actors, while the naïve subject performed a subsidiary act. We wanted to see how the teacher would respond if he were involved in the situation but did not actually give the shocks. In this situation only three subjects out of forty broke off. In a final group experiment the subjects themselves determined the shock level they were going to use. Two actors suggested higher and higher shock levels; some subjects insisted, despite group pressure, that the shock level be kept low; others followed along with the group.

Further experiments were completed using women as subjects, as well as a set dealing with the effects of dual, unsanctioned, and conflicting authority. A final experiment concerned the personal relationship between victim and subject. These will have to be described elsewhere, lest the present report be extended to monographic length.

It goes without saying that future research can proceed in many different directions. What kinds of response from the victim are most effective in causing disobedience in the subject? Perhaps passive resistance is more effective than vehement protest. What conditions of entry into an authority system lead to greater or lesser obedience? What is the effect of anonymity and masking on the subject's behavior? What conditions lead to the subject's perception of responsibility for his own actions? Each of these could be a major research topic in itself, and can readily be incorporated into the general experimental procedure described here.

LEVELS OF OBEDIENCE AND DEFIANCE

One general finding that merits attention is the high level of obedience manifested in the experimental situation. Subjects often expressed deep disapproval of shocking a man in the face of his objections, and others denounced it as senseless and stupid. Yet many subjects complied even while they protested. The proportion of obedient subjects greatly exceeded the expectations of the experimenter and his colleagues. At the outset, we had conjectured that subjects would not, in general, go above the level of 'Strong Shock'. In practice, many subjects were willing to administer the most extreme shocks available when commanded by the experimenter. For some subjects the experiment provides an occasion for aggressive release. And for others it demonstrates the extent to which obedient dispositions are deeply ingrained, and are engaged irrespective of their consequences for others. Yet this is not the whole story. Somehow, the subject becomes implicated in a situation from which he cannot disengage himself.

The departure of the experimental results from intelligent expectation, to some extent, has been formalized. The procedure was to describe the experimental situation in concrete detail to a group of competent persons, and to ask them to predict the performance of 100 hypothetical subjects. For purposes of indicating the distribution of break-off points judges were provided with a diagram of the shock generator, and recorded their predictions before being informed of the actual results. Judges typically underestimated the amount of obedience demonstrated by subjects.

In *Figure 3*, we compare the predictions of forty psychiatrists at a leading medical school with the actual performance of subjects in the experiment. The psychiatrists predicted that most subjects would not go beyond the tenth shock level (150 volts; at this point the victim makes his first explicit demand to be freed). They further predicted that by the twentieth shock level (300 volts; the victim refuses to answer) 3·73 per cent of the subjects would still be obedient; and that only a little over one-tenth of one per cent of the subjects would administer the highest shock on the board. But, as the graph indicates, the obtained behavior was very different. Sixty-two per cent of the subjects obeyed the experimenter's commands fully. Between expectation and occurrence there is a whopping discrepancy.

Why did the psychiatrists underestimate the level of obedience? Possibly, because their predictions were based on an inadequate conception of the determinants of human action, a conception that focuses on motives *in vacuo*. This orientation may be entirely adequate for the repair of bruised impulses as revealed on the psychiatrist's couch, but as soon as our interest turns to action in larger settings, attention must be paid to the situations in which motives are expressed. A situation exerts an important press on the individual. It exercises constraints and may provide push. In certain circumstances it is not so much the kind of person a man is, as the kind of situation in which he is placed, that determines his actions.

Many people, not knowing much about the experiment, claim that subjects who go to the end of the board are sadistic. Nothing could be more foolish as an overall characterization of these persons. It is like saying that a person thrown into a swift-flowing stream is necessarily a fast swimmer, or that he has great stamina because he moves so rapidly relative to the bank. The context of action must always be considered. The individual, upon entering the laboratory, becomes integrated into a situation that carries its own momentum. The subject's problem then is how to become disengaged from a situation which is moving in an altogether ugly direction.

The fact that disengagement is so difficult testifies to the potency of the forces that keep the subject at the control board. Are these forces to be conceptualized as

FIGURE 3   PREDICTED AND OBTAINED BEHAVIOR IN VOICE FEEDBACK

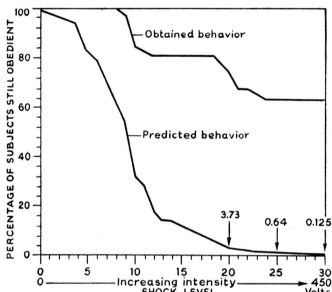

individual motives and expressed in the language of personality dynamics, or are they to be seen as the effects of social structure and pressures arising from the situational field?

A full understanding of the subject's action will, I feel, require that both perspectives be adopted. The person brings to the laboratory enduring dispositions toward authority and aggression, and at the same time he becomes enmeshed in a social structure that is no less an objective fact of the case. From the standpoint of personality theory one may ask: What mechanisms of personality enable a person to transfer responsibility to authority? What are the motives underlying obedient and disobedient performance? Does orientation to authority lead to a short-circuiting of the shame-guilt system? What cognitive and emotional defenses are brought into play in the case of obedient and defiant subjects?

The present experiments are not, however, directed toward an exploration of the motives engaged when the subject obeys the experimenter's commands. Instead, they examine the situational variables responsible for the elicitation of obedience. Elsewhere, we have attempted to spell out some of the structural properties of the experimental situation that account for high obedience, and this analysis need not be repeated here (Milgram, 1963). The experimental variations themselves represent our attempt to probe that structure, by systematically changing it and noting the consequences for behavior. It is clear that some situations produce greater compliance with the experimenter's commands than others. However, this does not necessarily imply an increase or decrease in the strength of any single definable motive. Situations producing the greatest obedience could do so by triggering the most powerful, yet perhaps the most idiosyncratic, of motives in each subject confronted by the setting. Or they may simply recruit a greater number and variety of motives in their service. But whatever the motives involved—and it is far from certain that they can ever be known—action may be studied as a direct function of the situation in which it occurs. This has been the approach of the present study, where we sought to plot behavioral regularities against manipulated properties of the social field. Ultimately, social psychology would like to have a compelling *theory of situations* which will, first, present a language in terms of which situations can be defined; proceed to a typology of situations; and then point to the manner in which definable properties of situations are transformed into psychological forces in the individual.[9]

POSTSCRIPT

Almost a thousand adults were individually studied in the obedience research, and there were many specific conclusions regarding the variables that control obedience and disobedience to authority. Some of these have been discussed briefly in the preceding sections, and more detailed reports will be released subsequently.

There are now some other generalizations I should like to make, which do not derive in any strictly logical fashion from the experiments as carried out, but which, I feel, ought to be made. They are formulations of an intuitive sort that have been forced on me by observation of many subjects responding to the pressures of authority. The assertions represent a painful alteration in my own thinking; and since they were acquired only under the repeated impact of direct observation, I have no illusion that they will be generally accepted by persons who have not had the same experience.

With numbing regularity good people were seen to knuckle under the demands of authority and perform actions that were callous and severe. Men who are in everyday life responsible and decent were seduced by the trappings of authority, by the control of their perceptions, and by the uncritical acceptance of the experimenter's definition of the situation, into performing harsh acts.

What is the limit of such obedience? At many points we attempted to establish a boundary. Cries from the victim were inserted; not good enough. The victim claimed heart trouble; subjects still shocked him on command. The victim pleaded that he be let free, and his answers no longer registered on the signal box; subjects continued to shock him. At the outset we had not conceived that such drastic procedures would be needed to generate disobedience, and each step was added only as the ineffectiveness of the earlier techniques became clear. The final effort to establish a limit was the Touch-Proximity condition. But the very first subject in

---

9. My thanks to Professor Howard Leventhal of Yale for strengthening the writing in this paragraph.

PAUL G. SWINGLE

this condition subdued the victim on command, and proceeded to the highest shock level. A quarter of the subjects in this condition performed similarly.

The results, as seen and felt in the laboratory, are to this author disturbing. They raise the possibility that human nature, or—more specifically—the kind of character produced in American democratic society, cannot be counted on to insulate its citizens from brutality and inhumane treatment at the direction of malevolent authority. A substantial proportion of people do what they are told to do, irrespective of the content of the act and without limitations of conscience, so long as they perceive that the command comes from a legitimate authority. If in this study an anonymous experimenter could successfully command adults to subdue a fifty-year-old man, and force on him painful electric shocks against his protests, one can only wonder what government, with its vastly greater authority and prestige, can command of its subjects. There is, of course, the extremely important question of whether malevolent political institutions could or would arise in American society. The present research contributes nothing to this issue.

In an article titled 'The Dangers of Obedience', Harold J. Laski wrote:

'. . . civilization means, above all, an unwillingness to inflict unnecessary pain. Within the ambit of that definition, those of us who heedlessly accept the commands of authority cannot yet claim to be civilized men.

'. . . Our business, if we desire to live a life, not utterly devoid of meaning and significance, is to accept nothing which contradicts our basic experience merely because it comes to us from tradition or convention or authority. It may well be that we shall be wrong; but our self-expression is thwarted at the root unless the certainties we are asked to accept coincide with the certainties we experience. That is why the condition of freedom in any state is always a widespread and consistent skepticism of the canons upon which power insists.'

REFERENCES

Buss, Arnold H. (1961). *The psychology of aggression.* New York and London: John Wiley.

Kierkegaard, S. (1843). *Fear and trembling.* English edition, Princeton: Princeton University Press, 1941.

Laski, Harold J. (1929). The dangers of obedience. *Harper's Monthly Magazine* **159**, June, 1–10.

Milgram, S. (1961). Dynamics of obedience: experiments in social psychology. Mimeographed report, *National Science Foundation*, January 25.

Milgram, S. (1963). Behavioral study of obedience. *J. abnorm. soc. Psychol.* **67**, 371–8.

Milgram, S. (1964). Issues in the study of obedience: a reply to Baumrind. *Amer. Psychol.* **19**, 848–52.

Miller, N. E. (1944). Experimental studies of conflict. In J. McV. Hunt (Ed.), *Personality and the behavior disorders.* New York: Ronald Press.

Scott, J. P. (1958). *Aggression.* Chicago: University of Chicago Press.

The preceding study illustrates very well the process of laboratory experimentation and indicates how meaningful and complex social problems may be studied under laboratory conditions.

Of course, the major challenge for any scientist is defining his problem in researchable terms. Milgram had to create a laboratory situation which permitted him to explore the obedience process. The independent variables of psychological proximity of the victim, proximity of the authority, and experimental environment had to be defined and experimental situations created which permitted manipulation of these variables. The dependent variable "obedience" was defined and measured in terms of switch closures; that is, the level of obedience was indicated by the closing of the switch which presumably delivered a specified level of shock to the victim.

Part of the planning phase of any laboratory experiment involves devising techniques for orienting the subjects for the purpose of the study. Subjects in Milgram's study had to be convincingly deceived so that they did not discover the true purpose of the study. The subjects had to be convinced that another's pain was directly related to their own behavior, and any suspicion regarding the naiveté of the "learner" had to be prevented.

Orienting the subject is typically accomplished by means of the "cover story." The cover story refers to the introductory remarks made by the experimenter which gives the subject the necessary details of the experiment. Frequently these details are misleading so that the subject is not oriented toward the true purpose of the experiment. In the preceding study, for example, Milgram informed the subjects that the experiment was concerned with the effects of punishment on memory and indicated that this area was in need of research because scientists knew very little about the effects of punishment on the memory process. The cover story must be understandable, it must be uniform (i.e., complementary to the procedures of the study itself), and it must communicate a realistic purpose.

A cover story which is not credible gives rise to what is referred to as a "transparent" experiment which, as the title implies, refers to a study in which the subjects are likely to be aware of the true purpose of the experiment. The cover story must be consistent with the procedures of the actual experiment. The experimenter's behavior must also, of course, be complementary to the cover story. In the previous study, for example, the subject, upon arriving at the laboratory was met by an experimental confederate, that is, a person who outwardly acts like a naive subject but is implicitly following the directions of the experimenter. The two persons (the subject and the confederate) entered the laboratory, were given the cover story by the experimenter and were then appointed to their respective roles in the experiment by means of a bogus drawing. Thus the subject was put in the position of the executant without being alerted to the fact that his switch-closing behavior was going to be observed and recorded.

One of the most important manipulations was that of leading the subject to perceive a "learner" experiencing authentic pain, the incidence and degree of which was directly related to the subject's switch-closing responses. The procedure which involves providing the subject with incorrect information about a situation is generally referred to as "false feedback." The subject heard screams, groans, grunts, and other exclamations indicative of pain, which he attributed to the learner. These sounds came from either a tape recorder or from a well-rehearsed confederate acting as though he were in pain. False feedback procedures are designed to lead a subject to believe that a certain situation exists regardless of whether or not the situation actually does exist. False feedback about a state or situation need not, of course, be limited to tape-recorded information nor the rehearsed behavior of a confederate. One may falsely inform a subject with information from any communication system which the subject believes to be reliable (e.g., printed material, experimenter's verbal report, and control panel indicator lights).

Laboratory experiments typically require extensive pilot work and rehearsal. The pilot or preliminary studies are designed to provide the experimenter with some indication of the feasibility of the study. The researcher is concerned with whether or not the situation is credible, and he is concerned with the strength of his treatment conditions. As Milgram reported, for example, he found that in the absence of protests and even with mild protests from the learner, subjects were virtually unconditionally obedient to the authority. This indicated that subjects would obey an authority to a greater extent than the experimenter had originally assumed. Thus stronger protests from the learner were necessary to prevent total obedience of all subjects which would, of course, obviate any differences resulting from the treatment conditions. The pilot study also indicates errors in procedures, incompatible instructions, and other technical problems which must be corrected to make the experimental situation a workable research tool.

In any experiment in which a confederate is used, a great deal of rehearsal is required. The confederate must rehearse his role so that his behavior is standard and consistent and, most importantly, so that his behavior is believable. The experimenter must also rehearse his part in the experiment. His delivery of the instructions must be consistent and standardized. This is particularly true in Milgram's study in which the stimulus for the subject's obedient response is the experimenter's command to push one of the switches. If the strength of this command varies from condition to condition, then one cannot say for certain whether it was the strength of the command, the nature of the appeal, or the independent variable condition which was responsible for the obedience.

One of the major advantages of laboratory experimentation, as previously stated, is the control which may be obtained over the variables affecting behavior. For example, in Milgram's study the screams, grunts, groans, and other indications of the learner's discomfort were tape recorded for some conditions and therefore identical from subject to subject. The victim was standardized, in a sense, because the same confederate took the part of the victim and therefore factors such as age, personality, and appearance of the confederate were relatively constant across groups. Finally, the environment within which the experiment took place was consistent from group to group and subject to subject. In short the experimenter is able, under laboratory conditions, to stabilize and standardize both the situation in which the behavior takes place and the behavior of other important people in the situation (e.g., the confederate).

In any research, the nature of the subject population and the method of obtaining a sample of this population is of critical importance. Milgram attempted to match his subjects with respect to such variables as age and occupation. Once subjects have been matched on those variables over which one may have some control, the assignment of subjects to treatment conditions must be completely random so that one may make the assumption that those uncontrolled variables which may affect the subject's behavior are randomly distributed throughout each treatment condition.

The results of any laboratory experiment are limited, often seriously, by the fact that the experiment took place in a laboratory and that frequently the subject is aware of the fact that it is an experiment. For example, in Milgram's study it is not unreasonable to assume that the experiments conducted at Yale University under the auspices and, presumably, with the approval of the university, gave rise to a situation in which the subjects were able to justify their behavior. The subject might assume that any experimenter working at Yale University would have to be responsible and knowledgeable and therefore would not allow the victim to be seriously injured. In an attempt to increase the generality of his findings to nonlaboratory situations, Milgram replicated the study in a different environment. Subjects in the Bridgeport study were not aware of the relationship between the experimenter and Yale University and therefore were not in a position to as easily rationalize their behavior nor to be as confident in their assumption that the experimenter had the training necessary to know what shock levels the human body can withstand without injury or severe pain.

Finally, there is one very important detail which every experimenter studying human behavior must consider. The reader will recall that Milgram deceived every subject in the experiment. All subjects were led to believe that they were participating in a study on memory, and many were also led to believe that they had severely hurt another person.

Psychological associations have strict codes of ethics which govern such situations. For important social research to be conducted it is often necessary to manipulate subjects without their awareness — to deceive them. It is just as imperative that every person's rights be guaranteed. Therefore, any time a subject is deceived the experimenter must dehoax the subject after the experiment. Typically, the experimenter sends out a letter to everyone who has participated in the experiment explaining what the study was about, what deceptions were involved, why the deceptions were necessary, and inviting the subjects to attend a question and answer session to be held at a convenient time in the near future.

Because of the nature of Milgram's experiment it was essential that each subject be dehoaxed and reassured before they were discharged from the laboratory. As Milgram reported, a very elaborate postexperimental dehoaxing treatment was devised to guarantee the wellbeing of each subject before he left the experimenter's presence.

The problem of ethical treatment of subjects is a very difficult one. It is obvious that the experimenter must determine whether or not he is infringing upon the rights of others and must make every effort to dehoax every subject. Experiments should not be started until the experimenter has satisfied himself that he can conduct the experiment in keeping with the established code of ethics.

Conformity and Compliance

You are at a club meeting; a member asks for a vote on a measure about which you are undecided; everyone else votes "yes"; you decide to vote with the group.

The above situation, which almost everyone has experienced, is an example of the influence a group may exert upon a person's decision. People tend to be acutely aware of the relationship between their expressed or explicit opinions, beliefs, behaviors, etc., and those characteristic of the group to which they belong. It is often psychologically "uncomfortable" to be in a position which is at variance with the expectations of persons with whom we feel some sort of allegiance or whose opinions we consider reasonable.

In short, groups exert social pressures upon members to be orthodox in behavior and attitude. The pressure may be extrinsic to the person, such as excommunication, loss of membership, or loss of rank within the group, or intrinsic to the person, such as not wanting to disappoint friends, not wanting to be "different," or being apprehensive of error when one's opinions are at variance with those of a respected colleague.

Similarity of behavior or opinion need not, of course, be indicative of conformity. The fact that most persons believe that the world is round and that most men wear ties at formal social functions simply indicates that there is a common fund of fact, opinion, and behavior peculiar to a given society. One would say, rather, that people are *uniform* in belief that the world is round and that tie wearing is *conventional*. Conventionality may vary in degree, however. In its less extreme forms, it is reasonable to maintain that people are simply making use of commonly agreed upon procedures to simplify social interaction. Shaking hands, saying "hello" to initiate conversation on a telephone, taking one's place at the end of a line at a ticket office, etc., are all examples of conventional behavior least indicative of conformity.

Conformity

The above suggests that one may best define conformity as a person's acceptance of or compliance with a group's (or society's) beliefs, attitudes, or actions owing to the social pressure felt by the individual resulting from the group's demands, threats, expectations, or authority. The definition implies that conformity is not evident unless the person in some way alters his behavior or attitudes as a direct consequence of direct or indirect social pressure.

There are several distinctions which may be made between different types of behavior that are classified as conformity. When one is threatened with loss of membership in a group, physical pain, etc., unless he complies by acting in a certain way, he may decide that it is expedient to simply *act* outwardly in the prescribed manner while personally maintaining his original point of view. Thus, the prisoner of war may sign the petition or "confession" to avoid or escape pain but not change his personal opinion at all. This type of behavior is referred to as "yielding."

If a person wants to join a particular group, discovers that the group favors placing lights on the city dump, and then decides that lighting the dump is a grand idea, we have a case of "norm acceptance." Norm acceptance is probably best described as true conformity in that the person totally complies with social pressure. The person acts as though he accepted the group norm and actually (inwardly) has accepted the group norm.

A third class of conformity is the negative case of norm acceptance, which might be called "counternorm acceptance" or "counterconformity." If a person despises a certain group and wants to maximize the psychological distance between himself and that group, he is very likely influenced by social pressure to accept the position most extremely opposite to that characteristic of the group. The counterconformist is, of course, influenced by the group's social pressure, but the direction of change of the norm or attitude is opposite to that of the conformist.

The experiment for this session will be a study of the effects of the perceived magnitude of the social pressure to accept a position on a subject about which the person, in most instances, is indifferent. The experiment will be conducted in the "field." That is, a commonplace situation (petition signing) is structured such that the experimental manipulation and response measurement are accomplished in a natural setting without the subject's being aware that he is involved in an experiment.

PAUL G. SWINGLE

In particular, the study is designed to explore the effects of increasing the size and status of the faction favoring a given position. The size of the faction is manipulated by varying the number of signatures already on a petition which is presented to a subject. The status of the group of signers is varied by attributing the signatures to either students or faculty members.

Previous research has indicated that conformity in laboratory-based decision-making situations may be increased by increasing the size of the group which unanimously holds a certain point of view or by increasing the status or authority of the members of the group. The present study attempts to determine the effects of these variables upon petition signing.

INSTRUCTIONS

Experimental Team Size: Two or three.

Subjects: This experiment will be conducted in the field at various locations in the university. Thus, the subjects will consist of a sample of those students who happen to be passing a specific place at the time of the experiment.

Apparatus: Petitions; clipboard; pencils.

Experimental Situation: Petitions are prepared which contain either none, one, or 10 signatures that are attributed to either students or faculty. Students at the university are stopped by one of the experimenters and asked to read and sign the petition. The frequency of signing the petitions is recorded.

Procedure

A. *In the Laboratory*

1. Duplicate at least 150 petitions of the form shown in Fig. 1.1.
2. Using a pencil (or pen, if that is what is to be used in the actual experiment) prepare the petitions, in laboratory class, as follows:
   a. Prepare 30 petitions with *one* signature with a check mark under the "Student" column (referred to in the following text as petition S_1).
   b. Prepare 30 petitions with *ten* signatures with a check mark under the "Student" column for each signature (referred to as S_{10}).
   c. Prepare 30 petitions with *one* signature with a check mark under the "Faculty" column (F_1).
   d. Prepare 30 petitions with *ten* signatures with a check mark under the "Faculty" column for each signature (F_{10}).

EXPERIMENT 1

We, the undersigned staff and students of _____
University, request that University officials place lights on the _____
_____ Building to add beauty to the campus at night.

| Name | | Faculty | Student |
| | | (Check one) | |

1.
2.
3.
4.
5.
.
.
.
.
.
.
.
23.
24.
25.

FIG. 1.1. Petition form.

[*Note:* At small institutions it may be necessary to use the names of actual faculty members, or at least some actual professors' names. The professors' permission must be obtained and their requirements satisfied before using their names. The reader's instructor will advise him as to whether or not bogus names are adequate.]

    e. Leave 30 petitions unsigned (referred to as B).

3. Divide the laboratory class into five experimental teams.

4. Select an hour during the school day at a time when at least two members of each experimental team are free; that is, select one time for the entire class so that all parts of the experiment are conducted simultaneously.

5. Select five locations at the university that have a reasonable amount of student traffic.

6. Assign one team to cover each location at the specified time.

7. Divide the 30 petitions equally among each team as follows:

6	S_1
6	S_{10}
6	F_1
6	F_{10}
6	B

8. Each team will divide the petitions between the two experimenters. Each active field experimenter receives 15 petitions to be distributed as follows:

3	S_1
3	S_{10}
3	F_1
3	F_{10}
3	B

9. Practice the in-the-field situation given below in the laboratory under the instructor's supervision. The procedure must be well rehearsed so that the behavior of each team is uniform.

B. *In the Field*

1. A few minutes before the specified experimental hour, the team of experimenters should arrive at their assigned locations.

2. Each experimenter should shuffle his petitions so that the order is random.

3. Be sure to have all materials. Clip the randomized (shuffled) petitions to the clipboard and have a pencil in hand.

4. At the assigned time, each experimenter will approach any student who is walking *alone* (do not approach students walking together) and state: "Please read and sign this petition." Hand the student a pencil and the clipboard.

5. Do not say anything more to the subject which might encourage or discourage his signing. If the subject refuses, simply say "thank you" and take the clipboard and pencil from him immediately.

6. Keep a tally sheet, such as that shown in Fig. 1.2, and record whether the student signs the petition or refuses to sign.

7. After the student passes, remove that petition, whether signed or not, from the top of the clipboard and record the subject's response on the tally sheet (Fig. 1.2).

8. Stop once you have approached and received responses (refusals or signatures) from 15 subjects.

Dehoaxing the Subjects: This experiment offers a good example of the ethical problems social scientists must face in the course of their

Experimenter's name _____ Team No. _____

Field location _____

Subject	Petition symbol (B, S_1, S_{10}, F_1, F_{10})	Signed	Refused
1.			
2.			
3.			
·			
·			
·			
13.			
14.			
15.			

FIG. 1.2. Tally sheet for recording subjects' responses to petition signing request.

research. In the experiment about 150 persons were misled and manipulated without their awareness or approval and the subjects' anonymity has obviously not been maintained.

Under these conditions the participants have the right to know the nature and purpose of the experiment. One might argue, however, that because of the trivial nature of the alleged purpose of the petition dehoaxing the subjects is an unnecessary bother. It would probably be very interesting for the class to discuss this topic to obtain some understanding of the differences of opinion. Students may also find that their own opinion changes after they have confronted the subjects during the experiment.

For the purposes of the present exercise, it should be sufficient to place a brief notice in the school paper, or notices on the bulletin boards, stating that the petition signing was part of a class experimental project and inviting all interested participants to attend a brief question and answer period during which the details of the project are explained.

Data Analysis

1. Combine the data from all five experimental teams and enter the number of signatures obtained on each type of petition, out of 30 approaches, on a form such as that shown in Table 1.1.

2. Plot a histogram of the totals.

TABLE 1.1

Total number of signatures obtained on each petition

B	S_1	S_{10}	F_1	F_{10}

Experimental Report

1. Do the data support expectations?
2. What is the effect of increasing the number of signatures on the petition?
3. Is there a status effect?
4. Do there seem to be any interactions (e.g., size of group effect may occur only in the low status condition)?

Reprinted from American Psychologist, 1955, Vol. 10, pp. 191–198, by permission of the author and the publisher.

CONFORMITY AND CHARACTER[1]

RICHARD S. CRUTCHFIELD

*Department of Psychology and
Institute of Personality Assessment and Research,
University of California, Berkeley*

DURING the Spring of 1953, one hundred men visited the Institute of Personality Assessment and Research at the University of California, Berkeley, to participate in an intensive three-day assessment of those qualities related to superior functioning in their profession.[2]

As one of the procedures on the final day of assessment, the men were seated in groups of five in front of an apparatus consisting of five adjacent electrical panels. Each panel had side wings, forming an open cubicle, so that the person, though sitting side by side with his fellow subjects, was unable to see their panels. The experimenter explained that the apparatus was so wired that information could be sent by each man to all the others by closing any of eleven switches at the bottom of his panel. This information would appear on the other panels in the form of signal lights, among five rows of eleven lights, each row corresponding to one of the five panels. After a warm-up task to acquaint the men with the workings of the apparatus, the actual procedure commenced.

Slides were projected on a wall directly facing the men. Each slide presented a question calling for a judgment by the person. He indicated his choice of one of several multiple-alternative answers by closing the appropriately numbered switch on his panel. Moreover, he responded *in order*, that is, as designated by one of five red lights lettered A, B, C, D, E, on his panel. If he were A, he responded first, if B, second, and so on. The designations, A, B, C, D, and E, were rotated by the experimenter from time to time, thus permitting each person to give his judgments in all the

[1] Adapted from the address of the retiring president of the Division of Personality and Social Psychology, American Psychological Association, New York City, September 4, 1954.

[2] The principal study reported here owes much to the collaboration of Dr. Donald W. MacKinnon, director of the Institute of Personality Assessment and Research, and of his staff. Mr. Donald G. Woodworth has contributed especially to the statistical analysis of data.

different serial positions. No further explanation about the purpose of this procedure was offered.

It may help to convey the nature of the men's typical experiences by giving an illustrative description of what happens concretely to one of the men. The first slide calls for a simple judgment of which of two geometrical figures is larger in area. Since his red light C is on, he waits for A and B to respond before making his response. And, as he is able to observe on the panel, his own judgment coincides with the judgments of A and B who preceded him, and of D and E who follow him. After judgments on several further slides in position C, he is then shifted to position D for more slides, then to A.

The slides call for various kinds of judgments—lengths of lines, areas of figures, logical completion of number series, vocabulary items, estimates of the opinions of others, expression of his own attitudes on issues, expression of his personal preferences for line drawings, etc. He is not surprised to observe a perfectly sensible relationship between his judgments and those of the other four men. Where clear-cut perceptual or logical judgments are involved, he finds that his judgments are in perfect agreement with those of the other four. Where matters of opinion are involved, and some differences in opinion to be expected, his judgments and those of the other four men are sometimes in agreement and sometimes not.

Eventually the man finds himself for the first time in position E, where he is to respond last. The next slide shows a standard line and five comparison lines, of which he is to pick the one equal in length to the standard. Among the previous slides he has already encountered this kind of perceptual judgment and has found it easy. On looking at this slide it is immediately clear to him that line number 4 is the correct one. But as he waits his turn to respond, he sees light number 5 in row A go on, indicating that that person has judged line number 5 to be correct. And in fairly quick succession light 5 goes on also in rows B, C, and D.

At this point the man is faced with an obvious conflict between his own clear perception and a unanimous contradictory consensus of the other four men. What does he do? Does he rely on the evidence of his own senses and respond independently? Or does he defer to the judgment 'of the group, complying with their perceptions rather than his own?

We will postpone for a moment the answer as to what he does, and revert to the description of our apparatus.

We have been describing the situation as if seen from the perspective of one of the men. Actually his understanding of the situation is wrong. He has been deceived. For the apparatus is *not* really wired in the way that he was informed. There actually is no connection among the five panels. Instead, they are all wired in an identical manner to a control panel where the experimenter sits behind the men. It is the experimenter who sends all the information which appears on the panels, and the wiring is in parallel in such a way that whatever signals are sent by the experimenter appear simultaneously and identically on all five panels. Moreover, the designations of serial order of responding—A through E—are identical at all times for the five panels, so that at a given moment, for instance, all five men believe themselves to be A, or at another time, E.

As we have just said, the responses actually made by the five men do not affect in any way the panels of the others. They do get registered individually on one part of the experimenter's control panel. The *latency* of each individual response to one tenth of a second is also recorded by timers on the control panel.

Hence, the situation as we have described it for our one illustrative man is actually the situation simultaneously experienced by all five men. They all commence in position C, and all shift at the same time to position D, and to A, and finally E. They all see the same simulated group judgments.

The entire situation is, in a word, contrived, and contrived so as to expose each individual to a standardized and prearranged series of group judgments. By this means the simulated group judgments can be made to appear sensible and in agreement with the individual, or, at chosen critical points, in conflict with his judgments.

Most of you will recognize at once the basic similarity of our situation to that invented by Asch (2) in his extremely important work of recent years on independence of individual judgment under opposing group pressure. In his method, ten subjects announced aloud and in succession their judgments of the relative length of stimulus lines exposed before the group. The first nine subjects were actually confederates of the experimenter, and gave uniformly false answers at preestablished points, thus placing pressure on the single naive subject.

For extensive research use, for instance in personality assessment, Asch's technique is handicapped by the severely unfavorable ratio of confederates to true subjects. The present technique, utilizing the electrical network described above, avoids this difficulty. There are no confederates required; all five subjects are tested simultaneously in a thoroughly standardized situation. The experimenter exercises highly flexible control of the simulated group judgments, and of the serial order of responding. Stimulus material to be judged can be varied as widely as desired by use of different slides.

Now at last come back to our man still sitting before his panel, still confronted with the spurious group consensus, still torn between a force toward independent judgment and a force toward conformity to the group. How he is likely to behave in the situation can best be described by summarizing the results for our study of 50 of the 100 men in assessment.

EFFECTS OF CONSENSUS

All of these men were engaged in a profession in which leadership is one of the salient expected qualifications. Their average age was 34 years. Their educational levels were heterogeneous, but most had had some college training.

Fifty of the men were tested in the procedure as described. Another 40 served as *control* subjects; they simply gave individual judgments of the slides without using the apparatus, and hence without knowledge of the judgments of others. The distribution of judgments of these control subjects on each slide was subsequently used as a baseline for evaluating the amount of group pressure influence on the experimental subjects.

Now as to results. When faced with the dilemma posed by this first critical slide, 15 of the 50 men, or 30 per cent, conformed to the obviously false group consensus. The remaining 70 per cent of the men maintained independence of judgment in face of the contradictory group consensus.

The first critical slide was followed by 20 others, all with the subjects responding in position E. The 20 slides involved a broad sampling of judgmental materials, exploring the question of what would happen to other kinds of perceptions, to matters of factual appraisal and of logic, of opinion and attitude, of personal preference—all under the same conditions of group pressure. Interpolated among them were occasional neutral slides, in which the group consensus was simulated as correct or sensible, in order to help maintain the subjects' acceptance of the genuineness of the apparatus and situation.

The results on several more of the critical slides will give a representative picture of what happens under group pressure. First, take another kind of perceptual judgment. A circle and a star are exposed side by side, the circle being about one third larger in area than the star. The false group consensus is on the *star* as the larger, and 46 per cent of the men express agreement with this false judgment.

On a simple logical judgment of completion of a number series, as found in standard mental tests, 30 per cent of the men conform to an obviously illogical group answer, whereas not a single control subject gives an incorrect answer.

As striking as these influence effects are, they are overshadowed by the even higher degree of influence exhibited on another set of items. These pertain to perceptual, factual, and logical judgments which are designed to maximize the *ambiguity* of the stimulus. There are three such examples: (*a*) two actually equal circles are to be judged for relative size; (*b*) a pair of words are to be judged as either synonyms or antonyms, though actually entirely unrelated in meaning and unfamiliar to all subjects; (*c*) a number series is to be completed which is actually insoluble, that is, for which there is no logically correct completion.

To take the third example, which gives the most pronounced influence effect of all 21 critical items, 79 per cent of the men conform to a spurious group consensus upon an arbitrarily chosen and irrational answer.

Influence effects are found, we see, on both well-structured and poorly-structured stimuli, with markedly greater effects on the latter.

Turning from perceptual and factual judgments to opinions and attitudes, it is clearly evident that here, too, the judgments of many of the men are markedly dependent upon a spurious group consensus which violates their own inner convictions. For example, among control subjects virtually no one expresses disagreement with the statement: "I believe we are made better by the trials and hardships of life." But among the experimental subjects exposed to a group consensus toward disagreement, 31 per cent of the men shift to expressing disagreement.

It can be demonstrated that the conformity behavior is not found solely for attitudes on issues like the foregoing, which may be of rather abstract and remote significance for the person. Among the control sample of men, not a single one expresses agreement with the statement: "I doubt whether I would make a good leader," whereas 37 per cent of the men subjected to group pressure toward agreement succumb to it. Here is an issue relating to appraisal of the self and hence likely to be of some importance to the person, especially in light of the fact already mentioned that one of the salient expected qualifications of men in this particular profession is that of leadership.

The set of 21 critical items ranges from factual to attitudinal, from structured to ambiguous, from impersonal to personal. With only two exceptions, all these items yield significant group pressure influence effects in our sample of 50 men. The very existence of the two exceptional items is in itself an important finding, for it demonstrates that the observed influences are not simply evidence of indiscriminate readiness to conform to group pressure regardless of the specific nature of the judgment involved. The character of the two exceptional items is significant, for they are the two most extremely personal and subjective judgments, namely, those in which the individual is asked which one of two simple line drawings *he prefers*. On these slides there is virtually no effective result of group pressure. Not more than one man of the 50 expresses agreement with the spurious group consensus on the nonpreferred drawing. Such personal preferences, being most isolated from the relevance of group standards, thus seem to be most immune to group pressure.

INDIVIDUAL DIFFERENCES

To what extent do the fifty men differ among themselves in their general degree of conformity to group pressure?

A total "conformity score" is readily obtainable for each individual by counting the number of the 21 critical items on which he exhibits influence to the group pressure. The threshold for influence for each item is arbitrarily fixed on the basis of the distribution of judgments by control subjects on that item.

Considering that we are dealing with a fairly homogeneous sample of limited size, the range of individual differences that we obtain is astonishingly large, covering virtually the entire possible scope of our measure. At the lower extreme, several of the men showed conformity on no more than one or two of the critical items. At the upper extreme, one man was influenced on 17 of the 21 items. The rest of the scores are well distributed between these extremes, with a mean score of about eight items and a tendency for greater concentration of scores toward the lower conformity end.

The reliability of the total score, as a measure of generalized conformity in the situation, is obtained by correlating scores on two matched halves of the items. The correlation is found to be .82, which when corrected for the combined halves gives a reliability estimate for the entire 21-item scale of .90.

To recapitulate, we find large and reliable differences among the 50 men in the amount of conformity behavior exhibited, and there appears to be considerable generality of this conformity behavior with respect to widely varied judgmental materials. Whether such conformity tendencies also generalize to other, quite different behavioral situations is a question for future research.

RELATIONS TO PERSONALITY VARIABLES

Assuming that we are, indeed, measuring conformity tendencies which are fundamental in the person, the question is what traits of character distinguish between those men exhibiting much conformity behavior in our test and those exhibiting little conformity. The assessment setting within which these men were studied provides an unusually fertile opportunity to explore this question, in light of the wide range of personality measurements available.

Correlational study of the conformity scores with these other variables of personality provides some picture of the independent and of the conforming person. As contrasted with the high conformist, the independent man shows more intellectual effec-tiveness, ego strength, leadership ability and maturity of social relations, together with a conspicuous absence of inferiority feelings, rigid and excessive self-control, and authoritarian attitudes.

A few correlations will illustrate. The assessment staff rating on "intellectual competence" correlates − .63 with conformity score, this being the highest relationship of any found. The *Concept Mastery Test*,[3] a measure of superior mental functioning, correlates − .51 with conformity. An "ego strength" scale, independently derived by Barron (3), correlates − .33, and a staff rating on "leadership ability," − .30 with conformity. Scales of Gough's *California Psychological Inventory* (6), pertaining to such dimensions as "tolerance," "social participation," and "responsibility," range in correlation from − .30 to − .41 with conformity.

And as for some of the positive correlates, the F scale (1), a measure of authoritarian attitudes, correlates + .39 with conformity, and a staff rating on amount of authoritarian behavior manifested in a standard psychodrama situation correlates + .35 with conformity.

The general appraisal of each man by the assessment staff in the form of descriptive Q sorts further enriches this picture. Those men exhibiting extreme independence in the situation as contrasted with those at the high conformity end are described more often in the following terms by the assessment staff, which was entirely ignorant of the actual behavior of the men in the group pressure procedure:

Is an effective leader.
Takes an ascendant role in his relations with others.
Is persuasive; tends to win other people over to his point of view.
Is turned to for advice and reassurance.
Is efficient, capable, able to mobilize resources easily and effectively.
Is active and vigorous.
Is an expressive, ebullient person.
Seeks and enjoys aesthetic and sensuous impressions.
Is natural; free from pretense, unaffected.
Is self-reliant; independent in judgment; able to think for himself.

In sharp contrast to this picture of the independent men is the following description of those high in conformity behavior:

With respect to authority, is submissive, compliant and overly accepting.

[3] Used with the kind permission of Dr. Lewis M. Terman.

Is conforming; tends to do the things that are prescribed.

Has a narrow range of interests.

Overcontrols his impulses; is inhibited; needlessly delays or denies gratification.

Is unable to make decisions without vacillation or delay.

Becomes confused, disorganized, and unadaptive under stress.

Lacks insight into his own motives and behavior.

Is suggestible; overly responsive to other people's evaluations rather than his own.

Further evidence is found in some of the specific items of personality inventories on which the answers of the high and low conformers are significantly different. Here are some illustrative items more frequently answered "True" by the independent subjects than by the conforming subjects:

Sometimes I rather enjoy going against the rules and doing things I'm not supposed to.

I like to fool around with new ideas, even if they turn out later to be a total waste of time.

A person needs to "show off" a little now and then.

At times I have been so entertained by the cleverness of a crook that I have hoped he would get by with it.

It is unusual for me to express strong approval or disapproval of the actions of others.

I am often so annoyed when someone tries to get ahead of me in a line of people that I speak to him about it.

Compared to your own self-respect, the respect of others means very little.

This pattern of expressed attitudes seems to reflect freedom from compulsion about rules, adventurousness (perhaps tinged with exhibitionism), self-assertiveness, and self-respect.

Turning to the opposite side of the picture, here are some illustrative items more frequently answered "True" by the extreme conformists, which reflect a rather rigid, externally sanctioned, and inconsistent, moralistic attitude.

I am in favor of very strict enforcement of all laws, no matter what the consequences.

It is all right to get around the law if you don't actually break it.

Most people are honest chiefly through fear of being caught.

Another set of items reveals a desire for clarity, symmetry, certainty, or. in presently popular phraseology, "an intolerance of ambiguity."

I don't like to work on a problem unless there is a possibility of coming out with a clear-cut and unambiguous answer.

Once I have made up my mind I seldom change it.

Perfect balance is the essence of all good composition.

Other items express conventionality of values:

I always follow the rule: business before pleasure.

The trouble with many people is that they don't take things seriously enough.

I am very careful about my manner of dress.

Anxiety is revealed in numerous items:

I am afraid when I look down from a high place.

I am often bothered by useless thoughts which keep running through my head.

I often think, "I wish I were a child again."

I often feel as though I have done something wrong or wicked.

And, finally, there are various expressions of disturbed, dejected, and distrustful attitudes toward other people:

When I meet a stranger I often think that he is better than I am.

Sometimes I am sure that other people can tell what I am thinking.

I wish that I could get over worrying about things I have said that may have injured other people's feelings.

I commonly wonder what hidden reason another person may have for doing something nice for me.

People pretend to care more about one another than they really do.

Although there is an unmistakable neurotic tone to many of the foregoing statements, one must be chary of inferring that those high on conformity are measurably more neurotic than the others. There does not in fact appear to be any significant correlation of the conformity scores with obvious standard measures of neuroticism as found, for instance, in scales of the Minnesota Multiphasic Personality Inventory. A similar negative finding has been reported by Barron (4) in his study of the personality correlates of independence of judgment in Asch's subjects.

In another area. attitudes concerning parents and children, differences between those high and low on conformity are especially interesting. The extreme conformists describe their parents in highly idealized terms, unrelieved by any semblance of criticism. The independents, on the other hand, offer a more balanced picture of praise and criticism.

Most of the men in the sample are fathers, and it is instructive to see that in their view of child-rearing practices, the conformers are distinctly more "restrictive" in their attitudes, and the independents distinctively more "permissive" (5).

Finally, there appears to be a marked difference in the early home background of the conformists and independents. The high conformers in this sample come almost without exception from stable homes; the independents much more frequently report broken homes and unstable home environments.

Previous theoretical and empirical studies seem to converge, though imperfectly, on a picture of the overconformist as having less ego strength, less ability to tolerate own impulses and to tolerate ambiguity, less ability to accept responsibility, less self-insight, less spontaneity and productive originality, and as having more prejudiced and authoritarian attitudes, more idealization of parents, and greater emphasis on external and socially approved values.

All of these elements gain at least some substantiation in the present study of conformity behavior, as objectively measured in our test situation. The decisive influence of intelligence in resisting conformity pressures is perhaps given even fuller weight in the present findings.

CONFORMITY BEHAVIOR IN DIFFERENT POPULATIONS

Two further studies have been made. The first was with 59 college undergraduates, mostly sophomores. Forty were females, 19 males. An additional 40 students served as control subjects.

Using the same procedures and the same items for judgment, the conformity results for this student sample were highly similar to those already reported for the adult men. Here again extensive group pressure effects are found on almost all items. And here again there are wide individual differences, covering virtually the entire score range.

The male students on the average exhibit just about the same level of conformity as do the adult men. The female students, on the other hand, exhibit significantly *higher* amounts of conformity than the male groups. This greater conformity among females is evident across the entire range of items tested. Interpretation of this sex difference in conformity will require further research.

But before mâle egos swell overly, let me hasten to report the results of a third study, just completed. Fifty women, all college alumnae in their early forties, were tested in the same group pressure procedure, again as part of a larger assessment setting, and under the auspices of the Mary Conover Mellon Foundation.[1] As in the previous populations, virtually the entire range of individual differences in conformity is exhibited by these

[1] The assessment was under the direction of Dr. R. Nevitt Sanford.

women. Some of them show no effect at all; others are influenced on almost all items. But the average conformity score for these 50 women is significantly *lower* than that found in the previous populations.

Thus we find our sample of adult women to be more independent in judgment than our adult men. The interpretation is difficult. The two groups differ in many particulars, other than sex. The women are highly selected for educational and socioeconomic status, are persons active in their community affairs, and would be characterized as relatively stable in personality and free of psychopathology. The adult men in our professional group are less advantageously selected in all these respects. Differences in intellectual level alone might be sufficient to account for the observed differences in conformity scores.

PSYCHOLOGICAL PROCESSES

Turn now to questions concerning the nature of the psychological processes involved in these expressions of conformity to group pressure. How, for instance, is the situation perceived by the individual? The most striking thing is that almost never do the individuals under this pressure of a false group consensus come to suspect the deception practiced upon them. Of the total of 159 persons already tested in the apparatus, and questioned immediately afterwards, only a small handful expressed doubt of the genuineness of the situation. Of these not more than two or three really seem to have developed this suspicion while in the actual situation.

Yet all the subjects are acutely aware of the sometimes gross discrepancies between their own inner judgments and those expressed by the rest of the group. How do they account for these discrepancies?

Intensive individual questioning of the subjects immediately following the procedure elicits evidence of two quite different tendencies. First, for many persons the discrepancies tend to be resolved through self-blame. They express doubt of their own accuracy of perception or judgment, confessing that they had probably misread or misperceived the slides. Second, for many other persons the main tendency is to blame the rest of the group, expressing doubt that they had perceived or read the slides correctly. This is not a neat dichotomy, of course. Most persons express something of a mixture of these explanations, which is not surprising in view of the fact that some slides may tend to favor one interpretation of the difficulty and other slides the opposite interpretation.

As might be predicted, there is a substantial relationship between conformity score and tendency to self-blame; or, putting it the other way, those who remain relatively independent of the group pressure are more likely to blame the discrepancies on poor judgments by the rest of the group.

But this is by no means a perfect relationship. There are many persons who, though retrospectively expressing doubt of the correctness of the group's judgment, did in fact conform heavily while in the situation. And what is even more striking is that a substantial number of the subjects—between 25 and 30 per cent—freely admit on later questioning that there were times when they responded the way the group did *even when they thought this not the proper answer*. It seems evident, therefore, that along with various forms of cognitive rationalization of the discrepancies, there occurred a considerable amount of what might be called deliberate conforming, that is, choosing to express outward agreement with the group consensus even when believing the group to be wrong.

Another noteworthy effect was the sense of increased psychological distance induced between the person himself and the rest of the group. He felt himself to be queer or different, or felt the group to be quite unlike what he had thought. With this went an arousal of considerable anxiety in most subjects; for some, manifest anxiety was acute.

The existence of these tensions within and between the subjects became dramatically manifest when, shortly after the end of the procedure, the experimenter confessed the deception he had practiced and explained the real situation. There were obvious and audible signs of relaxation and relief, and a shift from an atmosphere of constraint to one of animated discussion.

This is an appropriate point to comment on ethics. No persons when questioned after explanation of the deception expressed feelings that they had been ethically maltreated in the experiment. The most common reaction was a positive one of having engaged in an unusual and significant experience, together with much joking about having been taken in.

Undeniably there are serious ethical issues involved in the experimental use of such deception techniques, especially inasmuch as they appear to penetrate rather deeply into the person. My view is that such deception methods ethically require that great care be taken immediately afterwards to explain the situation fully to the subject.

These remarks on ethics of the method are especially pertinent as we move from study of judgmental materials which are noncontroversial to those which are controversial. In the studies of college students and of mature women, many new critical items were introduced and subjected to the pressure. They were intended to explore more deeply the conformity tendencies in matters of opinion and attitude. And they were so chosen as to pertain to socially important and controversial issues involving civil liberties, political philosophy, crime and punishment, ethical values, and the like.

Here are two salient examples. An expression of agreement or disagreement was called for on the following statement: "Free speech being a privilege rather than a right, it is proper for a society to suspend free speech whenever it feels itself threatened." Among control subjects, only 19 per cent express agreement. But among the experimental subjects confronted with a unanimous group consensus agreeing with the statement, 58 per cent express agreement.

Another item was phrased as follows: "Which one of the following do you feel is the most important problem facing our country today?" And these five alternatives were offered:

Economic recession
Educational facilities
Subversive activities
Mental health
Crime and corruption

Among control subjects, only 12 per cent chose "Subversive activities" as the most important. But when exposed to a spurious group consensus which unanimously selected "Subversive activities" as the most important, 48 per cent of the experimental subjects expressed this same choice.

I think that no one would wish to deny that here we have evidence of the operation of powerful conformity influences in the expression of opinion on matters of critical social controversy.

REINFORCEMENT OF CONFORMITY

There is one final point upon which I should like to touch briefly. That is the question of whether there are circumstances under which the power of the group to influence the judgments of the individual may be even more greatly reinforced, and if so, how far such power may extend.

One method has been tried as part of the study of college students. With half of the subjects, a further instruction was introduced by the experimenter. They were told that in order to see how well they were doing during the procedure, the experimenter would inform the group immediately after the judgments on each slide what the correct answer was. This was to be done, of course, only for those slides for which there was a correct answer, namely, perceptual judgments, logical solutions, vocabulary, etc. No announcement would be made after slides having to do with opinions and attitudes.

The experimenter here again deceived the subjects, for the answers he announced as correct were deliberately chosen so as to agree with the false group consensus. In short, the external authority of the experimenter was later added on as reinforcement to the group consensus.

The effect of this so-called "correction" method is striking. As the series of judgments goes on, these individuals express greater and greater conformity to the group pressure on slides which are of the same character as those for which earlier in the series the false group consensus was thus reinforced by the false announcement by the experimenter.

But the more critical issue is whether this enhanced power of the group generalizes also to judgments of an entirely unrelated sort, namely, matters of opinion and attitude, rather than of fact. In other words, will the group, through having the rightness of its judgment supported by the experimenter on matters of perception, logic, and the like, thereby come to be regarded by the individual as more right, or more to be complied with, on entirely extraneous matters, such as social issues?

The answer is absolutely clear. The enhanced power of the group does *not* carry over to increase the effective influence on expression of opinions and attitudes. The subjects exposed to this "correction" method do not exhibit greater conformity to group pressure on opinions and attitudes than that found in other subjects.

This crucial finding throws some light on the nature of the psychological processes involved in the conformity situation. For it seems to imply that conformity behavior under such group pressure, rather than being sheerly an indiscriminate and irrational tendency to defer to the authority of the group, has in it important rational elements. There is something of a reasonable differentiation made by the individual in his manner of reliance upon the group. He may be led to accept the superiority of the group judgment on matters where there is an objective frame of reference against which the group can be checked. But he does not, thereby, automatically accept the authority of the group on matters of a less objective sort.

CONCLUSION

The social psychologist is concerned with the character of conformity, the personologist with conformity of character. Between them they raise many research questions: the comparative incidence of conformity tendencies in various populations; the influence of group structure and the individual's role in the group on the nature and amount of conformity behavior; the effects of reward or punishment for conforming on habits of conformity; the genesis and change of conformity behavior in the individual personality; the determinants of extreme *anti*conformity tendencies.

Contributing to such questions we have what appears to be a powerful new research technique, enabling the study of conformity behavior within a setting which effectively simulates genuine group interaction, yet preserves the essential requirements of objective measurement.

REFERENCES

1. ADORNO, T. W., FRENKEL-BRUNSWIK, ELSE, LEVINSON, D., & SANFORD, R. N. *The authoritarian personality.* New York: Harper, 1950.
2. ASCH, S. E. *Social psychology.* New York: Prentice Hall, 1952.
3. BARRON, F. An ego-strength scale which predicts response to psychotherapy. *J. consult. Psychol.*, 1953, 17, 327–333.
4. BARRON, F. Some personality correlates of independence of judgment. *J. Pers.*, 1953, 21, 287–297.
5. BLOCK, J. Personality characteristics associated with fathers' attitudes toward child-rearing. *Child Develpm.*, 1955, in press.
6. GOUGH, H. G. *A preliminary guide for the use and interpretation of the California Psychological Inventory.* Privately distributed by the Institute of Personality Assessment and Research, Univer. of California, Berkeley, 1954. (Mimeo.)

Received September 4, 1954.

Reprinted from Southwestern Social Science Quarterly, 1956, Vol. 36, pp. 385–390, by permission of the authors and the publisher.

Social Forces in Petition-Signing

ROBERT R. BLAKE, JANE S. MOUTON,
and JACK D. HAIN
UNIVERSITY OF TEXAS

ONE APPROACH to social science involves the experimental analysis of phenomena, with investigations conducted under test-tube conditions to replicate situations occurring in real-life settings.[1] Two advantages result from transposing laboratory methods of experimentation to the natural setting where the phenomenon occurs. One is that increased confidence can be placed in the conclusions reached concerning the explanation of the phenomenon, since the method makes use of both control and systematic variation rather than depending upon procedures which allow for only *post hoc* explanations. A second advantage concerns the directness of the application of the findings. Since the social action investigated occurs under natural conditions and since participants are unaware that their behavior is being evaluated in a systematic way, there can be no question as to the validity of the conclusions reached for use in social engineering. The purpose of this paper is to demonstrate an experimental social analysis of a typical community phenomenon through a critique of the petition as a mechanism for inducing social change, and to evaluate the principles derived therefrom for application from the standpoint of social engineering.

The Problem

Pressures for change are often created by the petition. The petition is recognized as an effective means of exerting social pressure, owing to the generally accepted premise that the larger the number of signatures affixed, the more widespread the sentiment in favor of the proposal. But additional factors, unrecognized in the assertion that an endorsement indicates support, undoubtedly limit the validity of this assumption. One such factor is the way in which the request for support of the proposal is expressed at the time the

---

[1] Robert R. Blake, "Social Standards and Individual Conduct," *Southwestern Social Science Quarterly,* Vol. 35 (June, 1954), pp. 11–24; Robert R. Blake and Jane S. Mouton, "Present and Future Implications of Social Psychology for Law and Lawyers," *Journal of Public Law,* Vol. 3 (1955), 352–69; Robert R. Blake and Jane S. Mouton, "The Study of Social Conduct within the Framework of Adaptation-Level Theory," in Muzafer Sherif and M. O. Wilson (eds.), *Emerging Problems in Social Psychology* (third conference in social psychology, University of Oklahoma, in press).

PAUL G. SWINGLE

endorsement is sought. Given the same proposal, for example, a strong plea would be expected to elicit more signatures than a weak one. Another limiting factor involves the knowledge that other people are giving their endorsements or are refusing to do so. The former condition would be expected to produce more endorsements than the latter. The combination of these factors that would produce a high rate of endorsement would be a strong request plus the knowledge that others are also endorsing. A weak plea, together with the knowledge that others are refusing to endorse, would significantly decrease the rate.

The present experiment is designed to determine the validity of the foregoing predictions. To the extent that an endorsement rate is governed by the strength of the plea and the knowledge of the reactions of others, the unqualified assumption that an endorsement means support of a proposal is of strictly limited validity.

Experimental Design

Subjects and arrangements.—One hundred thirty-eight male students walking by the Student Union of the University of Texas served as subjects in the present study. As they passed, they were stopped and invited to sign a petition. The petition concerned a minor campus issue, selected because it represented a proposition toward which students were neither strongly in favor nor strongly opposed. The petition read: "We, the undersigned students of The University of Texas, request that University officials place lights on Littlefield Fountain to add to the beauty of the memorial." The petition carried no previous signatures. The option for the passer-by was to sign or to decline to do so.

Experimental Variations

Strength of the request.—In order to measure differences in signing due to the manner in which the request for the endorsement was stated, three pleas were used, each differing in its degree of compellingness. For the strong plea, the experimenter said, "Would you read and sign this petition, please?" A pencil was offered. The request of intermediate strength was, "Would you read and sign this petition?" A pencil was attached to the clip board but was not offered. The weak invitation was, "You don't want to sign this petition, do you?" No pencil was in view. The prediction is that the highest rate of endorsement would be obtained for the strongest request and the lowest rate for the weakest.

Knowledge of the reactions of others.—In order to measure the effect on the endorsement rate of representative attitudes toward the proposal, three conditions were set up whereby the passers-by were allowed to become aware of the reactions of others to the petition or were given no indication as to what others' reactions were. First, the passer-by was asked to read the petition just before a person assisting the experimenter had completed reading it. While the subject was waiting, he had the opportunity to observe the assistant's reaction to the petition. For one third of the passers-by, the assistant subsequently said, "Sure, I'll sign," wrote his name, and departed. For another third, the assistant returned the clip board, saying, "No, I'd rather not," then walked away. Presenting the clip board without providing any opportunity for knowing the reaction of another person served as the third condition. Responses from these three conditions were used as the basis for comparing the endorsement rate when the passer-by was unable to assess representative attitudes with the rates when he knew attitudes to be either favorable or unfavorable. The prediction is that the highest endorsement rate would be obtained when the subject knows that the person preceding him has signed and lowest when he knows that person refused to endorse the proposal.

Results

Differences in endorsement rate associated with request.—The three pleas were evaluated for the frequency of endorsement for each, under the condition where the passer-by had no opportunity to know the reaction of another person. With 16 subjects under each condition, 14 signed when the request was strong, 9 when it was of intermediate strength, and 6 when the request was weak. Data are shown in Table 1. Consistent with the prediction

TABLE 1

Reactions of Subjects to Three Degrees of Strength Used in the Request for Endorsement

Strength of Request	Sign	Refuse
Strong	14	2
Intermediate	9	7
Weak	6	10
Total	29	19

that the way the request for the support of a proposition is expressed will determine a person's readiness to sign, the X^2 of 8.54 ($2df$), which is significant beyond the 2 per cent level, shows that the rate of endorsement varied with the strength of the plea. The stronger the plea, the higher the endorsement rate.

Knowledge of reactions by others.—Knowledge of the reaction of others was evaluated for the frequency of endorsement produced by knowing either that another person signed the petition or that he refused to do so, using the request-condition of intermediate strength. These data are presented in Table 2. Of the 15 subjects under each condition, 14 people who were presented the petition just after they had seen another person sign it also endorsed it. When the petition was presented with the passer-by having no opportunity to see the reactions of another person, 8 of the 15 signed. Under the condition that another person was seen to refuse the petition, only 4 of the 15 subjects endorsed it. The X^2 of 18.86 $(2df)$, which is significant at the 1 per cent level, shows that the endorsement rate varied with the

TABLE 2

Reactions of Subjects to Different Behavior of an Assistant—Request of Intermediate Strength

Reactions of Assistant	Reactions of Subjects	
	Sign	Refuse
Sign	14	1
Absent	8	7
Refuse	4	11
Total	26	19

knowledge of the reactions by others. Consistent with the prediction that knowledge of the reactions of others to the petition will influence a person's readiness to endorse it, the rate of endorsement was found to be higher when others were known to have signed and lower when others were known to have refused to sign the petition.

Combination of strength of the request and knowledge of the reactions of others.—Results presented thus far show that for the same petition, the rate of endorsement varies with the way the request for support is expressed and with knowledge of the reactions by others to the petition. The rate of endorsement when both of these factors were varied simultaneously is evaluated in this section. The results are presented in Table 3.

TABLE 3

Reactions of Subjects to Different Behavior of an Assistant—Weak and Strong Requests

Reactions of Assistant	Strength of Request					
	Strong		Weak		Total	
	Sign	Refuse	Sign	Refuse	Sign	Refuse
Sign	15	0	11	4	26	4
Absent	12	3	6	9	18	12
Refuse	6	9	3	12	9	21
Total	33	12	20	25	53	37

The rate for the strong plea, presented in combination with the knowledge that another person signed, is shown in the upper-left corner of Table 3. With this combination of factors, all 15 subjects signed. At the opposite extreme, in the lower-right corner, when the weak plea was presented in combination with the assistant's refusal to endorse, 3 of the 15 subjects signed. Other values are intermediate.

Consistent with the predictions in the introduction, a decrease in the frequency of signing is associated with the two factors taken in combination. Column totals show a decrease in the endorsement rate when there is a decrease in the strength of the plea. This finding is consistent with the results in Table 1. With 45 cases for each condition, there were 33 endorsements for the strong, and 20 for the weak request. The X^2 of 7.76 ($1df$) is significant at approximately the 1 per cent level. Decreases in frequency of signing associated with the reactions of the assistant are shown in the rows where the totals are 26 when the assistant signed, 18 when no assistant was present, and 9 when the assistant refused. The X^2 of 17.67 ($2df$) is significant at the 1 per cent level. Finally, the interaction between variables produces an X^2 of 2.84 ($4df$). This value is not significant. The conclusion, then, is that rate of endorsement associated with the strength of the request is independent from that of knowledge of the reactions to the petition by others. This finding indicates that both factors combine to permit a better prediction than can be had if either is treated separately.

Summary

The purpose of this report is to demonstrate the use of experimental social analysis in studying a common phenomenon. The phenomenon was that of petition-signing. The experiment was conducted in a typical action-setting by asking 138 students passing the Student Union of the University of Texas to sign a petition requesting support for beautifying a campus memorial. Predictions that different rates of endorsement would be forthcoming were made in relation to the strength of the plea, the knowledge of the reactions of others to the proposal, and combinations of these two factors.

Results support predictions. With a standard petition, factors other than the content of the petition were found to influence the rate of endorsement. Whether or not the petition was signed is determined partly by the strength of the request for the endorsement, partly by the knowledge of the reactions of others, and partly by the pattern of combinations for these two factors. Since signing is a joint function of both and the two factors are independent, the adequacy of predicting an individual's readiness to endorse in any concrete setting can be increased by taking both into account.

The findings cast doubt on the validity of the unrestricted assertion that the larger the number of signatures for a petition, the more widespread the sentiment in favor of the proposed change. In order to interpret signatures on a petition in a manner consistent with social science knowledge, it is mandatory that endorsements be sought under conditions that are as nearly standardized as possible. Only when such conditions are satisfied can it be concluded that an endorsement represents a personal conviction to support the petition. The present experiment has shown how experimental analysis can produce results useful in social engineering by suggesting that petition signatures in themselves are uninterpretable unless the conditions employed in procuring the signatures, the strength of the request, and the background knowledge of the community attitudes toward the request are specified.

Reprinted from Journal of Social Psychology, 1961, Vol. 53, pp. 303–316, by permission of the authors and the publisher.

ON CONFORMITY WITH JUDGMENTS OF A MAJORITY OR AN AUTHORITY*

ABRAHAM S. LUCHINS AND EDITH H. LUCHINS[1]

A. INTRODUCTION

Among other experiments on conformity described in a previous report (6) was one in which the subject overheard several individuals judge the same stimulus to which he subsequently responded. The present report describes explorations of various social influences on such judgment situations. We were particularly interested in the relative effectiveness of a majority and an authority in obtaining agreement with correct and incorrect judgments. Therefore experimental variations were conducted in which an authority confirms or rejects the judgment of the majority.

B. GENERAL PROCEDURE AND SUBJECTS

The stimulus material consisted of five cards (2), each containing a drawing of a small square with two line segments, labeled 1 and 2, jutting out from the square at different angles. One of the line segments was one inch long throughout and the other was 15/16, 14/16, 12/16, 10/16, and 8/16 of an inch in the first through the fifth cards, respectively.

Serving as subjects were 120 college students, mostly freshmen. The control experiment was individually administered to 20 subjects and each of the experimental variations to 10 subjects. In the control experiment the cards were shown only to the subject, while in the variations they were also shown to three pre-instructed individuals (the experimenters' confederates). Experiments I through IV were conducted in Montreal, Canada, and the other experiments in Eugene, Oregon.

There were two experimenters present, one of whom did the actual administration while the other took notes in the back of the room. The initial instructions were essentially as follows, with the phrases in parentheses omitted in the control experiment.

---

* Received in the Editorial Office on April 17, 1959.
[1] The writers are indebted to Seymour J. Sofer, Morris Godel, Rob Roy, and David Sylwester, who served as "authorities" and collected the data on which this report is based.

> The purpose of this experiment is to test visual acuity as part of a new intelligence test being made by the psychology department. I am helping to standardize the test by gathering data as my lab. assignment. I will pass around some cards, one at a time. Look at each card for a few seconds (and pass it on). You are to note which of the two numbered lines on each card is shorter. Do not count the square as part of the line. Please state your answer (before you pass it on to the next person), saying it out loud so that I can hear it. Remember you are to tell me which of the two lines, No. 1 or No. 2, is the shorter one.

Subjects were also told that their responses would have no bearing on their school status.

After the experiment a conference was held with the subject in an attempt to have him explain why he responded as he did and how he reacted to the overheard responses and the right-wrong verdict.

C. Specific Procedures

1. One-Phase Experiments

a. Experiment O (control). As mentioned above the cards were shown only to the subject, with a judgment requested for each card.

b. Experiment I (affirmation of incorrect responses). For each card the three confederates responded before the subject, consistently giving the incorrect answer, i.e., naming the longer rather than the shorter line. After the subject had responded to a card, and before the next card was shown, the experimenter claimed that the incorrect response was "right" and the correct response "wrong." Thus the subject was said to be "wrong" if he did not agree with the confederates' responses which were consistently judged to be "right." Here the confederates' responses and the experimenter's verdict were both opposed to the objective evidence.

The experimenter was serving as the authority who knew what was right or wrong. It may be relevant to anticipate the qualitative findings and note here that in all the variations subjects usually did not question the experimenter's verdict and regarded him as the person "in the know."

c. Experiment II (rejection of correct responses). The procedure differed from Experiment I only in that the confederates consistently gave the objectively correct response. As in Experiment I, the experimenter claimed that the objectively correct response was "wrong" and the incorrect one was "right." Here the majority supported while the authority opposed the objective evidence.

d. Experiment III (affirmation of correct responses). The procedure differed from Experiment II only in that the experimenter judged the objectively correct response, which was consistently made by the confederates, to be "right" and the incorrect response to be "wrong." Here the majority and the authority were both in accord with the objective evidence.

e. Experiment IV (rejection of incorrect responses). The procedure differed from Experiment I only in that the incorrect responses, consistently made by the confederates, were judged to be "wrong." Here the authority supported while the majority opposed the objective evidence.

2. *Two-Phase Experiments*

Would subjects still show the influence of the overheard response and of the experimenter's verdict if they were given an opportunity to respond again to the cards, with the social forces not explicitly introduced? Variations were undertaken with new subjects to answer this question. In so doing we replicated the previous experiments. Each variation is divided into Phase B (where both the majority and the authority are involved, as in Experiments I through IV) and Phase C (where only the subject responds, as in the control experiment.

a. Experiment V. Phase B corresponded precisely to Experiment I. Immediately after Phase B, came Phase C in which the experimenter said that he was going to give the test again on an individual basis. A piece of paper was given to each person. The subject was told that since he had been last before, he would now be first. The subject was then shown each card for two or three seconds and asked to write his answer to each. This was Phase C. Responses were written in order that the subject would be able to make a "private" judgment, not overheard by the other subjects. We were interested in whether this "private" judgment would show the influence of the previous social pressures.

b. Experiments VI-VIII. The procedure differed from the above only in that the first phase of Experiments VI, VII, and VIII corresponded precisely to Experiments II, III, and IV, respectively.

3. *Three-Phase Experiments*[2]

How would responses be influenced if, prior to Phases B and C as described above, there was a phase in which the subject overheard the confederates, but wherein the experimenter gave no verdict?

a. Experiment IX. In the first phase, Phase A, the confederates gave

---

[2] Such experiments were also done with Oregon students in which, following Phase A, Phase B corresponded to Experiment II or IV. The data were lost in transit so that these variations remain to be replicated.

the incorrect response; the experimenter did not judge responses. Phase B corresponded to Experiment I, i.e., the confederates gave incorrect responses which were called "right" by the experimenter. Phase C involved "private" written judgments by the subject, as in the two-phase experiments.

b. Experiment X. In the first phase, Phase A, the confederates gave the correct responses while the experimenter gave no verdict. Phase B corresponded to Experimenter III, i.e., the confederates gave correct responses which were called "right." Phase C was as above.

D. RESULTS

1. *Correct Responses*

Table 1 gives the percentages of correct responses to each card, the mean on all five cards, and the mean on the last four cards. The latter mean is presented because the experimenter's verdict could not have influenced the subject's response to Card 1 the first time it was shown (not even the second time in the three-phase experiments).

a. One-phase experiments. Experiment O, the control experiment, yielded only four incorrect responses among the 20 subjects, all of them occurring on the first card where the difference between the two lines is only 1/16 of an inch. All of the experimental variations yielded more incorrect responses than the control experiment, indicative of deleterious influences of the social forces.

From Experiments I through IV, correct responses increased monotonically as revealed by four of the five cards and by the means based on all the cards (40, 68, 80, and 88 per cent) or on the last four cards (50, 75, 90, and 95 per cent). The results suggest that the deleterious effects of the social influences were strongest when both the majority and the authority supported incorrect judgments (Experiment 1). That every subject in this variation failed Card 1 indicates the influence of the overheard responses in this rather difficult judgment situation, but cannot be attributed to the experimenter's verdict, since the subject responded to this card before any verdict was made.

Experiments II and IV allow comparison of the relative effectiveness of the confederates' answers and of the experimenter's verdict. In Experiment II the overheard responses support correct judgments and the verdict supports incorrect judgments, while the reverse is the case in Experiment IV. That the latter yielded more correct responses suggests that the authority was a more potent social influence than the majority.

Note that Experiment III, where correct judgments were given by the

TABLE 1
PERCENTAGES OF CORRECT RESPONSES

Experiment Phase		Confed. communications	Experimenters verdict	Ss	1	2	3	4	5	Mean 5	Mean last 4
0		none	none	20	80	100	100	100	100	96	100
I		incorrect	right	10	0	40	60	40	40	40	50
II		correct	wrong	10	40	60	100	80	80	68	75
III		correct	right	10	40	80	100	100	100	80	90
IV		incorrect	wrong	10	60	30	100	50	100	88	95
V	B	incorrect	right	10	70	40	70	70	50	54	50
	C	none	none	10	50	90	70	70	70	60	63
VI	B	correct	wrong	10	60	70	90	90	70	80	85
VII	C	none	none	10	10	100	80	90	90	68	83
	B	correct	right	10	90	100	100	90	100	96	98
VIII	C	none	none	10	80	100	100	100	100	96	100
	B	incorrect	wrong	10	70	100	100	100	100	94	100
IX	C	none	none	10	100	100	100	100	100	100	100
	A	incorrect	none	10	70	60	60	100	100	78	80
	B	incorrect	right	10	60	70	60	80	80	70	73
X	C	none	none	10	70	60	50	70	60	62	60
	A	none	right	10	70	90	100	100	100	92	98
	B	correct	right	10	90	100	100	100	100	98	100
	C	none	none	10	80	100	100	100	100	96	100

confederates and were called right, did not yield more correct responses (but, in fact, somewhat fewer) than Experiment IV, where the confederates gave incorrect responses that were called wrong. In other words, when the majority and the authority were both in accord with the objective evidence, their combined effects were not as great as when only the authority supported the evidence. Qualitative data hint that this result may be an artifact of some subjects' reluctance to give the overheard response because of a disinclination to copy or follow the crowd.

One day after the one-phase experiments, the experimenter informally met about half of the subjects individually on the campus, and showed them the cards again. Almost everyone gave correct responses now. When asked why they had yesterday given different responses, some of the subjects claimed erroneously that the cards they saw yesterday were not the same as the ones they saw now. One wonders what would happen if the experiment had been readministered to them the next day with the confederates responding.

b. Two-phase experiments. In Phase B (where the confederates responded and a right-wrong verdict was given), percentages of correct responses increased monotonically from Experiments V through VII, as revealed by each of the last four cards and by their mean (50, 85, 98, 100 per cent). Thus, the results point to the same trend as in the one-phase experiments. Since the procedure in Phase B was precisely that used in the one-phase experiments, the present trend corroborates that which prevailed in Experiments I through IV. Again we find that the strongest deleterious effects occurred when both the majority and the authority opposed the objective evidence; the next strongest when the majority gave correct responses rejected by the authority; and still less when the majority gave incorrect responses rejected by the authority. As in the one-phase experiments, when the two social forces were opposed, the authority won out over the majority (cf. Experiments VI and VIII) and the two forces did not necessarily work in an accumulative manner (cf. Experiments VII and VIII).

In Phase C (where the subject wrote his answers and where the confederates' responses and the verdict were not used) correct responses increased monotonically from Experiments V through VIII, as shown by the last four cards, by their means (63, 83, 100, 100 per cent), and by the means based on all the cards (60, 68, 96, 100 per cent). This is the same trend that prevailed in Phase B and in the one-phase experiments, a finding which suggests that the previous experience with the confederates' responses and the experimenter's verdict influenced the subject's "private" written responses, and that the influences operated with the same relative strength and in the same direction as before, although not always with the same intensity.

Note that Phase C used the procedure of the control experiment. Yet there were only four errors, all on the first card, contributed by the 20 control subjects, as compared to 36 errors, with 14 on the first card, contributed by the 20 subjects in Experiments V and VI. This result attests to the strength of the persisting influence of the social forces when the authority, or the authority together with the majority, previously supported incorrect responses.

Comparison of Phase B and C in each experiment reveals little consistency in responses to a given card. Of the 20 interexperimental comparisons of responses to the five cards, six show an increase of correct responses from Phase B to Phase C, five show a decrease, and nine show no change.

Both Phase B and Phase C tended to yield more correct responses than the corresponding one-phase experiment. Of the 20 comparisons, Phase B showed more correct responses than the corresponding one-phase experiment in 11 cases, less in four cases, and the same in five cases. Of the 20 comparisons, Phase C has more correct responses than the corresponding one-phase experiments in 11 cases, less in three cases, and the same in six cases.

Why these differences in results were obtained is not known. Experiments I through IV were done with Montreal students and the other experiments with Oregon students. There seemed to be some differences among the two sets of students with regard to attitudes and assumptions concerning psychology in general and the experiment in particular. These differences, as well as subtle differences in the social atmosphere of the experimental sessions and possible cultural differences, may have contributed to differences in results. More detailed explorations of these areas should be of value in replication of the experiments.

c. Three-phase experiments. In Experiment IX correct responses decreased monotonically from Phases A to B to C on three of the five cards and as shown by the means based on all the cards (78, 70, 62 per cent) and on the last four cards (80, 73, 60 per cent). That correct responses decreased from Phase A (confederates give incorrect responses and no verdict is given) to Phase B (confederates give incorrect responses which are called right) suggests that the majority alone was less effective in fostering objectively incorrect responses, than when combined with an authority. That Phase C (subject alone responds) yielded the least correct responses suggests that the influence of the social forces not only persisted, even though they were no longer explicitly introduced, but was even stronger than before. While repeated experience with the cards might have been expected to make subjects more apt at judging them and thereby yielded increases in objectively correct responses, we see that the opposite trend prevailed.

In Experiment X, where correct responses were supported by the majority (Phase A) and by the majority as well as the authority (Phase B), such responses increased monotonically from Phase A to B to C as shown by the last four cards and by their means (98, 100, 100 per cent). Since the social forces here operated in a direction opposed to that in Experiment IX, it is not surprising that the direction of results is reversed and that correct responses are considerably higher than in Experiment IX.

Returning to Experiment IX, we compare it with Experiment V, where the social forces also were opposed to objective reality. Comparison of the first phases of both variations show that Experiment V tended to have less correct responses than Experiment IX (a mean of 54 per cent based on all five cards for Experiment V as compared to 78 per cent for Experiment IX). This finding reveals again that the authority and majority together were considerably more effective in fostering errors than the majority by itself. Comparison of the first phase of Experiment V with the second phase of Experiment IX indicates that, despite the fact that the procedures were identical, the former had considerably less correct responses (a mean of 54 per cent based on all five cards as compared to 70 per cent for Experiment IX), perhaps an artifact of the preceding Phase A. This finding again indicates that the social forces did not necessarily operate in an accumulative manner, i.e., exposure to the majority and then to the majority and authority was not more effective in fostering incorrect responses than simply exposure to the majority and authority. Finally, comparison of the last phases of both experiments reveals little difference in results.

2. Qualitative Data

We first survey the qualitative data for those variations (Experiments I, V, IX) where all the social pressures were opposed to the objective evidence. Responses to the cards gave little indication of the explanations subjects offered for their responses when questioned after the experiment. For example, of three subjects in Experiment I who gave the same responses as the confederates in every card (and therefore were consistently called "right" although actually incorrect), one subject claimed that he was not influenced by the overheard responses or the experimenter's verdict, another said that he was influenced "a little bit," while the third admitted to considerable influence, saying, "I did not want to be the dumb one." Even some subjects who gave objectively correct answers to all or most cards claimed that it was uncomfortable or disconcerting to disagree with the others so often and to be called "wrong." For example, of two subjects in Experiment I who agreed with the overheard response only in Card 1, one said that he repressed an urge to repeat the overheard response and always reported what he saw while the other said "I agreed on one card; you can't help it" and admitted being concerned about disagreeing and being called "wrong" in the subsequent cards.

Among reasons subjects gave for objectively incorrect responses were (a) the belief that the cards involved perceptual illusions, and therefore the line that looked shorter was actually longer, (b) perceptual errors, particularly in Cards 1 and 2, (c) being unsure or becoming confused, (d) errors made deliberately because of a desire to be playful or to thwart the experimenter, and (e) suspicion of the experiment or the confederates or the experimenter. It is not known whether a given explanation actually was behind a particular response or was a subsequent rationalization. The most prevalent explanation referred to perceptual illusions. For example, in Experiment V, Phase B, eight out of 10 subjects referred to a belief that perceptual illusions were involved. Six of these admitted, upon subsequent questioning, that they were influenced by the social pressures, saying, "My perceptions changed when I listened to them" or "I said it (the response to a card) because you told the others that they were right" or a similar statement. Of two subjects who in Phase C gave the objectively correct answer only in Card 3, one subject said she became confused and therefore followed the others while the other subject said that she was not influenced by the overheard responses but was guided by the belief that the cards showed optical illusions; neither subject could account for the discrepancy between her response to Card 3 and the proferred explanation.

In short, various explanations were given, with the same explanation being given for diverse patterns of responses and different explanations for the same pattern.

When the confederates' responses were opposed in direction to the experimenter's verdict (Experiments II, IV, VI, VIII) subjects' suspicions or curiosity seemed to be aroused somewhat more than when all the social pressures worked in the same direction. For example, of 10 incorrect responses made in Phase B of Experiment VI (where correct responses were made by the confederates but rejected by the experimenter) two were explained as due to suspicion of the test and three as due to curiosity about what would happen if the objectively incorrect answers were given (in Cards 4 and 5); two other errors were explained as due to perceptual errors and the remaining three errors were attributed to a belief that perceptual illusions were involved. In Phase C of this experiment, everyone of the 10 subjects contributed to the 16 objectively incorrect responses. Two subjects each gave such responses in the first two or three cards and said that they did so because they were suspicious of the test; one person who gave incorrect responses throughout Phase C, explained that she had previously been troubled by being called "wrong"; the others gave an incorrect response only in Card 1 (because they did not want to be called wrong or because of a possible perceptual illusion) but shifted to the correct answers when they discovered that the experimenter was not going to judge them on this trial.

When incorrect responses were given by the confederates and rejected by the experimenter, subjects generally appeared quite surprised that the confederates were repeatedly wrong. A few suspected that it was being done purposely, e.g., one asked the confederates, "What are you gals trying to do?" In Experiment IV (done in Montreal), some subjects volunteered to help the confederates; in Experiment VIII (done in Oregon), no one volunteered to help but some offered free advice concerning eyesight to the confederates, e.g., "You had better have your eyes examined." One Oregon subject grinned and seemed quite amused when the others were called wrong but puzzlement and discomfiture were the more usual reactions.

When the confederates and the experimenter supported objective reality (Experiments III, VII, X), only six errors occurred on a card other than the first. One was made by a subject who did not want to follow the crowd; two were made by two subjects who claimed later that they answered incorrectly just to see what would happen; and the others were made by subjects who suspected that the confederates were trying to mislead them. Incorrect responses to Card 1 were attributed mainly to perceptual errors. Most subjects in these variations said that they were not influenced and that they reported what they saw.

E. Suggestions for Future Research

In line with a variational approach (4), suggestions for research may be derived through variations of different factors, guided by the objective of maximizing or minimizing agreement with correct or incorrect judgments.

1. *Objective Evidence*

The strength of this factor may be heightened by providing subjects with rulers with which to measure the lines; it may be weakened by exposing the cards for shorter periods or at greater distances from the perceivers. The order of clarity of the material may be varied, e.g., by presenting the present cards in reverse order, from Card 5 to Card 1. Other material may be used, involving different degrees of clarity or ambiguity and various possibilities of structurization (3). Among material which may be used are descriptions of a person on the basis of which judgments are to be made concerning his personality (5) as well as so-called Einstellung series (1, 7), composed of such descriptions, or composed of volume-measuring problems, anagrams, mazes, etc.

2. *Majority*

This factor may be strengthened by using groups whose members agree to abide by the rule of the majority (either because of group decision or because of experimentally-introduced experiences). This factor may be varied through the use of fewer or more confederates or confederates who stand in various relationships of prestige or authority to the subject, or who belong or do not belong to the subject's peer group; it may be varied by having more than one naive subject present or by having a "confused" or non-unanimous majority, with some of the confederates agreeing with the evidence (or with the naive subject or subjects) while others disagree, and having this occur in every judgment situation or only some of them. The factor may also be varied by altering the order of responding, e.g., by letting the subject, in some trials or in all trials, respond before some or all of the confederates.

3. *Authority*

This factor may be strengthened by using subjects who agree to abide by the voice of the authority (because of group decision or because of previous-provided experiences in which they learn to rely on the experimenter or because of the nature of their relationship to the experimenter or to another person who serves as the authority). The factor may be varied by using material in which the experimenter, or another person serving as the authority, is known to be an expert or, at least, is known to be apt or not known to be inapt. An impersonal source may serve as the authority, e.g., a list of "right" answers. Material may be used which lends itself more or less adequately to the use of an authority. The nature of the relationship between the authority and the subject or between the authority and the majority may also be varied. The consequences of giving a response other than that wanted by the authority may be varied so that they are more or less serious than a verdict of "wrong," and so that there are consequences for subsequent action by the subject.

4. *Subjects*

This factor may be varied through the use of subjects who (because of different backgrounds or experimentally provided experiences) have diverse attitudes toward and assumptions about the experiment, the majority, the experimenter or other authority, the judgments and the motivations for being "right" or winning the authority's approval or the majority's approval. Experiments are needed in which the subject himself is an authority. For example, in a preliminary study, where the task was to give the next term in an arithmetical or geometrical series, there was no adverse influence on subjects' responses when the subjects were mathematics majors while the confederates were not specializing in mathematics; when these roles were reversed, there was considerable influence on responses. Experiments of this sort are needed to learn more about the role of the expert in conformity situations.

5. *Conditions of testing*

Conditions of testing may be varied by telling subjects, just before Phase C that the others (the confederates) will not see his written responses and that these will not be judged by the experimenter in the others' presence. On the other hand, in another variation, subjects may be told, just before Phase C, that the others will see his written responses and/or that his written responses will be judged in the others' presence. Another variation is to introduce a phase, in lieu of or in addition to the present Phase C, in which the subject alone responds, but orally rather than in written form. Still another variation is to have a phase in which the subject responds (in written or oral form) after the confederates leave the room. Phase C or subsequent retesting may be done in a place other than that in which the previous testing took place, in an attempt to intensify the difference between test and retest conditions.

F. SUMMARY

Experiments with 120 college subjects explored various social influences on judgments of the relative lengths of two line segments. Five cards were used, each containing a drawing of a small square with two line segments, labeled 1 and 2, jutting out from the square at different angles. One line segment was one inch long throughout while the other was 15/16, 14/16, 12/16, 10/16, and 8/16 of an inch in Cards 1 through 5, respectively. The announced task was to name the shorter of the two lines in each card.

In a control experiment only the subject judged the lines. In the one-phase experiments the subject overheard three pre-instructed individuals (the experimenters' confederates) respond to a card before it was shown to him; after the subject responded, and before the next card was presented, the experimenter labeled responses as "right" or "wrong." In the two-phase experiments, after the just-described procedure, the cards were readministered to the subject who responded in writing without overhearing the confederates although they were present; no right-wrong verdict was given by the experimenter. The three-phase experiments began with a phase in which the subject overheard the confederates but no right-wrong verdict was used; the subsequent administrations of the cards were as in the two-phase experiments.

The 20 control subjects contributed only four errors, all on the first card, where the difference in length between the two lines is smaller than on the other cards. Every experimental variation, regardless of whether the confederates gave correct or incorrect responses and regardless of what verdict the experimenter gave, yielded more incorrect responses than the control experiment, suggestive of a negative influence of the social forces even when they were both in accord with the objective evidence. In each set of experiments, the fewest correct responses occurred when both the majority (the confederates) and the authority (the experimenter) opposed the objective evidence, i.e., when the confederates consistently gave incorrect responses and such responses were called "right." The next strongest deleterious effects occurred when the authority opposed and the confederates supported the objective evidence; less deleterious effects occurred when these roles were reversed. This result indicates that when the majority and authority operated in opposing directions, the authority tended to have the stronger influence. When the majority and the authority were both in accord with the objective evidence, their combined effects were not as great (in terms of yielding correct responses) as when only the authority supported the evidence while the majority was opposed to it, suggesting that the social forces did not operate in an accumulative manner. That correct responses decreased from a phase in which the confederates gave incorrect responses and no verdict was given, to a phase in which the confederates' incorrect responses were called right, suggests that the majority alone was less effective in fostering incorrect responses than when combined with an authority.

When the subject responded in writing, his "private" judgments suggested that the social influences, although no longer explicitly introduced, were still operating in the same direction and with the same relative strength as before, although not always with the same intensity.

When subjects were questioned after the experiment, they attributed their objectively incorrect responses to perceptual errors, to a belief that optical illusions were involved (a prevalent response), to a desire not to disagree or not to be called wrong (another frequent response), to becoming confused or unsure of themselves, to suspicion of the experimenter or the confederates or the experiment, to a desire not to copy when the confederates gave correct responses, to deliberate attempts to name what was wrong in order to see what would happen or in order to be playful or to thwart the experimenter. While some subjects admitted being influenced by the confederates and the experimenter, others (even some who gave incorrect responses in every card) insisted that they were not influenced or were only slightly influenced. It is not known if subjects' explanations were merely rationalizations.

Suggestions were made for future research in terms of variations of the objective evidence, the majority, the authority, the subjects, and conditions of testing.

REFERENCES

1. LUCHINS, A. S. Mechanization in problem solving. *Psychol. Monog.*, 1942, **54**, 1-95.
2. ————. On agreement with another's judgments. *J. Abnorm. & Soc. Psychol.*, 1945, **39**, 97-111.
3. ————. On the description of the stimulus field in social psychology. *Psychol. Rev.*, 1950, **57**, 27-30.
4. ————. A variational approach to phenomena in social psychology. In *Emerging Problems in Social Psychology*, M. Sherif and M. O. Wilson, *Eds.* Norman, Oklahoma: Univ. Book Exchange, 1957.
5. ————. Primacy-recency in impression formation. In *The Order of Presentation in Persuasion*, Carl I. Hovland et al., *Eds.* New Haven: Yale Univ. Press, 1957.
6. LUCHINS, A. S., & LUCHINS, E. H. On conforming with true and false communications. *J. Soc. Psychol.*, 1955, **42**, 283-304.
7. ————. Rigidity of Behavior. Eugene, Oregon: Univ. Oregon Press, 1959.

Department of Psychology
University of Miami
Coral Gables 46, Florida

Dissonance and Attitude Change

We often find ourselves in situations which necessitate expressing opinions contrary to private beliefs or behaving in a manner that is inconsistent with our private opinions or characteristic mode of behavior. A nondrinker, for example, may find it socially expedient to have a drink when at a social function. A prejudiced businessman may find it necessary to be friendly toward Negroes to attract their business. A clergyman may discourage Negroes from attending his church to retain certain white parishioners' support.

There are, of course, endless examples of people behaving contrary to their personal convictions, and one might wonder if such behavior affects one's original attitudes. Does the bigot, for example, become more tolerant if he must publicly express opinions which lead others to think he is tolerant (e.g., a prejudiced politician seeking Negro support)? The answer seems to be "yes." Many researchers have found that one's delivering a short talk or writing an essay advocating a position opposite his own, in general does result in changes in the role player's attitudes in the direction advocated in the talk or essay. This effect seems to be magnified by several variables such as effort, volition (i.e., the subject's felt freedom to refuse participation), and social support.

There are several alternative explanations to account for this phenomenon. One might argue, for example, that simple rehearsal of the opposing point of view is sufficient for attitude change in that it forces the subject to review and pay attention to (perhaps for the first time) the bases for views opposing his own.

A second explanation is based upon dissonance theory. The reader may recall Festinger's theory of cognitive dissonance which maintains that persons are psychologically uncomfortable when they entertain logically inconsistent cognitions. People who espouse opinions contrary to their own may be considered to be in a state of dissonance. If one believes, for example, that a particular minority group should be segregated from the nation's majority but publicly states the opposite, these two cognitions (public *vs.* private opinions) are in an obverse relationship. The cognitive consistency (consonance) principle maintains that either the individual's public or his private attitude must change unless, of course, he can justify the logic of the inconsistency (e.g., being well paid to espouse views opposite one's own or seeking election).

It is very difficult in most experimental situations, to determine which of the above two hypotheses is, in fact, correct. The laboratory experiment for this session is a test of the dissonance interpretation. Subjects will be asked to espouse attitudes at variance to their own. The dissonance experienced by subjects will be manipulated, whereas the rehearsal factor will be kept constant. After the experimental manipulation the subject's private attitude will be measured.

The "Before–After" and the "After–Only" Experimental Design

If an experimenter is concerned with the effects of a certain experimental manipulation upon a subject's attitude, the obvious design might seem to be that of measuring the subject's attitude both before and after the experimental treatment and then simply examining the two measures to determine if any change is apparent. Although there is much to recommend this design, there is one basic difficulty with administering the same or a similar attitude measuring instrument to the same subject as part of an experiment. The basic difficulty is, of course, that the subject remembers that his attitudes have previously been "measured." This, in turn, may result in the subject's disguising any true attitude change. Measuring attitudes before the experimental treatment may also alert the subjects to the fact that the experimenter's interest has something to do with attitudes. This type of situation, which might be called a "transparent experiment," may result in subjects resisting the effects of the experimenter's manipulations, biasing or falsifying their responses, etc.

A design which, in part, controls for some of the above biases is the "after-only." This design, as the name implies, involves measuring the subject's attitude only after exposure to the experimental treatment. Thus, the subject is less likely to be alerted to the experimenter's purpose and less likely to be resistant to the effects of the manipulations.

The after-only design is, however, based upon two assumptions: First, that the attitude in question is of a nature that permits the experimental variable to have an effect. If, for example, one were interested in increasing the subject's assurance that the world was round, the experiment is likely doomed to failure since virtually

100% of the potential experimental subjects are 100% sure that the world is, in fact, round. In short, without prior measurements, the experimenter must have an understanding of his subject population so that he is reasonably certain of the relative intensity and complexity of the attitude being manipulated and also certain that the change anticipated is possible.

Second, the experimenter must take precautions against any biased population sampling so that the crucial assumption of comparable populations in each group is not violated. That is, if the attitude is measured only after the experimental manipulation one must be sure that the different groups did not differ, with respect to the attitude in question, before the manipulation. If the samples did differ at the outset one may not conclude that any difference observed at the end of the experiment resulted from the experimental manipulation.

INSTRUCTIONS

Experimental Team Size: Entire laboratory class with three or four main participants.

Subjects: Arrange for one group of at least 14 naive subjects, preferably all of the same sex, for the experimental sample. Also, make arrangements to test an additional seven or more control subjects. This is usually quite easy to arrange at most universities by asking introductory psychology students to volunteer. Some universities have a general pool of student subjects from which you might draw. The instructor will give the method for obtaining subjects and assign someone to be responsible for obtaining the experimental sample.

Apparatus: Paper; pencils; watch with second hand; attitude scales.

Experimental Situation: Experimental subjects are asked to write a short essay on a topic, but taking a position opposite to their own personal opinion. After the essay is completed, the subjects are divided into two groups. Each subject in group A is required to deliver a one-minute presentation of the important points made in his essay in front of the entire lab class. Each subject in group B is required to deliver his main points for one minute to only one person. After the presentations, the subjects complete an attitude measurement scale to assess the effects of the dissonance produced by the class presentation upon attitude change in the direction of the communication.

Control Subjects: Control subjects are asked to complete the questionnaire without any experimental manipulation (i.e., no essay writing nor rehearsal). The questionnaire may be administered to control subjects at a time more convenient than the experimental session since it only requires a minute or so to complete. It might be possible, for example, to obtain permission from a professor to administer the questionnaire to a small class during the last few minutes of the class period.

Procedure: Experimental Group

1. Duplicate a sufficient number of attitude scales (Fig. 2.1).

S # _____

Please answer the following questions:

1. At what age do you think persons should be permitted to drive?

_____ years old.

2. Out of every 100 automobile accidents, how many do you think were *caused* by persons under 21?

_____ out of 100.

3. Out of every 100 automobile accidents, how many do you think *involve* persons under 21?

_____ out of 100.

FIG. 2.1. Attitude scale.

2. Arrange to have subjects arrive at a specified laboratory time.

3. Have two class members take charge of seating the subjects in a separate room. Do not permit talking, and take care not to disclose the experimental manipulations. That is, keep the subjects unaware of the fact that the laboratory class is waiting nearby and offer no other information. Respond to any questions of procedure, purpose, and so on, with the simple statement: "The instructions I shall give in a moment will answer your questions."

4. After all subjects are seated, pass out sheets of paper and pencils and give the following instructions to the entire group:

"We are interested in the quality of essays that can be written arguing in favor of specific positions. We are varying the amount of time to write such essays and your group, today, will have just 15 minutes. When I say 'go,' write the most persuasive argument you can on the topic I mention, regardless of whether or not you personally favor such a position. Any questions?"

At this time, the experimenter should answer any questions on the essay writing procedure. Do not mention anything about what will happen later, and do not mention the topic.

5. After the subjects are ready, state:

"The topic is 'Why I favor raising the legal age for driving an automobile to 21.' You may begin."

6.   a. Allow exactly 15 minutes for the subjects to write.

     b. During the 15-minute session the experimenters will randomly assign the subjects to experimental conditions as follows:

On a separate piece of paper for each subject present in the room, write the following code: A_1, A_2, A_3, ..., $A_{1/2n}$ and B_1, B_2, B_3, ..., $B_{1/2n}$. The letter refers to experimental group A or B and the numbers indicate the order in which the subjects receive the manipulation. Mix up the 14 (or more, if there are more than 14 subjects) pieces of paper.

7. After exactly 15 minutes tell the subjects to stop.

8. Have one experimenter draw one number and give it to each subject. Do not permit any talking among the subjects.

Group A Subjects

1. Leaving one experimenter with the group at all times, have the second experimenter take subject A_1 (with his essay) out of the room, *but not into the laboratory*. Once in private the experimenter gives subject A_1 the following instructions:

"We are only interested in the points you consider most important in your essay. Please read it through once more."

2. Wait until the subject has finished, then state:

"I would like you to state your major points to a group of people who will record them. You will have exactly one minute to state the major arguments. You don't mind, do you?"

(*Important:* Although the subject has been given the opportunity to refuse, the experimenter should act as though he takes it for granted that the subject will talk before the group. Subjects are likely to become very anxious at this time because of the anticipated "public" presentation. Since this is the major manipulation creating considerable dissonance owing to the greater effort, anxiety, fear, etc., associated with the presentation of a counternorm argument, it is imperative that the experimenter must not say or do anything which might destroy the effect. The experimenter must only repeat what has been said in the instructions should the subject ask further questions.)

Bring the subject into the laboratory in front of the class and tell him to begin. The class should have pencils and paper in front of them and simulate note taking during the presentation.

3. After exactly one minute, stop the subject, take him from the room, and in a *separate* room (i.e., not with other subjects) give him the attitude measure with the following instructions:

"Thank you very much for your help. Before you leave, we would like to have some indication of your personal attitude on the driving age issue since it may have affected the major points you made. Please fill out this questionnaire."

4. Leaving subject A_1 to fill out the questionnaire, the experimenter calls subject A_2 and follows the same group A procedure.

5. Collect and code all the essays and questionnaires from the subjects.

Group B Subjects

1. Have the third experimenter take subject B_1 out of the room. When in private, the following instructions should be given:

"We are only interested in the points you consider most important in your essay. Please read it through once more."

2. Wait until the subject has finished, then state:

"I would like you to tell me the major points, which I will record. You will have exactly 1 minute to state the major arguments."

3. The experimenter should then take a pencil and paper, tell the subject to please begin and simulate note taking. Allow exactly 1 minute, then stop the subject.

4. Take the subject to a separate room and follow the same procedure (item 3) as for group A (attitude measurement).

5. Leaving subject B_1, repeat the process for subject B_2, and so on.

6. Collect and code all essays and questionnaires from each subject.

7. After all subjects are finished, explain the study in detail and answer all questions.

(*Note:* It is most important that subjects not be allowed to communicate. The procedures should be well established under the instructor's supervision before any subjects are used. The greatest source of error in this experiment is the experimenter's interaction with the subjects. Procedure, instructions, and even the experimenter's assumed mood must be well rehearsed in the laboratory before the study begins.)

Data Analysis

Content of essays. Divide the class into groups of two. Have each group of students read the essays and record in a table, similar in form to Table 2.1, the number of points the subject makes favoring increasing the driving age. Record each point whether good or bad, but do not record the same point twice (i.e., the subject may say the same thing in different ways). Each class group must read and score the essays independently of the other class groups so that one team does not bias the other team's ratings.

TABLE 2.1

NUMBER OF POINTS MADE IN ESSAY FAVORING INCREASING THE DRIVING AGE

Subject	No. of points	Subject	No. of points
A_1	X_{a1}	B_1	X_{b1}
A_2	X_{a2}	B_2	X_{b2}
A_3	X_{a3}	B_3	X_{b3}
.	.	.	.
.	.	.	.
.	.	.	.
A_n	X_{an}	B_n	X_{bn}

Reliability of content analysis. Whenever responses are being measured, the reliability of the measurement instrument should be determined. For example, if one were measuring the speed of runners in a race with a stopwatch, the watch should be tested against a known standard time interval. If a 10-second standard interval were sometimes recorded as 9 seconds and other times as 12 seconds, one would conclude that the watch was not a reliable instrument for measuring the speed of the runners. The same principle holds when judges are rating a subject's responses. Instead of comparing the raters against some known standard, which is frequently not possible, one usually determines the degree of agreement between two or more independent judges.

In the present case, several teams have rated the content of the subjects' essays. To determine whether the teams have made reliable judgments one could statistically determine the degree of agreement between each team.

For the purposes of the present exercise, a graphic method will be used. For each subject, plot the ratings (i.e., number of points made in the essay in favor of increasing the driving age) of each class-rating team in a form similar to Fig. 2.2. The reliability of the ratings is indicated by the shape of the curve in the graphs. A perfectly flat line (e.g., if all rating teams rated subject A_1's essay as containing four points) would indicate perfect intergroup reliability. The more the line deviates from a flat line, the poorer the reliability.

EXPERIMENT 2

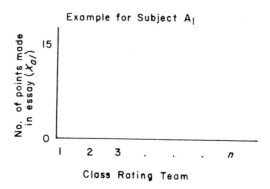

FIG. 2.2. Example for subject A_1.

It would be useful to have a class discussion during which several teams, whose rating of a particular subject greatly differs from the class average (i.e., those rating teams whose judgments shown on the reliability curve are very high or low relative to the other teams), explain their ratings to determine if the differences are because of error or real differences of opinion.

For the purpose of the present experimental exercise, any reliability curve which exceeds a range of plus or minus one point from a straight line should be reevaluated by every rating team. For example, if the ratings of the points made in a subject's essay range from, say, three to five points (i.e., a line at the four-point level with no single points exceeding five or less then three), need not be reevaluated.

Pool the class data, compute the mean of the group judgments, and enter in a table such as Table 2.2 (where TP stands for total points made by group).

For example, take all the class groups' ratings of the number of points made in subject A_1's essay:

X_{a1} Class rating group 1
X_{a1} Class rating group 2
X_{a1} Class rating group 3

.

.

.

X_{a1} Class rating group n

——————

ΣX_{a1}

Mean $X_{a1} = \Sigma X_{a1}/n$

where n is the number of rating groups.

Attitude Measurement. Record the subjects' responses and compute averages for each question as shown in Tables 2.3, 2.4, and 2.5 (where TQ stands for group total for each question).

Plot a histogram of the average group A score for each question, the group B score for each question and the control group score (from Tables 2.3, 2.4, and 2.5) in a form similar to Fig. 2.3.

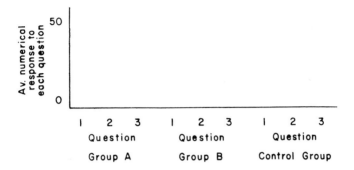

FIG. 2.3. Form for histogram.

TABLE 2.2
POOLED DATA

Subjects	Group A	Group B
1	$\Sigma X_{a\,1/n}$	$\Sigma X_{b\,1/n}$
2		
3		
.		
.		
.		
n		
TP		

From Table 2.2, divide each experimental group in two halves, according to the number of points made in their essays. Rank the subjects in each group, starting with one for the subject who makes the fewest points. Count up one-half of the ranks in each group and designate as group A—low and group B—low. The remaining halves designate as group A—high and group B—high. Record the mean total questionnaire scores for each group as in Table 2.6.

Plot a histogram of the data in Table 2.6.

TABLE 2.3
GROUP A

Questions	Subjects						TQ	$\bar{X}$
	1	2	·	·	·	n		
1								
2								
3								

TABLE 2.4
GROUP B

Questions	Subjects						TQ	$\bar{X}$
	1	2	·	·	·	n		
1								
2								
3								

TABLE 2.5
CONTROL GROUP

Questions	Subjects						TQ	$\bar{X}$
	1	2	·	·	·	n		
1								
2								
3								

TABLE 2.6
NUMBER OF POINTS MADE IN ESSAY

	Top half	Bottom half
Group A		
Group B		

Experimental Report

1. Did the experimental manipulation have the expected effect upon attitudes? That is, are the experimental groups more inclined toward negative opinion of under-21 drivers than are the control subjects?

2. Do the trends support the notion that increased effort, anxiety,

etc., associated with the presentation of the subject's argument increase attitude change in the direction of the argument?

3. Does any question on the scale appear to be more sensitive (show more change) than the others?

4. Is there a relationship between the number of points made on the essay and attitude change?

5. Is there any reason to believe that the groups differed before the experiment started with respect to the attitude in question? (Compare TP for group A vs. TP for group B in Table 2.2.)

Reprinted from Journal of Experimental Social Psychology, 1965, Vol. 1, pp. 103–120, by permission of the author and the publisher.

The Effect of Effort and Improvisation on Self-Persuasion Produced by Role-Playing[1]

Philip G. Zimbardo

One of the more reliable findings in the area of attitude change is the greater modification of attitudes following role-playing than following passive exposure to persuasive communications. "Role-playing" is the blanket term for a wide variety of procedures in which a subject is induced to enact the behavior of another person (usually someone disliked) or to assume and publicly espouse a set of opinions with which he disagrees.

Although there has been considerable variability in the operational use of role-playing (from classroom debate to psychodrama), all of the studies share the minimal requirement of the technique that the subject become involved in the attempt to render, sincerely and convincingly, the attitude position of another person. This essential abstracted from the traditional method (cf. Bronfenbrenner and Newcomb, 1948; Sarbin, 1954; Moreno, 1958) may indeed be the most useful one for influencing attitudes. Unfortunately, however, there has been little systematic evaluation of the variables involved in the complex process of role-playing, probably because the assumed therapeutic value of the technique and its popularity in educational and industrial circles have made for its uncritical acceptance as a whole.

The self-persuasion which occurs as a consequence of effective role-playing is also interesting because it does not fit the typical attitude-change model. In the self-persuasion paradigm the target of one's persuasion attempt is the communicator himself. The change in attitude is thus the result of a person's communication to himself of a counternorm position. There is ample anecdotal evidence to support the generalization that attitude change occurs when one behaves in a manner discrepant with

[1] This research has been supported by a grant from the Quartermaster Food and Container Institute for the Armed Forces, QM Research and Engineering Command, U. S. Army. It has also received supplementary support from the Yale Attitude Change Program under the direction of Irving L. Janis. The views or conclusions contained in this report are solely those of the author and are not to be construed as necessarily reflecting the views or endorsement of the Department of Defense.

his private attitudes and values. However, the question arises of why anyone *would* engage in behavior that is contrary to his beliefs. Moreover, the question becomes more perplexing in the light of the large body of field and laboratory evidence demonstrating that people do not voluntarily expose themselves to ideas, situations, or communications which disagree with their attitudes (cf. Lipset *et al.*, 1954; Festinger, 1957).

The inevitable answer to which we are led is that some external force must induce behavioral compliance: either a reward providing positive incentive for engaging in discrepant behavior, or a punishment for failure to do so. Therefore, although in self-persuasion situations there is no external communicator, there is, nevertheless, some external control over the subject's reinforcement schedule.

One of the few systematic attempts to explore the variables in role-playing which influence attitude change has been the series of studies by Janis and the Yale Attitude Change Program (cf. Janis and King, 1954; King and Janis, 1956; Hovland *et al.*, 1953). In an attempt to understand their empirical finding that "overt verbalization induced through role-playing tends to augment the effectiveness of a persuasive communication," they isolate the variable of *improvisation* as a major determinant in the acceptance of new ideas.

Subjects who were required to improvise a speech contrary to their own position adjusted their attitudes to conform with their role behavior more than did subjects who were required to read a prepared speech opposing their own position, although both the improvised and prepared speeches contained similar arguments and conclusions.

To account for this finding and a related one of Kelman (1953), the experimenters offer the cognitive explanation that attitude change results when a person incorporates new statements into the "repertoire of responses" associated with his attitude position. Therefore, attitude change is facilitated when a given overt response is supported by implicit responses, and is impeded when implicit responses interfere with the overt response: "Improvised role-playing might have been successful in helping to overcome resistance by reducing the intensity of those internal responses which normally interfere with the acceptance of persuasive messages" (King and Janis, 1956, p. 183). The "improvisation-interfering response hypothesis" thus stresses the importance of self-stimulation, since in thinking of new supporting arguments the person is forced to consider "cogent illustrations," "impressive appeals," "convincing thought-sequences," and "vivid anticipations."

In explaining the importance of "the improvisation factor as a crucial one in determining the effects of active participation" (Hovland *et al.*, 1953, p. 233), a related line of argument is also advanced. The act of improvising a speech discrepant with one's position is viewed as an internal debate in which the subject constructs a communication designed to attack the defenses and weaknesses he knows best while offering arguments most understandable to him. In short, improvisation provides an opportunity to "hand-tailor the material to suit" his own resisting self.

This formulation has recently been questioned. "The concept of improvisation is not yet well defined either conceptually or empirically. Although the effects of improvisation are said to be self-persuasion through good arguments and reduced resistance to change through suppression of interfering responses, . . . the conditions that produce such improvisation have not been clearly stated" (Brehm and Cohen, 1962, p. 252). Festinger's theory of cognitive dissonance (1957) subsumes role-playing under the area "forced public compliance." The knowledge that one's public behavior does not follow from his relevant private attitudes creates in him the motivational state of dissonance. If the discrepant role-playing behavior is entirely *justifiable* in light of the magnitude of the force used to induce the compliance (i.e., a large reward, serious threat, or some positive aspect of the inducing agent), then this third cognition is consonant with the overt behavior, and there should be little change in attitude. However, what if the inducement to comply is just sufficient to force the performance of the act, but not strong enough either to justify the behavior completely or to deny volition in the decision? The perception of one's overt behavior, being constrained by reality, is difficult to alter; consequently, the now-dissonant private attitude, much less resistant, is changed. This theory maintains that the attitude change occasioned by role-playing is a dissonance-reducing device, designed to make private attitudes consonant with public behavior.

It follows that the extent of the change in attitude will be governed by those variables which control the magnitude of the dissonance. One such variable, which may be central to an understanding of role-playing effects, is the amount of *effort* required in the performance of discrepant behavior. This variable, absent from the original formulation of the theory (Festinger, 1957), has since been regarded a major determinant of dissonance (cf. Cohen, 1959, 1960; Festinger and Aronson, 1960; Aronson, 1961; Brehm and Cohen, 1962). For example, Lawrence and Festinger (1962) employ a dissonance theory explanation to account for their findings that resistance to extinction *increases* as the effort required to perform a learned task increases: "The information that the animal has concerning the expenditure of energy and effort is dissonant with continuing to engage in the action . . . the greater the effort required, the greater would be the magnitude of dissonance. . . ." Consequently, the organism "will develop some extra attraction for the activity or its consequences in order to give itself additional justification for continuing to engage in the behavior" (p. 156).

Aronson (1961) has attempted to demonstrate that the degree of effort expended in attempting to obtain a series of goal objects results in the development of an extra attraction for the stimulus color associated with the unrewarded trials. Cohen (1959) manipulated "mental effort" also in human subjects by leading them to expect different degrees of concentration necessary to understand a communication. His results revealed that for subjects with a moderate discrepancy between their initial attitudes and the discrepant stand taken in the communication, attitude change was greatest under low effort conditions, but when the discrepancy was large, then the predicted dissonance effect of greater change with greater effort was obtained. Unfortunately, an unambiguous interpretation of attitude change in terms of differential effort cannot be made from this study, because attitude discrepancy was a correlational variable rather than an independently manipulated one. Therefore, the effects of effort may be a consequence of unknown sources of variance associated with systematic differences in initial attitude.

The present study may be viewed in part as a test of the general derivation from dissonance theory that the amount of attitude change toward an object or goal is a function of the magnitude of the barriers or aversive stimuli to be overcome in attaining the goal. The major hypothesis to be tested is that the greater the physical effort required in publicly reading and understanding a communication discrepant from one's own attitude, the greater will be the resulting dissonance and consequent attitude change in the direction advocated by the role performance. Thus, changing one's attitude (at least the affective component of attitude) may be equated with the concept of "developing an extra attraction" for the consequences of the effortful activity, i.e., liking or approving of its conclusion or its recommendation for action. Effort, then, may function to increase dissonance by serving as a barrier to goal attainment, or as an aversive stimulus to be endured in the process of making goal responses. It may also operate by increasing the salience and irrevocability of the discrepant public performance.

A second aim of the present study is to come to terms with the improvisation explanation of self-persuasion in role-playing. According to a dissonance theory formulation, the effects of improvisation upon attitude change can be traced to the increased effort that improvisation requires, the value of improvisation being a consequence of its mediating motivational properties rather than the "cognitive-intellectual" aspects of improvisation having to do with its content or quality per se.

METHOD

Two experiments were performed,[2] the first of which was designed primarily to assess the feasibility and efficacy of the manipulation of effort, and will be presented only in summary fashion. A detailed exposition of experimental procedures and data analyses will be reserved for the second study.

Experiment One

Procedure

As part of an alleged survey from a national research institute, all students in the introductory psychology course at University College of New York University ($N = 150$) indicated their attitudes toward 10 topics of local and national interest. The attitude topic chosen for experimental manipulation was "the letter versus numerical grading system in college" because it was rated as involving and yielded a wide range of opinions. The majority of students favored the numerical grading system (0–100) and 20 students were randomly selected from among this group to serve as experimental subjects (Ss). Each S in the experiment was told he was participating in a study of the determinants of verbal behavior and would, therefore, be asked to perform some verbal tasks under special experimental conditions. The major task was to read a prepared speech as convincingly and as perfectly as possible. The speech was a 300-word communication strongly in favor of a system of letter grades as final course evaluations.

Effort Manipulation

The amount of effort required to read the communication aloud was manipulated by varying the interval of delay between speaking and hearing. Pretesting with a specially designed delayed auditory feedback apparatus (DAF) had established that 0.3-second delay produced considerable speech disruption, while a delay of 0.01 second had only negligible effects on speech. A consequence of the longer delay was an increased amount of perceived effort expended in order to overcome speech (and even thought) disruption. Accordingly, half of the Ss were randomly assigned to the High Effort condition (long feedback delay), while half were put in the Low Effort condition (minimal feedback delay). An attempt to check on the effectiveness of the manipulation was made by asking Ss to indicate on a 5-point scale their impression of how hard it was to read the report, as well as by observation and interview of each subject.

Attitude change. Immediately after two successive public readings of the report

---

[2] The author wishes to express his gratitude to his undergraduate honors students who assisted with the testing of the Ss: Ken Fink, Shep Siegel, and Leslie Wolfson; and to Robert Formica, Mat Weisenberg, and Ira Firestone, who made valuable analytic contributions. No effects attributable to experimenter differences were found in either study, except on the measure of psychological effort, which was slightly higher for Ss run by the author.

(to increase comprehension of its content), S's opinion was elicited toward the critical topic of grading as well as three "control" topics (i.e., no communication, but measured in the initial survey and after the DAF experience). A 7-point attitude scale was used which ranged from "extremely in favor" to "extremely against" the issue. Attitude change is the net difference between pre- and postcommunication attitude ratings on the critical and control topics.

Results

Comprehension. There were no differences between groups in the learning of the content of the communication as measured by a recall test on which both groups correctly recalled a mean of 4.4 items out of a possible 6.

Effort. Although observation of the Ss' experimental behavior (e.g., straining neck muscles, clenching fists) as well as their spontaneous interview comments clearly indicated that greater effort was expended by those in the longer delay condition, the self-report scale does not reveal a significant difference. On the 5-point scaled question of how hard it was to read the report, the Long Delay group mean is 3.0, while it is 2.2 for the Short Delay group ($t = 1.65$, $df = 18$, $p = .13$).[3] It was expected that the obtained difference in the predicted direction could be increased by use of a scale not so narrow in its range, and by removing the ambiguity of its wording (the possible confounding of the mechanics of delivery with the understanding of the content).

Attitude change. (a) There were no differences between the two effort conditions in attitude change on any of the three control topics (starting an honor system, increasing the proportion of coeds,. establishing a free city university). In fact, the mean change for each of the control topics was approximately zero. (b) On the experimental topics, the act of publicly reading a communication contrary to one's private beliefs produced in both effort conditions an amount of attitude change significantly greater than chance ($p < .01$). (c) The effectiveness of the persuasive communication was increased by having it publicly read under conditions which *maximized* the amount of effort necessary to comprehend the communication and make it comprehensible. While the mean change for the Low Effort treatment was $+1.60$ units, the mean change for the High Effort treatment was $+2.30$. This difference, in the predicted direction, falls short of statistical significance ($t = 1.67$, $df = 18$, $p = .13$). These trends in the expected direction, though not significant, encouraged a more thorough attack on the problem and led to a second experiment the following academic year.

[3] All probability values reported are for two-tailed tests of significance.

Experiment Two

General Design

A before-after attitude change design was again utilized in which *S*s publicly presented a speech which advocated a position discrepant from their own. Half of the *S*s again read a prepared speech, while half improvised a speech from a prepared outline of arguments. The effort involved in presenting the speech was manipulated so that half of the *S*s in each communication condition were randomly assigned to a High Effort condition (i.e., long interval of delayed feedback), with the rest of the *S*s in a Low Effort condition (i.e., short interval of delay). This basic 2×2 factorial design was supplemented by a fifth group which served as a no-communication control. Since every *S* also listened passively to a persuasive communication as well as presented one actively, this variable could be tested by within-group comparisons.

Method

Subjects

Eighty undergraduate students at University College fulfilled part of a requirement of their introductory psychology course by participating for 1 hour in this experiment. Sixty were in the experimental group (16 females and 44 males),[4] while 20 were in the control group (5 females and 15 males). They were selected from among a population of 300 students given a survey questionnaire similar to that used in the first experiment. These *S*s held positions which varied from "mildly" to "strongly against" the admission of Red China into the U.N.—the topic to be influenced by active communication. In addition, their initial attitudes were similar to those of the *S*s in experiment 1 on the issue of numerical grading—the topic to be influenced by passive communication.

Procedure

The general atmosphere of the experimental setting was designed to convey the impression of a psychological aptitude-testing study. The *S* was told that he was participating in a study designed to develop a test for verbal and oral aptitudes, and toward that end we were experimenting with several special procedures and new techniques. The *S* was ushered into a soundproof room and a headset of earphones and microphone was attached. The *E* gave the instructions from an adjacent room while observing *S* through a one-way vision screen and recording his performance.

---

[4] The sex ratio of this study, as in the first, is representative of the ratio of approximately three males to each female in the college. Since sex did not contribute in a significant way to the variance of attitude change scores, the data for the two sexes were combined.

The *S* was given two tasks: the first to listen to a tape-recorded speech alleged to be from another student and analyze several aspects of it, and then to present a speech himself. The first speech concerned the issue of "letter grading versus numerical grading" and advocated a position contrary to *S*'s own attitude on the issue. The *S* listened to the same communication used in experiment 1, then judged how logical, interesting, and convincing it was. This is the *Passive Exposure condition*. It served several functions in the design. First, it further disguised the true purpose of the experiment by enhancing its specious psychometric rationale, and by minimizing the salience of the particular attitude issue used later in the oral speeches. This condition also provides data against which to compare: (1) the results of experiment 1 (employing the same topic, but with different *S*s under Active Participation conditions), as well as (2) the results of the Active Participation treatment to be presented below (employing the same *S*s but with a different topic). Because the order of presentation of these two exposure conditions was held constant and was not counterbalanced, unequivocal interpretation of these data cannot be made.

The *Active Participation condition* followed, and *S*s in all four experimental groups received these instructions:

> Verbal aptitude is made up of many components, one of which is oral presentation. I would now like you to be an active participant rather than the passive judge of a speech. I want you to present a speech in your natural speech style. Your talk will be tape-recorded for purposes of analysis and so that others may evaluate your performance. Present it as convincingly and sincerely as possible. Present it in such a way that it is comprehensible to you and your audience. When you are finished you will be asked some questions about it. You will be given two minutes now to rehearse the speech silently, and when I signal, begin and continue talking despite any experimental variations you may perceive.

The Communication and Attitude Measurement

In order to determine student knowledge on the experimental topic, 10 additional *S*s from the same population were asked to list all the positive implications of admission of Red China to the U.N. The median number of arguments given was 11, while 20 different arguments in all were advanced.

An outline of 8 arguments was prepared from this sampling, including some major and some minor points. In the *Improvisation* condition, *S* had to prepare a convincing speech from this outline. He was told to organize a coherent speech using the points given as well as adding examples and additional arguments. There was thus some opportunity afforded for improvising a speech which advocated a discrepant attitude position.

In the *Read* condition, *S* simply read a 400-word communication which contained the same 8 arguments embellished with appropriate examples and presented as a formal speech.[5]

When he had finished making his speech, *S* was told that the oral part of the study was completed, but that his assistance was requested "in helping us to evaluate this pilot stage of our study and in aiding with the planning of some details of our final

---

[5] A better procedure would be to match *S*s and then have one member of a pair improvise a speech while the second member reads a written version of this improvised speech, thereby controlling exactly for content and varying only improvisation.

study." He could do this by completing a questionnaire about speech topics which he felt may have relevance for college students. The postcommunication attitude measurement was taken after S had indicated from among a list of 10 topics those which would be best suited for use with students at New York University. The S was then asked to indicate on a 7-point attitude scale how he felt personally about each of the issues. "Admission of Red China to the U.N." and "use of a numerical grading system" were the first opinions elicited, while the other issues similarly varied between those of national or local interest.

Effort Manipulation

Effort was manipulated by having one group, Low Effort, receive only slightly delayed feedback, the delay being less than 0.01 second, while the High Effort group had a delay of 0.25 second interpolated between their speaking and hearing. Parametric studies of DAF have established these delay periods as requiring little effort and considerable effort, respectively (for a summary of this literature, see Smith, 1962, and Yates, 1963). Smith notes, for example, that "Both errors and increased effort in speaking occurred at times of uncertain or precarious control of articulation as governed by the delay period."

The Ss then completed rating scales designed to evaluate the experimental conditions and manipulations, and finally answered a recall test of 8 questions covering the 8 points in both the prepared outline and complete speech.

Extensive interviews with the Ss revealed that none of them perceived the purpose of the experiment or the hypotheses, and that attitude and attitude change were, at best, weak "demand characteristics" relative to the power of the DAF experience and the psychological testing cues. To the inevitable inquiry of how well they had done on the test, all Ss were told they did quite well. The true purpose and deceptions were not revealed to the Ss in order to maintain the validity of our procedures in a school without an honor system.

RESULTS

Assessment of the Experimental Conditions and Manipulations

Comprehension. The majority of Ss in each group learned and retained most of the prepared arguments. This is not surprising, since the arguments were first read silently, then presented orally by all Ss. The group means, which do not differ among themselves, ranged from 6.7 to 7.1 correctly recalled arguments.

Effort. The manipulation of effort through DAF variations produced a marked effect. The Ss in the Long Delay condition perceived that they had expended significantly more *physical* effort (mean $= 66.0$) in presenting their speech than did Ss in the Short Delay condition (mean $= 32.5$) ($F = 17.29$, $df = 1,55$, $p < .001$). This difference becomes somewhat attenuated when Ss describe how much *psychological* effort they expended in presenting the speech (mean for High Effort $= 72.7$, Low Effort mean $= 57.5$, $p < .10$). Thus, added to the effects of DAF on physical effort are the effects of the psychometric testing atmosphere which probably raised achievement motivation and thereby increased in all Ss the amount of psychological effort expended in order to do well.

Contrary to expectation, there were no differences in effort between the Read and Improvise conditions even approaching statistical significance.

Role-playing. The majority of Ss in all conditions reported that they advocated the speech position *sincerely* and *convincingly*. There were no differences between groups on either of these measures, the absolute levels being quite high. There were also no treatment differences in the perception of how *fair* and unbiased the speeches were. In general, they were recognized as being intentionally persuasive and slightly one-sided. One of the expected differences which emerged as a consequence of role-playing was that Ss who read the prepared, organized speech felt its arguments were more *logical* than those who had to improvise a speech ($F = 11.41$, $df = 1{,}55$, $p < .01$).

Neither effort nor type of delivery produced a significant difference in the extent to which the Ss were *satisfied* with how well they had performed. However, while three of the groups showed almost identical, moderately low degrees of satisfaction (mean of 39 out of 100), the Read, No-Delay group was most satisfied with their performance (mean = 61.7) and significantly more so than any of the other groups ($p < .05$, by Duncan's Multiple Range Test; cf. Edwards, 1960).

Analysis of the tape-recorded speeches of Ss in the *Improvisation* condition indicated that only 20 Ss out of the 28 with scorable tapes were able to improvise at least one new argument or introduce examples to augment the prepared arguments. Separate analyses, therefore, will be presented for the entire Improvisation treatment, and then for those Ss who fulfilled the task requirement.

The Effect of the Treatments upon Attitude Change

When the mean change of the four Active Exposure treatments is compared with the control group mean ($-.75$) by the use of Dunnett's test (cf. Edwards, 1960), the attitude change for each of the experimental subgroups is significant beyond the .01 level. The Passive Exposure groups also differed significantly from the mean of their control group ($-.67$), but the probability level is about .05 in each case. Thus, the arguments used in the speeches were effective in significantly altering attitudes of Ss exposed to them compared with those control Ss with similar initial attitudes but no exposure to the communication.

Effort and Attitude Change

The major purpose of this study was to examine the effect upon attitude change of the amount of effort exerted in presenting a speech which advocates a discrepant position. The conclusion to be drawn from Table 1 is that attitude change increases with increased effort expended in role-playing. The greater attitude change by High Effort than by Low Effort Ss approaches significance ($t = 1.69$, $df = 57$, $p = .10$). This finding then replicates the trend ($p = .13$) of more change under effortful conditions observed in the first study. Combining these probabilities from the two samples drawn from statistically independent populations yields a significant two-tailed probability value of .03 (by means of Stouffer's technique, as reported in Mosteller and Bush, 1954, pp. 328–331).

If we now consider not the magnitude of change but rather the frequency of net proportion of Ss who change (the difference between positive and negative change),[6] significant results emerge. For the combined data from the two experiments there is a net change of 80% for the High Effort group and 50% for the Low Effort group. The obtained critical

TABLE 1

MEAN ATTITUDE CHANGE AS A FUNCTION OF EFFORT AND COMMUNICATION DELIVERY

Active communication delivery		Effort (in active speech)	
		Low	High
Read	1st speech passive	.67	.79
	2nd speech active	1.80	2.14[b]
		(1.60)[a]	(2.30)
Improvise	1st speech passive	1.00	.71
	2nd speech active	1.40	2.00

[a] Means for conditions in experiment 1.

[b] $n = 15$ in each experimental group, except for this group in which one S was eliminated from the data analysis due to a congenital speech disturbance.

ratio of 2.3 ($p = .02$) increases our confidence that effort had a real effect upon attitude modification. The difference between the Read and Improvise groups was not significant.

Since there were no differences between the two effort groups on any of the no-communication control topics or in response to the communication to which they were passively exposed prior to manipulation of DAF, it may be concluded that the observed attitude change findings are relatively specific ones related to the experimental treatment.

Active Participation versus Passive Exposure

Actively role-playing a discrepant position has a much greater effect upon attitude change than does being passively exposed to a persuasive speech. More Ss change their attitude in the direction advocated on the

[6] See Hovland, Lumsdaine, and Sheffield (1949) in Appendix B for a discussion of this measure.

active topic than on the passive one (76% versus 46%, $p < .01$) and they change more than twice as much ($t = 3.02$, $df = 58$, $p < .01$).[7]

Because this within-group comparison confounds type of exposure with attitude topic, it is preferable to compare the effects of active and passive exposure to the same topic. Unfortunately, this may be done only by comparison of attitude change by Active Ss in the first experiment with Passive Ss in the second experiment, thereby holding constant the topic (numerical grading). Again, a greater percentage of Active Participation Ss change positively (75%, $p < .06$) and change a greater amount ($t = 2.41$, $df = 77$, $p < .02$).

TABLE 2

MEAN PERCEIVED EFFORT AND ATTITUDE CHANGE AS A FUNCTION OF ACTUAL
IMPROVISATION AND DELAYED FEEDBACK (WITHIN THE
IMPROVISATION CONDITION)

Group	Feedback delay	N	Effort	Attitude change
Improvised	Long	(9)	74.4	2.2
	Short	(11)	37.9	1.4
	Mean	(20)	54.3	1.76
Did not improvise	Long	(5)	52.0	1.5
	Short	(3)	17.7	1.2
	Mean	(8)	39.1	1.39
	Mean long delay	(14)	66.4	1.95
	Mean short delay	(14)	33.6	1.36

Improvisation

It was expected that, within the Active Participation treatment, improvising a speech would result in greater attitude change than would reading a prepared speech, and that this effect could be traced to the role of effort involved in improvisation. The data do not support this expectation, since the similar mean attitude change for both the Read and Improvisation conditions does not allow rejection of the null hypothesis.

However, if an internal analysis of the data for effort and attitude change is performed according to actual improvisation rather than experimental treatment, trends consistent with our expectations are apparent. In Table 2 it can be seen that Ss who do improvise expend somewhat more effort than those who do not ($F = 3.42$, $df = 1,24$, $p <$

[7] It was necessary to use Edwards' correction for t-test comparisons when the variances differ significantly (1960, p. 107), since the variability was greater within the Active than Passive Exposure condition.

.10), and also show slightly, though not significantly, more attitude change. However, differences in Delay conditions within each Improvisation group have a greater effect on effort ($F = 9.32$, $p < .01$) than do differences between Improvisation groups within each Delay condition. The slightly greater attitude change between Delay conditions than between Improvisation groups is not statistically significant.

If we now consider attitude change within these cells, it is interesting to observe that the Improvisation-Delay group which shows most effort also shows most opinion change, +2.2 units, while the other groups all change less and approximately the same amount. Within the group of Ss who actually improvised ($n = 20$), 89% of those in the Long Delay condition changed positively, while only 54% of the Short Delay Ss changed their attitudes similarly. Tape recordings. of the improvised speeches were judged separately for their content and delivery by two independent judges. There were no significant differences between the two Improvisation groups (High and Low Effort) in the quality of the arguments or the examples presented to support the admission of Red China to the U.N. However, as might be expected, a difference did emerge on a measure of how well the improvised speech was delivered. The Low Effort Ss were judged to be somewhat better orators than the High Effort Ss (means of 4.9–3.6, respectively, on a 7-point scale; $t = 1.79$, $df = 26$, $p < .10$). These findings make it difficult to interpret the attitude change results solely as a consequence of Ss in the two conditions convincing themselves because of what they said or how well they said it.

It should also be noted that the results are not explainable in terms of different durations of exposure to the communication as a consequence of the greater difficulty in the High Effort condition. The Ss in this condition took on the average only 20 seconds longer than the Low Effort Ss to deliver their speeches ($p > .30$).

DISCUSSION

It may be concluded from this study that conditions which demand greater effort for the performance of a role increase the effectiveness of role-playing in changing attitudes; therefore, in terms of the derivation of our initial hypothesis, a dissonance theory analysis of this situation appears justified. Moreover, the use of delayed auditory feedback proved to be an effective technique for modifying attitudes and one deserving of further attention. The manipulation of effort by means of DAF variations poses some problems of theoretical interpretation also worthy of investigation.

A thorough examination of the literature relating effort to behavior in both animal and human Ss reveals that the relationship is complex and equivocal. Thus, in the present study, as with most others in this area, the same results may be explained by alternative theories which assume different mechanisms, or on the other hand, similar motivational explanations may lead to contrary predictions.

Although the data are generally in accord with the predictions derived from a dissonance theory analysis, alternative explanations can be readily advanced due to the ambiguous theoretical status of the variable of effort, as well as to its special conditions of manipulation in this study. Explanations can be advanced in terms of anxiety (see Korobow, 1955), frustration-aggression, inhibition (see Koch, 1954, p. 143), stimulus intensity dynamism, variations in the S_D value of proprioceptive feedback (see Lewis, 1963), interfering responses (see Kelman, 1953), and distraction (see Festinger and Maccoby, 1964).

Unfortunately, space limitations do not permit a thorough analysis of each of these alternatives. However, in most instances where these approaches gave rise to clear-cut predictions, available internal data in the present study cast doubt upon their adequacy. One explanation which does demand somewhat fuller treatment in this discussion is what might be termed "the sweet smell of effortful success" notion (Chapanis and Chapanis, 1964) which has been explicitly advanced as an alternative to the dissonance theory conception of effort.

The major premise of this position is that if, as a consequence of a history of cultural conditioning, greater reinforcement is associated with increased effort, then effort will come to elicit mediating evaluative responses. In other words, effort may influence behavior and attitudes in its function as a determinant of habit strength. The stimulus of effort will itself become a reinforcer, as in the saying, "Effort is its own reward." The extent to which such pithy sayings abound in our culture serves to remind us of the Puritan value placed upon work—regardless of its material consequences.

In this connection, it is interesting to note that in a study by Child (1946), some children who chose a more effortful rather than a less effortful task offered the following reasons: "It's more fun when it's harder to do." "I thought that the prize might be a little better since it was harder to do." "The easy things are baby things." "It's just better to do a little work for something you get." "I don't know whether I could reach it [the difficult one] and I wanted to find out if I could."

Thus with human Ss, at least, effort may influence behavior and attitudes through prior learned associations with reward for effort per se. This reward need not be extrinsic, need not even be in the form of social approval. The successful completion of an effortful task is intrinsically rewarding because it involves the satisfaction associated with mastery of the environment, and with increases in feelings of personal competence. Chapanis and Chapanis (1964), in attacking previous dissonance-oriented experiments dealing with effort, base their criticism on similar notions. They note that overcoming obstacles leads to pleasurable feelings of success, a consequent greater evaluation of the object overcome and "thus effort would be confounded with *feeling of success*" (p. 5). Such a pleasure-through-effort explanation is certainly tenable in most human studies but cannot be used indiscriminately as an explanation for all studies which manipulate effort. For example, such an explanation is not adequate to handle the results of Cohen's (1959) effort experiment in which the effect of effort on attitudes is not simple, but interacts with the degree of communicator-recipient attitude discrepancy. Moreover, in a comprehensive field experiment of role-playing effects, Jansen and Stolurow (1962) found least effort was associated with greater liking and satisfaction. In fact, the authors note that *discomfort* on the part of the *S*s is associated with largest changes in attitudes and perceptions.

The inadequacy of this explanation for the present results is apparent when we consider two points. First, that the group which was most satisfied with their performance was the Read, No-Delay group which exerted the least effort. In addition, satisfaction was neither related to actual speech performance nor to attitude change. Second, the novelty of the DAF experience for all of our *S*s meant that there were no prior standards of performance to use as a reference for establishing competence. In fact, Cohen and Zimbardo (1962) easily manipulated *S*s' perception of how well or poorly they had performed precisely because of the absence of standards of success.

Improvisation

Although the present study follows closely in many aspects of general design and procedure the study from which the improvisation notion first arose (Janis and King, 1954), it failed to detect what King and Janis call "one of the most salient features of an improvised performance: the spontaneous additions and elaborations of the arguments contained in the communications" (1956, p. 183).

Contrary to this statement is the clearly observable difficulty of manipulating improvisation in a brief experimental situation just because the task of inventing arguments and finding examples for a position that is not one's own places so great a burden upon the subject. Beyond this empirical observation, moreover, lies more substantial experimental evidence that calls to question the statement of King and Janis that a "substantial" percentage of their *S*s improvised. The figures that they do present report that only 47% of the *S*s in the Improvisation condition thought that they had sincerely advocated the role. In the present study 28% of the Ss were unable to improvise even to the minimal essential of providing a single new argument, while a mere third of the Ss improvised to an extent that might be considered significant. This evidence is bolstered by the data offered in a recent study by Greenbaum (1963) which showed that only 34% of those Ss asked to improvise managed to provide any new arguments, even with the quite familiar issue of civil defense and ample time for preparation (7 minutes). Jansen and Stolurow were led by their study (1962) to conclude that "the relative ineffectiveness of improvisation might be explained by the fact that improvising is not an activity which can be done on request, but has to be developed with great care and can be expected to appear only after careful preparation" (p. 22).

With this conclusion McGuire (1962) would concur. His concern is to explain why active participation is *not* better than passive for one who is required to defend his own position against persuasive counterattack. He argues that subjects perform badly in the Active Participation condition because, having little experience with such a task, they are unable to learn material that would support their beliefs. McGuire's research is centered upon a special kind of attitude, the belief in cultural truisms. However, his argument—that one does not under normal circumstances defend this kind of belief, and consequently has no practice in the skills required for such a defense—would hold as well for the present research, for one has as little practice in improvising counternorm arguments. Thus, it would appear that successful improvisation demands experience, adequate preparation, intelligence, and perhaps even a special "aptitude for role-taking" (Sarbin and Jones, 1955).

In the present study, as well as the one cited earlier by Greenbaum (1963), quality of improvisation bore no relation to attitude change, while Jansen and Stolurow (1962) demonstrated that attitude change was significantly *less* when Ss improvised than when they imitated the improvisation of another person. Finally, Stanley and Klausmeier's (1957) attempt to replicate the King and Janis finding also yielded negative conclusions, even after internal analyses according to age, sex, and Ss' initial opinions. The failure of the present study to achieve the improvisation effect then is not unusual, but rather is in keeping with the results obtained by other researchers and forces a reconsideration in some detail of the study by King and Janis.

In conclusion then, "The improvisation hypothesis asserts that people tend to be especially impressed by their own persuasive efforts when they are stimulated to think up new arguments and appeals in order to do a good job of convincing others" (King and Janis, p. 178). The results of the present study cause us to re-evaluate such a statement and dictate that attention should be centered upon the role of "persuasive effort" per se, as well as upon the intellectual stimulation aspect of invention of arguments. The need for systematic theoretical and empirical appraisal of the role of effort upon attitudes and other socially significant behaviors is certainly called for.[8]

SUMMARY

Opinion change increased as the amount of effort expended to deliver a persuasive counternorm speech was increased. In two experiments physical effort was manipulated by varying the interval of delay in auditory feedback. No differences were found between Ss who improvised a speech advocating a discrepant attitude position and those who merely read the speech sincerely. The theory of cognitive dissonance appears to offer adequate and parsimonious explanation of the results.

REFERENCES

ARONSON, E. The effect of effort on the attractiveness of rewarded and unrewarded stimuli. *J. abnorm. soc. Psychol.*, 1961, **63**, 375–380.

BREHM, J. W., AND COHEN, A. R. *Explorations in cognitive dissonance.* New York: Wiley, 1962.

BRONFENBRENNER, U., AND NEWCOMB, T. M. Improvisations: An application of psychodrama in personality diagnosis. *Sociatry*, 1948, **1**, 367–382.

CHAPANIS, NATALIA P., AND CHAPANIS, A. Cognitive dissonance: Five years later. *Psychol. Bull.*, 1964, **61**, 1–22.

CHILD, I. Children's preference for goals easy or difficult to obtain. *Psychol. Monogr.*, 1946, **60**, No. 4.

COHEN, A. R. Communication discrepancy and attitude change: A dissonance theory approach. *J. Pers.*, 1959, **27**, 386–396.

COHEN, A. R. Attitudinal consequences of induced discrepancies between cognitions and behavior. *Publ. Opin. Quart.*, 1960, **24**, 297–318.

COHEN, A. R., AND ZIMBARDO, P. G. An experiment on avoidance motivation. Study described in J. W. Brehm and A. R. Cohen, *Explorations in cognitive dissonance.* New York: Wiley, 1962. Pp. 143–151.

EDWARDS, A. L. *Experimental design in psychological research.* (Rev. ed.) New York: Rinehart, 1960.

FESTINGER, L. *A theory of cognitive dissonance.* New York: Row, Peterson, 1957.

FESTINGER, L., AND ARONSON, E. The arousal and reduction of dissonance in social contexts. In D. Cartwright and A. Zander (Eds.), *Group Dynamics.* (2nd ed.) New York: Row, Peterson, 1960. Pp. 214–231.

---

[8] It is surprising to note that Hess (1962) reports as one of the most reliable findings in ethology the positive effect of effort on imprinting. The strength of imprinting during the critical period is a function of the logarithm of effort expended by the duckling in following the imprinting object. In another study, ducklings who had to overcome aversive stimulation (painful shocks) for following a model imprinted more strongly than those not presented such a barrier. Both results are in clear agreement with the dissonance theory formulation presented here.

PAUL G. SWINGLE

Festinger, L., and Maccoby, N. On resistance to persuasive communications. *J. abnorm. soc. Psychol.*, 1964, **68**, 359–366.

Greenbaum, C. W. The effects of choice and reinforcement on attitude change in a role-playing situation. Unpublished doctoral dissertation, New York Univer., 1963.

Hess, E. H. Ethology: An approach toward the complete analysis of behavior. In *New directions in psychology*. New York: Holt, Rinehart and Winston, 1962. Pp. 157–266.

Hovland, C. I., Lumsdaine, A. A., and Sheffield, F. D. *Experiments on mass communication*. Princeton, N. J.: Princeton Univer. Press, 1949.

Hovland, C. I., Janis, I. L., and Kelley, H. H. *Communication and persuasion*. New Haven, Conn.: Yale Univer. Press, 1953.

Janis, I. L., and King, B. T. The influence of role playing on opinion change. *J. abnorm. soc. Psychol.*, 1954, **49**, 211–218.

Jansen, Mathilda J., and Stolurow, L. M. An experimental study of role playing. *Psychol. Monogr.*, 1962, **76**, No. 31. (Includes a bibliography of role-playing theory and experiments.)

Kelman, H. Attitude change as a function of response restriction. *Human Relat.*, 1953, **6**, 185–214.

King, B. T., and Janis, I. L. Comparison of the effectiveness of improvised versus non-improvised role-playing in producing opinion changes. *Human Relat.*, 1956, **9**, 177–186.

Koch, S. Clark L. Hull. In W. Estes *et al.* (Eds.), *Modern learning theory*. New York: Appleton-Century-Crofts, 1954. Pp. 1–176.

Korobow, N. Reactions to stress: A reflection of personality trait organization. *J. abnorm. soc. Psychol.*, 1955, **51**, 464–468.

Lawrence, D. H., and Festinger, L. *Deterrents and reinforcement*. London: Tavistock, 1962. (Includes a bibliography of effort studies.)

Lewis, M. The psychological effect of effort. Unpublished paper, Fels. Res. Inst., 1963. (Includes a bibliography of effort studies.)

Lipset, S. M., Lazarsfeld, P. F., Barton, A. H., and Linz, J. The psychology of voting: An analysis of political behavior. In G. Lindzey (Ed.), *Handbook of social psychology*. Vol. II. Cambridge, Mass.: Addison-Wesley, 1954. Pp. 1124–1175.

McGuire, W. J. Immunization against persuasion. Unpublished manuscript, Columbia Univer., 1962.

Moreno, J. L., Moreno, Z., and Moreno, J. The discovery of the spontaneous man. *Psychodrama group Psychother. Monogr.*, 1958, No. 34.

Mosteller, F., and Bush, R. B. Selected quantitative techniques. In G. Lindzey (Ed.), *Handbook of social psychology*. Vol. I. Cambridge, Mass.: Addison-Wesley, 1954. Pp. 289–334.

Sarbin, T. R. Role theory. In G. Lindzey (Ed.), *Handbook of social psychology*. Vol. I. Cambridge, Mass.: Addison-Wesley, 1954. Pp. 223–255.

Sarbin, T. R., and Jones, D. S. An experimental analysis of role playing. *J. abnorm. soc. Psychol.*, 1955, **51**, 231–241.

Smith, K. U. *Delayed sensory feedback and behavior*. Philadelphia, Pa.: Saunders, 1962. (Includes a bibliography of delayed feedback.)

Stanley, J. C., and Klausmeier, H. J. Opinion constancy after formal role playing. *J. soc. Psychol.*, 1957, **46**, 11–18.

Yates, A. Delayed auditory feedback. *Psychol. Bull.*, 1963, **60**, 213–231.

Received June 23, 1964

Reprinted from Journal of Personality, 1959, Vol. 27, pp. 407–417, by permission of
the authors and the publisher.

Verbalization and reactions to cognitive dissonance[1]

JACOB M. RABBIE, JACK W. BREHM,[2] AND ARTHUR R. COHEN
Yale University

When an individual is induced to take a stand at variance with
his private attitude, he may subsequently show attitude change in the
direction of that induced stand (Cohen, Brehm, & Fleming, 1958;
Festinger & Carlsmith, 1959; Janis & King, 1954; Kelman, 1953;
King & Janis, 1956). An explanation of this phenomenon has been
offered by Festinger (1957).

According to this explanation, when an individual is forced to do
or say something inconsistent with his attitudes he will experience
"cognitive dissonance." The greater is the amount of force, the less
will be the amount of dissonance. Dissonance is said to have motivational characteristics such that the greater is its magnitude, the
more will the individual try to reduce or eliminate it. One way of
reducing dissonance is by changing one's attitudes so that they more
nearly coincide with what one is doing or has done. Thus a change
in private attitude toward the position a person has been induced to
support will reduce the dissonance consequent to taking that position.
Previous research has generally dealt with situations in which the
individual has actually taken the discrepant position. Dissonance
theory does not, however, necessarily demand that the discrepant
verbal statement actually be made. Though the theory is somewhat
ambiguous on this point, it would appear that mere commitment to
making the statement should be sufficient to produce dissonance.
Indeed, it is possible that verbalizing the stand could qualify attitude
change resulting from dissonance. Logically then, the effect could
be either to increase or decrease attitude change. An increase could

[1] This report was prepared as part of the Yale Communications Research Program which is under the general direction of Carl I. Hovland. It was supported by
the Rockefeller Foundation and the Bell Telephone Laboratories. The senior
author would also like to thank the Netherlands Organization for Pure Research
(Z.W.O.) for their support.
[2] Now at Duke University.

occur, for example, from the facilitating effect of thinking of arguments consistent with the dissonance-reducing private attitude. A decrease could occur from embarrassment about being inconsistent with one's initial attitude. The present study was designed to test the idea that the decision to take a discrepant stand on an issue is sufficient to create dissonance, and to examine the possible effects of verbalization on subsequent dissonance reduction.

The evidence on the effect of verbalization of an attitude discrepant from that privately held is unclear. The studies by Cohen, et al. (1958), Janis and King (1954, 1956), and Kelman (1953) found that Ss who wrote the greatest number of original arguments tended to show the greatest amount of attitude change. However, the study by Festinger and Carlsmith (1959) found that the condition producing most attitude change (high dissonance) also produced relatively inferior verbalization of the discrepant position.

An unpublished study by Brehm[3] points up this inconsistency. Junior high school students were offered prizes for writing essays in favor of shorter summer vacations. It was found that in those conditions in which attitude change (and presumably dissonance) was slight, there was a positive trend between number of arguments an S wrote and how much he changed his attitude. On the other hand, in those conditions in which attitude change (and presumably dissonance) was great, there was a negative relationship between these same measures. In other words, under high dissonance conditions, Ss who wrote many arguments discrepant from their initial attitudes changed their opinions less than those who wrote few such arguments.

A negative relationship between number of arguments written and amount of attitude change could occur for any of several reasons. Generally, it could occur because of some personality difference among Ss that simultaneously affected writing of arguments and attitude change, or because the writing of arguments affected subsequent attitude change, or because attitude change immediately after the decision affected the number of arguments subsequently written.

The present experiment was designed to test two related hypotheses in order to throw some light on this general problem of the effect of verbalizing discrepant attitudes.

[3] Brehm, J. W. Forced verbal compliance and attitude change. Unpublished manuscript.

Verbalization and dissonance

1. The decision to take a discrepant position on an issue is sufficient to produce dissonance and consequent attitude change in the direction of the position taken.

2. Verbalizing the discrepant position will tend to inhibit attitude change produced by dissonance.

To test these hypotheses, the present study was designed to create two degrees of dissonance where individuals' attitudes toward the issue were measured (*a*) before and (*b*) after verbalization of the discrepant attitude.

METHOD

An after-only design was employed. Under the guise of a "survey," the *S*s were asked to write essays against their private attitudes on an issue of high importance to them. To create low dissonance in half of the *S*s the *E* strongly justified writing the discrepant essay and to create high dissonance in the other half, *E* barely justified it. In order to examine the effect on attitude change of verbalizing the discrepant stand, attitudes of half of each of the above groups were measured before writing the essay while attitudes of the rest were measured after writing the essay.

Subjects

Sixty freshmen at Yale University were assigned to the experimental conditions on a random basis.

Procedure

The *E* introduced himself to the *S* as a member of the "Research Communication Center of Yale University" which was conducting a survey for the Yale administration.

*S*s were told that the administration was quite concerned about some aspects of athletic competition between schools and was seriously considering eliminating athletic competition altogether. The administration was also worried about the recent stress on the development of the natural sciences and was thinking of making the study of Latin and Greek obligatory for all students.

The request to write the essay was introduced as follows:

> It is our experience that the best way to get all relevant arguments on both sides of an issue is to ask people to write a strong essay favoring only *one* side. We already have enough essays in support of continuing athletic competition between schools. What we really need now are more essays in favor of eliminating interschool competition. You can, if you really want, write in favor of keeping athletic competition, but as I said before, we already have enough of these. I understand that you may have different views on the matter, but as you can see, it it very interesting for us to know what kind of arguments people bring up in their essays if they have different opinions about it.

Manipulation of the Magnitude of Dissonance.

The amount of dissonance is an inverse function of the amount of force used to obtain compliance. To create high force and low dissonance, reasons may be given that would lead a person to take a discrepant stand on the issue. Higher dissonance may be created by not giving the individual these reasons. Thus high justification equals low dissonance while low justification equals high dissonance.

In the High Justification (HJ) condition, *E* said:

> By writing against athletic competition between schools you will help the Research Communication Center in its scientific study of this new method as a way of arriving at solutions to age-old controversies such as those between labor and management or between nations in international affairs. You will help me since I must have more essays against athletic competition between schools in order to use this study for my doctoral dissertation. I am completely dependent upon you. Most every one has written on the side I asked them to, so I hope you will do the same.

In the Low Justification (LJ) condition these instructions were omitted. *S*s were simply asked to write the discrepant essay.

The decision was dramatized by having the *S* choose between sheets labeled "Strongly Against Athletic Competition between Schools" and "In Favor of Athletic Competition between Schools." It should be clear that all *S*s whose data were analyzed in the present experiment wrote against their position.[4]

Manipulation of the Time of Attitude Measurement.

In the Attitude-Essay condition the *S* was told immediately after he had made his decision:

> Now that you have made the decision to write an essay *against* athletic competition between schools, I would like to get your answers on a couple of questions. You see, this part of the study has nothing to do with the survey proper. I mean by this that the information you give on the questionnaire will not be made available to the administration, but will only be used for scientific purposes. We want to know to what extent a person's general attitude toward an interview situation like this will affect the quality and the number of arguments he writes in the essay. In this way only are we able to assess the validity of the method we have used. We would therefore appreciate it very much if you could answer this questionnaire as accurately and as truthfully as you can. Please give your own personal opinion about these things.

The first part of the questionnaire, designed to measure *S*'s attitude toward the elimination issue and an irrelevant issue, was then completed. Finally, the essay was written and the second part of the questionnaire, designed to

[4] Because students were strongly against elimination of interschool athletics, many refused to write in favor of it. Since these *S*s were approximately equally divided among the four experimental conditions, no serious bias is expected from this selection factor. The proportion of students contacted who refused was 46 per cent.

measure the success of the Justification manipulation and alternative avenues of dissonance reduction, was completed.

In the Essay-Attitude condition, the S was asked to write the essay immediately after he made his decision. After he finished the essay, he was asked to fill out both parts of the questionnaire.

While Ss were asked to take 10 minutes to write the essay, they were not interrupted and generally took about 20 minutes.

The attitude issues were chosen on the basis of pretest data obtained from a comparable group of Yale undergraduates. These data showed a very strong bias on both issues, especially against the elimination of athletic competition between schools. These issues were selected because all Ss were on one side of the issue. Moreover, since both issues were highly involving, it was extremely difficult for the Ss to reduce dissonance by belittling their importance. Also, since these attitudes were presumably highly resistant to change, any attitude change due to the experimental manipulations should be a convincing demonstration of the hypotheses.

The Questionnaire

The first part was designed to measure Ss' private attitude toward the central issue, elimination of athletic competition, and toward an irrelevant issue, the obligatory mastery of Latin and Greek. For both questions, answers were indicated along an 81-point response scale, each tenth point identified by labels running from "Dislike Extremely" (0) to "Like Extremely" (7.0).

The second part of the questionnaire contained a check on the justification manipulation. Ss were asked, "To what extent did you feel obliged to write on the side suggested by the Interviewer?"

Additional questions were included to check alternative avenues of dissonance reduction. Ss were asked: "To what extent did you dissociate yourself from the arguments given in the essay?"; "How fair do you think it is for us to ask students to give arguments which may be used against them?"; "How satisfied were you with the essay if you consider it as an academic exercise?" It was assumed that a positive response to each of these questions indicated reduction of the dissonance produced by the discrepant stand, in addition to or instead of reduction through attitude change.

RESULTS

Evidence on the effectiveness of the justification manipulation

Data from the obligation question show that the justification manipulation was successful. The over-all mean for the HJ condition is 1.22, for the LJ, 2.12. The difference is significant beyond the 5 per cent level by t test for both Attitude-Essay and Essay-Attitude conditions.[5]

Effect of Decision on Attitude Change

The first hypothesis to be tested by this study was that the decision to take a discrepant stand is sufficient to create dissonance and

[5] All p values reported in this paper are for both tails of the distribution.

consequent attitude change in the direction of that stand. Thus, within the Attitude-Essay condition, where attitudes were measured immediately after the decision, there should be greater attitude change in the LJ than in the HJ condition. The relevant data are presented in Table 1. Analysis of the average attitude scores shows

TABLE 1
MEAN ATTITUDE SCORES AND MEAN VARIANCES

	Attitude-Essay		Essay-Attitude	
	Score	S_M^2	Score	S_M^2
Athletic elimination issue				
HJ................................	.87[a]	.0206	.94	.0627
LJ................................	1.44	.0539	1.29	.1979
Obligatory Latin and Greek issue				
HJ................................	1.78	.1170	1.93	.3196
LJ................................	3.29	.3083	2.54	.2682

[a] The higher the score, the more positive is the attitude.

that the score for LJ, 1.44, is indeed greater than the score for HJ, .87, significant at the 5 per cent level. It may be concluded that the decision alone is sufficient to create dissonance.

Effect of Verbalizing on Attitude Change

The second hypothesis was that the writing of the essay has an inhibiting effect on attitude change. Thus the attitude score for Ss in the Essay-Attitude condition should be smaller than that for Ss in the Attitude-Essay condition. However, analysis of the data revealed no such effect. The mean scores for the LJ (1.29) and HJ (.94) conditions are practically identical to those in the Attitude-Essay condition. They are not significantly different from each other, however, due to greater variance of response in this condition. Thus, while the Essay-Attitude condition fails to produce a significant difference in attitudes between Ss in the HJ and LJ conditions, it also fails to be different from the Attitude-Essay condition in amount of attitude change produced. We may conclude there is no evidence for either an inhibiting or a facilitating effect from verbalizing the discrepant stand.

The present data may also be inspected for a relationship within conditions between number of arguments written and amount of attitude change. Dividing all experimental Ss into approximately equal groups of those who changed their attitudes in the direction of the discrepant stand and those who did not, we find an inverse relationship between number of arguments and attitude score. Some positive attitude change was shown by 56 per cent of those writing four or more arguments and by 86 per cent of those writing three or fewer arguments. This difference is significant by chi-square at the 2 per cent level. The trend is in the same direction for both Attitude-Essay and Essay-Attitude conditions. Thus, the internal evidence is consistent with that of the study by Brehm (see footnote 3). For Ss within conditions, regardless of when they wrote the essay, the greater the number of arguments written (i.e., the greater the strength of verbalization of the discrepant stand), the less is the amount of attitude change.

Alternative Modes of Reducing Dissonance.

The after questionnaire included questions about the degree of dissociation, satisfaction with the essay, the fairness of this kind of survey, and the likability of the Interviewer. There were no significant differences between the HJ and LJ groups for any of these questions. If we can assume that the questions indicate the most obvious other means for dissonance reduction in this situation, the data suggest that attitude change may be a more appropriate way to reduce dissonance than ways unrelated to behavior with regard to the specific issue. Thus, having taken a stand against one's own position, the easiest way to reduce dissonance may be to change one's attitude.

Specificity of the Dissonance Effect.

In order to obtain some information on the extent to which the dissonance effect is specific to attitudes toward elimination of athletics, a second question was asked concerning an irrelevant attitude. This concerned the S's views about the obligatory mastery of Latin and Greek.

The ts for these data show a difference between the High and Low Just conditions at beyond the 5 per cent level for the Attitude-Essay condition and insignificant though in the same direction for the Essay-Attitude condition. Thus, it appears that the dissonance effect was not specific to the relevant attitude.

JACOB M. RABBIE, JACK W. BREHM, AND ARTHUR R. COHEN

DISCUSSION

Whether the discrepant position was or was not verbalized made no difference in subsequent attitudes. At the same time within experimental conditions there was a negative relationship between number of arguments written (strength of verbalization) and the final attitude regardless of whether the attitude was measured before or after the verbalizing. Thus our experimental conditions produced the within-condition phenomenon we set out to explain, but failed to support the hypothesis that the act of verbalizing tends to inhibit attitude change resulting from dissonance. These same data also suggest rejection of the hypothesis that verbalizing facilitates attitude change resulting from dissonance. What, then, might still explain the inverse relation between attitude change and number of arguments written?

A possibility is that individuals vary in their perception of the magnitude of force used to induce them to take the discrepant stand. The more force perceived, the greater will be the number of arguments written, but the less will be the magnitude of dissonance and consequent attitude change. If this explanation were correct, we would expect to find a positive relationship between the number of arguments written and the extent to which the S felt obliged toward the E. The data show no relationship.

Another possible hypothesis is that attitude change reduces the pressure to write arguments in favor of the discrepant stand. In other words, once the individual has made the decision to take the discrepant stand, the ensuing dissonance can be reduced by attitude change *or* by actually verbalizing the stand. To the extent that an individual does one, he need not do the other. This hypothesis cannot be tested by the present study, however, since there is no manipulation of attitude change independent of magnitude of dissonance.

There also remains untested the general hypothesis that a personality variable is simultaneously affecting both the number of arguments written and the amount of attitude change. It may be, for example, that persons of low intelligence can write only few arguments but are highly prone to use attitude change as a method of reducing dissonance. Those of high intelligence, on the other hand, may be able to write many arguments but reduce dissonance by rationalization or other methods rather than by attitude change.

Verbalization and dissonance

Attitude Change on the Irrelevant Issue

This study also presented evidence on the specificity of the dissonance effect. It was expected that no differences between conditions would occur on the irrelevant issue, the obligatory mastery of Latin and Greek. However, a reliable difference was found between the HJ and LJ treatments of the Attitude-Essay condition. The general pattern of attitudes was quite similar to that for the relevant issue. What explanation can be offered for this finding?

One possible reason for the similarity in pattern among the conditions is that the major effects are due primarily to sampling error. If attitudes toward the relevant and irrelevant issues were positively correlated in the sample, and if sampling error produced an unusually large mean difference for one issue, a similar difference would be likely to occur for the other issue. Since this explanation assumes a positive correlation between attitudes on the two issues, its plausibility can easily be further checked. Ss in each experimental condition were split at approximately the median attitude on each issue. The resulting two by two tables showed no evidence of a positive relationship between the two attitudes. Thus, although the results could still be due solely to sampling error, this explanation derives no special cogency from the similarity of outcome for the relevant and irrelevant issues.

A second possible reason for the similarity of attitudes for the two issues is that Ss were making an implicit decision to take a discrepant stand on the irrelevant issue. If our interpretation of the main effects for the relevant issue is correct, then making a decision to support a discrepant stand is sufficient to produce attitude change. Thus if our experimental procedure tended to produce an implicit decision in regard to the irrelevant issue, then subsequent attitudes should be similar to those for the relevant issue. Let us therefore inspect the procedure to see whether or not such implicit decisions might have frequently been made.

First of all, the E said he was gathering information on both issues. Some Ss may have immediately decided to support the discrepant stand on the irrelevant issue before learning that it was only the relevant issue on which further essays were needed. And second, the irrelevant issue may often have been seen as the lesser of two evils. Pretest attitudes on the two issues support this view. It might even be fair to say that if an S was willing to take a discrepant stand on the

JACOB M. RABBIE, JACK W. BREHM, AND ARTHUR R. COHEN

relevant issue, he was also willing to do so on the irrelevant issue. Several students actually asked permission to write on the irrelevant issue instead of on the relevant one. Thus it seems likely that many Ss did in fact make an implicit (or even explicit) decision to take a discrepant stand on the irrelevant issue. The dissonance created by such a decision would be subject to the experimental manipulations and would therefore produce the same differential amounts of attitude change between conditions as did that for the relevant issue. It therefore seems likely that the similarity of attitudes for the relevant and irrelevant issues is due to our failure to eliminate or minimize decisions in regard to the irrelevant issue. If this interpretation is correct, the data for the irrelevant issue further supports the hypothesis that the decision to take a stand discrepant from one's private opinion is sufficient to produce dissonance and consequent attitude change.

SUMMARY

It has been shown that when an individual is induced to support a position discrepant from his private attitude, he tends to show attitude change toward that position. This phenomenon has been explained by Festinger's theory of cognitive dissonance. It has also been found that under certain conditions, the greater the number of arguments written by an individual in favor of the discrepant stand, the less is his attitude change. This phenomenon is not readily explained by dissonance theory. The purpose of the present study was to show that (a) the decision to take the discrepant stand is sufficient to produce dissonance and consequent attitude change, and (b) the more the individual verbalizes in favor of the discrepant stand, the more inhibited will be his attitude change.

Sixty college students were individually asked to write essays against their private attitudes. High and low dissonance was created by giving them few or many justifications for taking the discrepant stand. Attitudes of half of the subjects in each of these conditions were measured before they wrote the discrepant essay (but after the decision) while those of the other half were measured after they wrote the essay.

The results indicated that the decision to take a discrepant position is sufficient to produce dissonance and consequent attitude change in the direction of that position. However, verbalizing the discrepant stand before or after attitude measurement neither inhibited nor facilitated the attitude change. Within conditions there was a

Verbalization and dissonance

negative relationship between attitude change and strength of verbalization of the discrepant stand. Alternative hypotheses were suggested.

REFERENCES

COHEN, A. R., BREHM, J. W., & FLEMING, W. H. Attitude change and justification for compliance. *J. abnorm. soc. Psychol.*, 1958, **56**, 276-278.

FESTINGER, L. *Theory of Cognitive Dissonance.* Evanston: Row, Peterson and Company, 1957.

FESTINGER, L., & CARLSMITH, J. M. Cognitive consequences of forced compliance. *J. abnorm. soc. Psychol.*, 1959, **58**, 203-211.

JANIS, I. L., & KING, B. T. The influence of role playing in opinion change. *J. abnorm. soc. Psychol.*, 1954, **49**, 211-218.

KELMAN, H. Attitude change as a function of response restriction. *Human. Relat.*, 1953, **6**, 185-214.

KING, B. T., & JANIS, I. L. Comparison of the effectiveness of improvised versus non-improvised role-playing in producing opinion changes. *Hum. Relat.*, 1956, **9**, 177-186.

Manuscript received December 15, 1958.

Observer Bias

In an area as complex as social behavior, the problem of scientific objectivity is critical. When one is dealing with a physical dimension such as length, for example, objectivity is comparatively easy to achieve. If a table is measured and one is then asked to measure the table, the *independent* assessments of the table's length should be almost identical within a small margin of error, say, one-sixteenth of an inch. Even if one were careless in his scientific approach and said "This table is 6 feet long; measure it to see if you agree" gross error in the final assessment of the table's length is unlikely. The fact that one was informed of the measurement of the table may influence him to accept a measurement of 5 ⅞ feet as 6 feet, but would not lead him to accept a measurement of 4 feet 2 inches as agreeing with a measurement of 6 feet.

When measuring human behavior the situation is quite different. If one must depend upon observers' judgments for measurements of behavior, objectivity is critical. Take, for example, two observers or judges looking at a picture of a grimacing face. The facial features resulting from the grimace may lead one judge to believe that the picture was taken when the individual was smiling. The second judge might interpret the features as indicative of surprise, horror, or excitement. If, however, both judges were told that the picture was taken at the exact moment the individual was informed of a death in his family both judges would tend to interpret the facial expression as indicative of sorrow. It is apparent, then, that when people attempt to make judgments about others, any added information such as what they are expected to observe may result in the observer's basing his judgments in part upon the previous information.

Blind and Double Blind Experiments

To control the contaminating effects of bias, researchers frequently design experiments utilizing the blind or double blind technique. If, for example, one wanted to test the effects of a new drug upon the behavior of patients residing in a ward in a mental institution, one would need some measure of the patient's behavior on the ward before and after administration of the drug.

The procedure might include, first, having someone rate each patient's ward behavior on some scale; second, administering the drug to one-half the patients; third, having another rating of ward behavior after a suitable period of time and then comparing the before and after ratings. A blind design would simply involve not telling the judge which patients had the drug and which patients had not. A double blind would involve keeping everyone except the experimenter (i.e., patient, judge, and drug administator) unaware as to which patients received the drug and which did not. This could be accomplished by having the drug administrator give some patients the drug and some patients a placebo without either the drug administrator or the patient having knowledge of whether placebo or drug were administered. The double blind technique controls differences in the treatment a patient receives, except for the drug, in that exactly the same thing happens to all patients.

The experiment for the laboratory session is a demonstration of the powerful effects of previous information (bias) upon an observer's ratings. Two observers are given equivalent, but opposite, information regarding what they might expect to observe, while another subject is not provided with such information.

INSTRUCTIONS

Experimental Team Size: Three.

Subjects: Arrange for exactly three volunteer subjects (friends, students, family members, etc.) to take part in the project which takes about 20 minutes.

Apparatus: One table; five chairs; two place cards (3 × 5 in. file cards, one with the number 1 and the other with the number 2 printed on it); pencils; subjects' response sheets; watch or clock.

Experimental Situation: Two of the three team members will hold a 15-minute discussion on any topic they choose which will be observed by the three subjects. The two speakers are seated at a table 7 feet or more from the subjects' chairs. A place card in front of each speaker identifies him as speaker 1 or speaker 2.

Procedure

1. Form teams of three members each.

2. Prepare response sheets (e.g., mimeographed) for each subject following the model shown in Fig. 3.1.

3. The experiment should be conducted in a room at the dormi-

tories, a group member's home, a free classroom, etc. The entire procedure must, however, be practiced in the laboratory until it runs smoothly. Two teams may work together in the laboratory, for the purposes of rehearsal, alternating as subjects and experimental team. The team serving as subjects should be very critical of the experimental team's behavior so that after several rehearsals each team may conduct a well-organized experiment.

Keep a tally of the number of aggressive remarks made by each speaker. Simply make one check mark (√) in the appropriate column for each aggressive remark.

	Speaker 1	Speaker 2	Speaker 1	Speaker 2
1		26		
2		27		
3		28		
.		.		
.		.		
.		.		
.		.		
23		48		
24		49		
25		50		

FIG. 3.1. Subject's response sheet.

4. Decide which two team members will hold the conversation. The only restriction is that the discussants must be of the same sex. The discussants should practice the 15-minute conversation alone until both are confident that the conversation can be maintained with a minimum of awkwardness. Each discussant should try to behave as naturally as possible.

5. The two team members will decide on a topic for discussion (e.g., a novel, baseball, or a current political event).

6. Divide the subjects into three groups of one subject each and designate them as subject A, B, and C, respectively.

7. Give each subject his or her instructions in private.

8. Instructions to subjects:

General instructions given to all subjects

"We are interested in how well people can judge aggressive remarks in social situations. When we go into the experimental room you will observe a discussion between two persons. I will give you a checklist upon which you will record the number of aggressive remarks made by each speaker. Simply place a check mark in the appropriate column to indicate each aggressive remark you observe."

Specific instructions to subject A

"The speaker with the number 1 in front of him (her) has been told to act verbally aggressive during the conversation, and we wish to see whether this is noticeable to a neutral observer. Please remain silent while in the experimental room."

Specific instructions to subject B

"The speaker with the number 2 in front of him (her) has been told to act verbally aggressive during the conversation, and we wish to see whether this is noticeable to a neutral observer. Please remain silent while in the experimental room."

Specific instructions to subject C

"Both speakers are going to act naturally, and we wish to see whether any aggressive behavior is observed. Please remain silent while in the experimental room."

9. Bring the subjects into the experimental room, seat them in a row facing the two seated speakers. Seat the subjects in order (that is, A next to B next to C) to facilitate distribution and collection of response sheets. The subjects should be at least 7 feet away from the speakers and at least 2 feet apart, to discourage conversation. Do not permit any conversation between subjects.

10. Code the response sheets by placing a letter A on the top of subject A's sheet, B on the top of subject B's sheet, etc. Give a response sheet to each subject, following the above code.

11. After the subjects are seated and all materials distributed the discussants should start their conversation.

12. After exactly 15 minutes tell the subjects to stop and collect their response sheets.

13. The study should at this time be explained in detail to the subjects. Explain all manipulations and their purpose to every subject.

TABLE 3.1

Number of aggressive remarks recorded

Subject	Speaker 1	Speaker 2
A		
B		
C		

Data Analysis

1. Record the total number of aggressive remarks recorded by each subject in tabular form such as in Table 3.1.

2. Draw a histogram of the above data as shown in Fig. 3.2.

3. Combine data: Pool the data from all experimental teams in the class in a table as shown in Table 3.2.

4. Compute the mean score for each subject total.

5. Draw a histogram of the above mean scores, following the model in item 2.

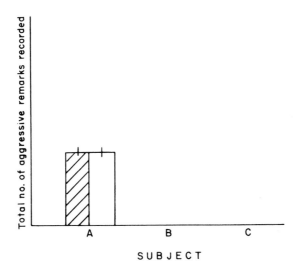

FIG. 3.2. Form for histogram. The shaded area indicates speaker 1, and the unshaded area indicates speaker 2.

TABLE 3.2
POOLED DATA: NUMBER OF AGGRESSIVE REMARKS
ATTRIBUTED TO THE DISCUSSANTS

Subject	Speaker 1 Experimental Team								Total	Speaker 2 Experimental Team								Total
	1	2	3	4	5	6	7	8		1	2	3	4	5	6	7	8	
A																		
B																		
C																		

EXPERIMENT 3

Experimental Report

1. Do the data support expectations? Does A tend to see speaker 1 as verbally aggressive while B reports the reverse?

2. Do the data support the expectation of no differences in the control condition?

Reprinted from American Psychologist, 1962, Vol. 17, pp. 776–783, by permission of the author and the publisher.

ON THE SOCIAL PSYCHOLOGY OF THE
PSYCHOLOGICAL EXPERIMENT:

WITH PARTICULAR REFERENCE TO DEMAND CHARACTERISTICS
AND THEIR IMPLICATIONS [1]

MARTIN T. ORNE [2]

Harvard Medical School

> *It is to the highest degree probable that the subject['s] . . . general attitude of mind is that of ready complacency and cheerful willingness to assist the investigator in every possible way by reporting to him those very things which he is most eager to find, and that the very questions of the experimenter . . . suggest the shade of reply expected . . . . Indeed . . . it seems too often as if the subject were now regarded as a stupid automaton . . . .*
>
> A. H. PIERCE, 1908 [3]

SINCE the time of Galileo, scientists have employed the laboratory experiment as a method of understanding natural phenomena. Generally, the experimental method consists of abstracting relevant variables from complex situations in nature and reproducing in the laboratory segments of these situations, varying the parameters involved so as to determine the effect of the experimental variables. This procedure allows generalization from the information obtained in the laboratory situation back to the original situation as it occurs in nature. The physical sciences have made striking advances through the use of this method, but in the behavioral sciences it has often been difficult to meet two necessary requirements for meaningful experimentation: reproducibility and ecological validity. It has long been recognized that certain differences will exist between the types of experiments conducted in the physical sciences and those in the behavioral sciences because the former investigates a universe of inanimate objects and forces, whereas the latter deals with animate

organisms, often thinking, conscious subjects. However, recognition of this distinction has not always led to appropriate changes in the traditional experimental model of physics as employed in the behavioral sciences. Rather the experimental model has been so successful as employed in physics that there has been a tendency in the behavioral sciences to follow precisely a paradigm originated for the study of inanimate objects, i.e., one which proceeds by exposing the subject to various conditions and observing the differences in reaction of the subject under different conditions. However, the use of such a model with animal or human subjects leads to the problem that the subject of the experiment is assumed, at least implicitly, to be a *passive responder* to stimuli—an assumption difficult to justify: Further, in this type of model the experimental stimuli themselves are usually rigorously defined in terms of what *is done* to the subject. In contrast, the purpose of this paper will be to focus on what the human subject *does* in the laboratory: what motivation the subject is likely to have in the experimental situation, how he usually perceives behavioral research, what the nature of the cues is that the subject is likely to pick up, etc. Stated in other terms, what factors are apt to affect the subject's reaction to the well-defined stimuli in the situation? These factors comprise what will be referred to here as the "experimental setting."

Since any experimental manipulation of human subjects takes place within this larger framework or setting, we should propose that the above-mentioned factors must be further elaborated and the parameters of the experimental setting more carefully defined so that adequate controls can be de-

[1] This paper was presented at the Symposium, "On the Social Psychology of the Psychological Experiment," American Psychological Association Convention, New York, 1961.
    The work reported here was supported in part by a Public Health Service Research Grant, M-3369, National Institute of Mental Health.
[2] I wish to thank my associates Ronald E. Shor, Donald N. O'Connell, Ulric Neisser, Karl E. Scheibe, and Emily F. Carota for their comments and criticisms in the preparation of this paper.
[3] See reference list (Pierce, 1908).
[4] Ecological validity, in the sense that Brunswik (1947) has used the term: appropriate generalization from the laboratory to nonexperimental situations.

signed to isolate the effects of the experimental setting from the effects of the experimental variables. Later in this paper we shall propose certain possible techniques of control which have been devised in the process of our research on the nature of hypnosis.

Our initial focus here will be on some of the qualities peculiar to psychological experiments. The experimental situation is one which takes place within the context of an explicit agreement of the subject to participate in a special form of social interaction known as "taking part in an experiment." Within the context of our culture the roles of subject and experimenter are well understood and carry with them well-defined mutual role expectations. A particularly striking aspect of the typical experimenter-subject relationship is the extent to which the subject will play his role and place himself under the control of the experimenter. Once a subject has agreed to participate in a psychological experiment, he implicitly agrees to perform a very wide range of actions on request without inquiring as to their purpose, and frequently without inquiring as to their duration.

Furthermore, the subject agrees to tolerate a considerable degree of discomfort, boredom, or actual pain, if required to do so by the experimenter. Just about any request which could conceivably be asked of the subject by a reputable investigator is legitimized by the quasi-magical phrase, "This is an experiment," and the shared assumption that a legitimate purpose will be served by the subject's behavior. A somewhat trivial example of this legitimization of requests is as follows:

A number of casual acquaintances were asked whether they would do the experimenter a favor; on their acquiescence, they were asked to perform five push-ups. Their response tended to be amazement, incredulity and the question "Why?" Another similar group of individuals were asked whether they would take part in an experiment of brief duration. When they agreed to do so, they too were asked to perform five push-ups. Their typical response was "Where?"

The striking degree of control inherent in the experimental situation can also be illustrated by a set of pilot experiments which were performed in the course of designing an experiment to test whether the degree of control inherent in the *hypnotic* relationship is greater than that in a waking relationship.[5] In order to test this question, we tried to develop a set of tasks which waking subjects would refuse to do, or would do only for a short period of time. The tasks were intended to be psychologically noxious, meaningless, or boring, rather than painful or fatiguing.

For example, one task was to perform serial additions of each adjacent two numbers on sheets filled with rows of random digits. In order to complete just one sheet, the subject would be required to perform 224 additions! A stack of some 2,000 sheets was presented to each subject—clearly an impossible task to complete. After the instructions were given, the subject was deprived of his watch and told, "Continue to work; I will return eventually." Five and one-half hours later, the *experimenter* gave up! In general, subjects tended to continue this type of task for several hours, usually with little decrement in performance. Since we were trying to find a task which would be discontinued spontaneously within a brief period, we tried to create a more frustrating situation as follows:

Subjects were asked to perform the same task described above but were also told that when finished the additions on each sheet, they should pick up a card from a large pile, which would instruct them on what to do next. However, every card in the pile read,

You are to tear up the sheet of paper which you have just completed into a minimum of thirty-two pieces and go on to the next sheet of paper and continue working as you did before; when you have completed this piece of paper, pick up the next card which will instruct you further. Work as accurately and as rapidly as you can.

Our expectation was that subjects would discontinue the task as soon as they realized that the cards were worded identically, that each finished piece of work had to be destroyed, and that, in short, the task was completely meaningless.

Somewhat to our amazement, subjects tended to persist in the task for several hours with relatively little sign of overt hostility. Removal of the one-way screen did not tend to make much difference. The postexperimental inquiry helped to explain the subjects' behavior. When asked about the tasks, subjects would invariably attribute considerable meaning to their performance, viewing it as an endurance test or the like.

Thus far, we have been singularly unsuccessful

[5] These pilot studies were performed by Thomas Menaker.

in finding an experimental task which would be discontinued, or, indeed, refused by subjects in an experimental setting.[6,7] Not only do subjects continue to perform boring, unrewarding tasks, but they do so with few errors and little decrement in speed. It became apparent that it was extremely difficult to design an experiment to test the degree of social control in hypnosis, in view of the already *very high degree of control in the experimental situation itself.*

The quasi-experimental work reported here is highly informal and based on samples of three or four subjects in each group. It does, however, illustrate the remarkable compliance of the experimental subject. The only other situations where such a wide range of requests are carried out with little or no question are those of complete authority, such as some parent-child relationships or some doctor-patient relationships. This aspect of the experiment as a social situation will not become apparent unless one tests for it; it is, however, present in varying degrees in all experimental contexts. Not only are tasks carried out, but they are performed with care over considerable period of time.

Our observation that subjects tend to carry out a remarkably wide range of instructions with a surprising degree of diligence reflects only one aspect of the motivation manifested by most subjects in an experimental situation. It is relevant to consider another aspect of motivation that is common to the subjects of most psychological experiments: high regard for the aims of science and experimentation.

A volunteer who participates in a psychological experiment may do so for a wide variety of reasons ranging from the need to fulfill a course requirement, to the need for money, to the unvoiced hope of altering his personal adjustment for the better, etc. Over and above these motives, however, college students tend to share (with the experimenter) the hope and expectation that the study in which they are participating will in some material way contribute to science and perhaps ultimately to human welfare in general. We should

[6] Tasks which would involve the use of actual severe physical pain or exhaustion were not considered.

[7] This observation is consistent with Frank's (1944) failure to obtain resistance to disagreeable or nonsensical tasks. He accounts for this "primarily by S's unwillingness to break the tacit agreement he had made when he volunteered to take part in the experiment, namely, to do whatever the experiment required of him" (p. 24).

expect that many of the characteristics of the experimental situation derive from the peculiar role relationship which exists between subject and experimenter. Both subject and experimenter share the belief that whatever the experimental task is, it is important, and that as such no matter how much effort must be exerted or how much discomfort must be endured, it is justified by the ultimate purpose.

If we assume that much of the motivation of the subject to comply with any and all experimental instructions derives from an identification with the goals of science in general and the success of the experiment in particular,[8] it follows that the subject has a stake in the outcome of the study in which he is participating. For the volunteer subject to feel that he has made a useful contribution, it is necessary for him to assume that the experimenter is competent and that he himself is a "good subject."

The significance to the subject of successfully being a "good subject" is attested to by the frequent questions at the conclusion of an experiment, to the effect of, "Did I ruin the experiment?" What is most commonly meant by this is, "Did I perform well in my role as experimental subject?" or "Did my behavior demonstrate that which the experiment is designed to show?" Admittedly, subjects are concerned about their performance in terms of reinforcing their self-image; nonetheless, they seem even more concerned with the utility of their performances. We might well expect then that as far as the subject is able, he will behave in an experimental context in a manner designed to play the role of a "good subject" or, in other words, *to validate the experimental hypothesis.* Viewed in this way, the student volunteer is *not* merely a passive responder in an experimental situation but rather he has a very real stake in the successful outcome of the experiment. This problem is implicitly recognized in the large number of psychological studies which attempt to conceal the true purpose of the experiment from the subject in the hope of thereby obtaining more reliable data. This maneuver on the part of psychologists is so widely known in the college population that even if a psy-

[8] This hypothesis is subject to empirical test. We should predict that there would be measurable differences in motivation between subjects who perceive a particular experiment as "significant" and those who perceive the experiment as "unimportant."

chologist is honest with the subject, more often than not he will be distrusted. As one subject pithily put it, "Psychologists always lie!" This bit of paranoia has some support in reality.

The subject's performance in an experiment might almost be conceptualized as problem-solving behavior; that is, at some level he sees it as his task to ascertain the true purpose of the experiment and respond in a manner which will support the hypotheses being tested. Viewed in this light, the totality of cues which convey an experimental hypothesis to the subject become significant determinants of subjects' behavior. We have labeled the sum total of such cues as the *"demand characteristics of the experimental situation"* (Orne, 1959a). These cues include the rumors or campus scuttlebutt about the research, the information conveyed during the original solicitation, the person of the experimenter, and the setting of the laboratory, as well as all explicit and implicit communications during the experiment proper. A frequently overlooked, but nonetheless very significant source of cues for the subject lies in the experimental procedure itself, viewed in the light of the subject's previous knowledge and experience. For example, if a test is given twice with some intervening treatment, even the dullest college student is aware that some change is expected, particularly if the test is in some obvious way related to the treatment.

The demand characteristics perceived in any particular experiment will vary with the sophistication, intelligence, and previous experience of each experimental subject. To the extent that the demand characteristics of the experiment are clear-cut, they will be perceived uniformly by most experimental subjects. It is entirely possible to have an experimental situation with clear-cut demand characteristics for psychology undergraduates which, however, does not have the same clear-cut demand characteristics for enlisted army personnel. It is, of course, those demand characteristics which are perceived by the subject that will influence his behavior.

We should like to propose the heuristic assumption that a subject's behavior in any experimental situation will be determined by two sets of variables: (*a*) those which are traditionally defined as experimental variables and (*b*) the perceived demand characteristics of the experimental situation. The extent to which the subject's behavior is related to the demand characteristics, rather than to

the experimental variable, will in large measure determine both the extent to which the experiment can be replicated with minor modification (i.e., modified demand characteristics) and the extent to which generalizations can be drawn about the effect of the experimental variables in nonexperimental contexts [the problem of ecological validity (Brunswik, 1947)].

It becomes an empirical issue to study under what circumstances, in what kind of experimental contexts, and with what kind of subject populations, demand characteristics become significant in determining the behavior of subjects in experimental situations. It should be clear that demand characteristics cannot be eliminated from experiments; all experiments will have demand characteristics, and these will always have some effect. It does become possible, however, to study the effect of demand characteristics as opposed to the effect of experimental variables. However, techniques designed to study the effect of demand characteristics need to take into account that these effects result from the subject's *active* attempt to respond appropriately to the *totality* of the experimental situation.

It is perhaps best to think of the perceived demand characteristics as a contextual variable in the experimental situation. We should like to emphasize that, at this stage, little is known about this variable. In our first study which utilized the demand characteristics concept (Orne, 1959b), we found that a particular experimental effect was present only in records of those subjects who were able to verbalize the experimenter's hypothesis. Those subjects who were unable to do so did not show the predicted phenomenon. Indeed we found that whether or not a given subject perceived the experimenter's hypothesis was a more accurate predictor of the subject's actual performance than his statement about what he thought he had done on the experimental task. It became clear from extensive interviews with subjects that response to the demand characteristics is not merely conscious compliance. When we speak of "playing the role of a good experimental subject," we use the concept analogously to the way in which Sarbin (1950) describes role playing in hypnosis: namely, largely on a nonconscious level. The demand characteristics of the situation help define the role of "good experimental subject," and the responses of the subject are a function of the role that is created.

We have a suspicion that the demand characteristics most potent in determining subjects' behavior are those which convey the purpose of the experiment effectively but not obviously. If the purpose of the experiment is not clear, or is highly ambiguous, many different hypotheses may be formed by different subjects, and the demand characteristics will not lead to clear-cut results. If, on the other hand, the demand characteristics are so obvious that the subject becomes fully conscious of the expectations of the experimenter, there is a tendency to lean over backwards to be honest. We are encountering here the effect of another facet of the college student's attitude toward science. While the student wants studies to "work," he feels he must be honest in his report; otherwise, erroneous conclusions will be drawn. Therefore, if the subject becomes acutely aware of the experimenter's expectations, there may be a tendency for biasing in the opposite direction. (This is analogous to the often observed tendency to favor individuals whom we dislike in an effort to be fair.) [9]

Delineation of the situations where demand characteristics may produce an effect ascribed to experimental variables, or where they may obscure such an effect and actually lead to systematic data in the opposite direction, as well as those experimental contexts where they do not play a major role, is an issue for further work. Recognizing the contribution to experimental results which may be made by the demand characteristics of the situation, what are some experimental techniques for the study of demand characteristics?

As we have pointed out, it is futile to imagine an experiment that could be created without demand characteristics. One of the basic characteristics of the human being is that he will ascribe purpose and meaning even in the absence of purpose and meaning. In an experiment where he knows some purpose exists, it is inconceivable for him not to form some hypothesis as to the purpose, based on some cues, no matter how meager; this will then determine the demand characteristics which will be perceived by and operate for a particular subject.

Rather than eliminating this variable then, it becomes necessary to take demand characteristics into account, study their effect, and manipulate them if necessary.

One procedure to determine the demand characteristics is the systematic study of each individual subject's perception of the experimental hypothesis. If one can determine what demand characteristics are perceived by each subject, it becomes possible to determine to what extent these, rather than the experimental variables, correlate with the observed behavior. If the subject's behavior correlates better with the demand characteristics than with the experimental variables, it is probable that the demand characteristics are the major determinants of the behavior.

The most obvious technique for determining what demand characteristics are perceived is the use of postexperimental inquiry. In this regard, it is well to point out that considerable self-discipline is necessary for the experimenter to obtain a valid inquiry. A great many experimenters at least implicitly make the demand that the subject not perceive what is really going on. The temptation for the experimenter, in, say, a replication of an Asch-group pressure experiment, is to ask the subject afterwards, "You didn't realize that the other fellows were confederates, did you?" Having obtained the required, "No," the experimenter breathes a sigh of relief and neither subject nor experimenter pursues the issue further.[10] However, even if the experimenter makes an effort to elicit the subject's perception of the hypothesis of the experiment, he may have difficulty in obtaining a valid report because the subject as well as he himself has considerable interest in appearing naive.

Most subjects are cognizant that they are not supposed to know any more about an experiment than they have been told and that excessive knowledge will disqualify them from participating, or, in the case of a postexperimental inquiry, such knowledge will invalidate their performance. As we pointed out earlier, subjects have a real stake in viewing their performance as meaningful. For this reason, it is commonplace to find a pact of ignorance resulting from the intertwining motives of both experimenter and subject, neither wishing to create a situation where the particular subject's performance needs to be excluded from the study.

[9] Rosenthal (1961) in his recent work on experimenter bias, has reported a similar type of phenomenon. Biasing was maximized by ego involvement of the experimenters, but when an attempt was made to increase biasing by paying for "good results," there was a marked reduction of effect. This reversal may be ascribed to the experimenters' becoming too aware of their own wishes in the situation.

[10] Asch (1952) himself took great pains to avoid this pitfall.

For these reasons, inquiry procedures are required to push the subject for information without, however, providing in themselves cues as to what is expected. The general question which needs to be explored is the subject's perception of the experimental purpose and the specific hypotheses of the experimenter. This can best be done by an open-ended procedure starting with the very general question of, "What do you think that the experiment is about?" and only much later asking specific questions. Responses of "I don't know" should be dealt with by encouraging the subject to guess, use his imagination, and in general, by refusing to accept this response. Under these circumstances, the overwhelming majority of students will turn out to have evolved very definite hypotheses. These hypotheses can then be judged, and a correlation between them and experimental performance can be drawn.

Two objections may be made against this type of inquiry: (a) that the subject's perception of the experimenter's hypotheses is based on his own experimental behavior, and therefore a correlation between these two variables may have little to do with the determinants of behavior, and (b) that the inquiry procedure itself is subject to demand characteristics.

A procedure which has been independently advocated by Riecken (1958) and Orne (1959a) is designed to deal with the first of these objections. This consists of an inquiry procedure which is conducted much as though the subject had actually been run in the experiment, without, however, permitting him to be given any experimental data. Instead, the precise procedure of the experiment is explained, the experimental material is shown to the subject, and he is told what he would be required to do; however, he is not permitted to make any responses. He is then given a postexperimental inquiry as though he had been a subject. Thus, one would say, "If I had asked you to do all these things, what do you think that the experiment would be about, what do you think I would be trying to prove, what would my hypothesis be?" etc. This technique, which we have termed the pre-experimental inquiry, can be extended very readily to the giving of pre-experimental tests, followed by the explanation of experimental conditions and tasks, and the administration of postexperimental tests. The subject is requested to behave on these tests as though he had been ex-

posed to the experimental treatment that was described to him. This type of procedure is not open to the objection that the subject's own behavior has provided cues for him as to the purpose of the task. It presents him with a straight problem-solving situation and makes explicit what, for the true experimental subject, is implicit. It goes without saying that these subjects who are run on the pre-experimental inquiry conditions must be drawn from the same population as the experimental groups and may, of course, not be run subsequently in the experimental condition. This technique is one of approximation rather than of proof. However, if subjects describe behavior on the pre-inquiry conditions as similar to, or identical with, that actually given by subjects exposed to the experimental conditions, the hypothesis becomes plausible that demand characteristics may be responsible for the behavior.

It is clear that pre- and postexperimental inquiry techniques have their own demand characteristics. For these reasons, it is usually best to have the inquiry conducted by an experimenter who is not acquainted with the actual experimental behavior of the subjects. This will tend to minimize the effect of experimenter bias.

Another technique which we have utilized for approximating the effect of the demand characteristics is to attempt to hold the demand characteristics constant and eliminate the experimental variable. One way of accomplishing this purpose is through the use of simulating subjects. This is a group of subjects who are not exposed to the experimental variable to which the effect has been attributed, but who are instructed to act *as if* this were the case. In order to control for experimenter bias under these circumstances, it is advisable to utilize more than one experimenter and to have the experimenter who actually runs the subjects "blind" as to which group (simulating or real) any given individual belongs.

Our work in hypnosis (Damaser, Shor, & Orne, 1963; Orne, 1959b; Shor, 1959) is a good example of the use of simulating controls. Subjects unable to enter hypnosis are instructed to simulate entering hypnosis for another experimenter. The experimenter who runs the study sees both highly trained hypnotic subjects and simulators in random order and does not know to which group each subject belongs. Because the subjects are run "blind," the experimenter is more likely to treat the two groups of subjects identically. We have found that simulating subjects are able to perform with great effectiveness, deceiving even well-trained hypnotists. However, the simulating group is not exposed to the experimental condition (in this case, hypnosis) to which the given effect under investigation is often ascribed. Rather, it is a group faced with a problem-solving task: namely, to utilize whatever cues are made available by the experimental context and the experimenter's concrete behavior in order to behave as they think that hypnotized subjects might. Therefore, to the extent that simulating subjects are able to behave identically, it is possible that demand characteristics, rather than the altered state of consciousness, could account for the behavior of the experimental group.

The same type of technique can be utilized in other types of studies. For example, in contrast to the placebo control in a drug study, it is equally possible to instruct some subjects not to take the medication at all, but to act as if they had. It must be emphasized that this type of control is different from the placebo control. It represents an approximation. It maximally confronts the simulating subject with a problem-solving task and suggests how much of the total effect could be accounted for by the demand characteristics—assuming that the experimental group had taken full advantage of them, an assumption not necessarily correct.

All of the techniques proposed thus far share the quality that they depend upon the active cooperation of the control subjects, and in some way utilize his thinking process as an intrinsic factor. The subject does *not* just respond in these control situations but, rather, he is required *actively* to solve the problem.

The use of placebo experimental conditions is a way in which this problem can be dealt with in a more classic fashion. Psychopharmacology has used such techniques extensively, but here too they present problems. In the case of placebos and drugs, it is often the case that the physician is "blind" as to whether a drug is placebo or active, but the patient is not, despite precautions to the contrary; i.e., the patient is cognizant that he does not have the side effects which some of his fellow patients on the ward experience. By the same token, in psychological placebo treatments, it is equally important to ascertain whether the subject actually perceived the treatment to be experimental or control.

Certainly the subject's perception of himself as a control subject may materially alter the situation.

A recent experiment [11] in our laboratory illustrates this type of investigation. We were interested in studying the demand characteristics of sensory deprivation experiments, independent of any actual sensory deprivation. We hypothesized that the overly cautious treatment of subjects, careful screening for mental or physical disorders, awesome release forms and, above all, the presence of a "panic (release) button" might be more significant in producing the effects reported from sensory deprivation than the actual diminution of sensory input. A pilot study (Stare, Brown, & Orne, 1959), employing preinquiry techniques, supported this view. Recently, we designed an experiment to test more rigorously this hypothesis.

This experiment, which we called Meaning Deprivation, had all the *accoutrements* of sensory deprivation, including release forms and a red panic button. However, we carefully refrained from creating any sensory deprivation whatsoever. The experimental task consisted of sitting in a small experimental room which was well lighted, with two comfortable chairs, as well as ice water and a sandwich, and an optional task of adding numbers. The subject did not have a watch during this time, the room was reasonably quiet, but not soundproof, and the duration of the experiment (of which the subject was ignorant) was four hours. Before the subject was placed in the experimental room, 10 tests previously used in sensory deprivation research were administered. At the completion of the experiment, the same tasks were again administered. A microphone and a one-way screen were present in the room, and the subject was encouraged to verbalize freely.

The control group of 10 subjects was subjected to the identical treatment, except that they were told that they were control subjects for a sensory deprivation experiment. The panic button was eliminated for this group. The formal experimental treatment of these two groups of subjects was the same in terms of the objective stress—four hours of isolation. However, the demand characteristics had been purposively varied for the two groups to study the effect of demand character-

[11] This experiment is described in a paper in preparation by M. T. Orne and K. E. Scheibe: The Contribution of Nondeprivation Factors in the Production of Sensory Deprivation Effects.

istics as opposed to objective stress. Of the 14 measures which could be quantified, 13 were in the predicted direction, and 6 were significant at the selected 10% alpha level or better. A Mann-Whitney U test ha , been performed on the summation ranks of all measures as a convenient method for summarizing the overall differences. The one-tailed probability which emerges is $p = .001$, a clear demonstration of expected effects.

This study suggests that demand characteristics may in part account for some of the findings commonly attributed to sensory deprivation. We have found similar significant effects of demand characteristics in accounting for a great deal of the findings reported in hypnosis. It is highly probable that careful attention to this variable, or group of variables, may resolve some of the current controversies regarding a number of psychological phenomena in motivation, learning, and perception.

In summary, we have suggested that the subject must be recognized as an active participant in any experiment, and that it may be fruitful to view the psychological experiment as a very special form of social interaction. We have proposed that the subject's behavior in an experiment is a function of the totality of the situation, which includes the experimental variables being investigated and at least one other set of variables which we have subsumed under the heading, demand characteristics of the experimental situation. The study and control of demand characteristics are not simply matters of good experimental technique; rather, it is an empirical issue to determine under what circumstances demand characteristics significantly affect subjects' experimental behavior. Several empirical techniques have been proposed for this purpose. It has been suggested that control of these variables in particular may lead to greater reproduci-

bility and ecological validity of psychological experiments. With an increasing understanding of these factors intrinsic to the experimental context, the experimental method in psychology may become a more effective tool in predicting behavior in nonexperimental contexts.

REFERENCES

ASCH, S. E. *Social psychology.* New York: Prentice Hall, 1952.

BRUNSWIK, E. *Systematic and representative design of psychological experiments with results in physical and social perception.* (Syllabus Series, No. 304) Berkeley: Univer. California Press, 1947.

DAMASER, ESTHER C., SHOR, R. E., & ORNE, M. T. Physiological effects during hypnotically-requested emotions. *Psychosom. Med.* 1963, 25, 334–343.

FRANK, J. D. Experimental studies of personal pressure and resistance: I. Experimental production of resistance. *J. gen. Psychol.*, 1944, 30, 23–41.

ORNE, M. T. The demand characteristics of an experimental design and their implications. Paper read at American Psychological Association, Cincinnati, 1959. (a)

ORNE, M. T. The nature of hypnosis: Artifact and essence. *J. abnorm. soc. Psychol.*, 1959, 58, 277–299. (b)

PIERCE, A. H. The subconscious again. *J. Phil., Psychol., scient. Meth.*, 1908, 5, 264–271.

RIECKEN, H. W. A program for research on experiments in social psychology. Paper read at Behavioral Sciences Conference, University of New Mexico, 1958.

ROSENTHAL, R. On the social psychology of the psychological experiment: With particular reference to experimenter bias. Paper read at American Psychological Association, New York, 1961.

SARBIN, T. R. Contributions to role-taking theory: I. Hypnotic behavior. *Psychol. Rev.*, 1950, 57, 255–270.

SHOR, R. E. Explorations in hypnosis: A theoretical and experimental study. Unpublished doctoral dissertation, Brandeis University, 1959.

STARE, F., BROWN, J., & ORNE, M. T. Demand characteristics in sensory deprivation studies. Unpublished seminar paper, Massachusetts Mental Health Center and Harvard University, 1959.

PAUL G. SWINGLE

Reprinted from Journal of Personality and Social Psychology, 1966, Vol. 3, pp. 20–27, by permission of the authors and the publisher.

DATA DESIRABILITY, EXPERIMENTER EXPECTANCY, AND THE RESULTS OF PSYCHOLOGICAL RESEARCH [1]

ROBERT ROSENTHAL, PAUL KOHN, PATRICIA M. GREENFIELD,

AND NOEL CAROTA

19 male Es employing a Taffel-type task conducted a verbal conditioning experiment with 60 female Ss. ½ the Es were led to expect their Ss to show verbal conditioning, and ½ were led to expect no verbal conditioning. ½ the Es in each of these groups were led to feel that it would be desirable if their Ss showed conditioning, and ½ were led to feel that it would be undesirable. Those Es who (a) both wanted and expected, and (b) neither wanted nor expected their Ss to show increased use of I and WE pronouns obtained significant conditioning (p = .001). Those Es who (a) wanted but did not expect, and (b) expected but did not want increased use of I and WE pronouns obtained no significant conditioning (p = 1.00). Ss high in need for social approval arrived earlier at the site of the experiment, were less "aware" of the contingency but were no more likely to show conditioning. Ss' ratings of Es' behavior during the experiment showed significant differences between Es in different experimental conditions, between Es who were 1st vs. later born, and between Es who were high vs. low in need for social approval.

A series of experiments has recently been reported which suggests that for a variety of experimenters, subjects, and situations, the experimenter's expectancy or hypothesis may be a significant partial determinant of the results he obtains (Rosenthal, 1964). In most of our studies, the particular data experimenters were led to expect were presumably also desired by them. The effects of experimenter expectancy have therefore been confounded with those of desirability. This seems reasonable from the standpoint of ecological validity. "Real" experimenters ordinarily want to obtain data they expect and do not want to obtain data they do not expect. Nevertheless one can think of research situations wherein experimenters expect to obtain data they do not consider desirable for any of several reasons (e.g., Milgram, 1963). Moreover, one can also think of situations wherein experimenters do not really expect to obtain data which would be highly desirable (i.e., "long-shot" studies).

The general purpose of the present investigation, then, was to study the separate and combined effects on research findings of the

[1] This investigation was supported by Research Grants G-24826 and GS-177 from the Division of Social Sciences of the National Science Foundation.

experimenter's expectancy of certain results and the desirability to the experimenter of those results. A more specific purpose of the present study was to learn whether experimenters' expectancies and desires might be partial determinants of the results of studies of verbal conditioning. An earlier study did show that the experimenter's expectancies might be determinants of the degree of his subjects' awareness that they had undergone a conditioning procedure. That study did *not*, however, vary the experimenter's expectancy of whether conditioning would or would not occur; nor did it involve any manipulation of the outcome desirability of either subjects' awareness or subjects' conditioning scores (Rosenthal, Persinger, Vikan-Kline, & Fode, 1963).

Accordingly, half our experimenters were led to expect that their subjects would show verbal conditioning while the remaining experimenters were led to expect no verbal conditioning. Half the experimenters in each of these groups were led to feel that their subjects' verbal conditioning would reflect well on the experimenter while the remaining experimenters were led to feel that their subjects' verbal conditioning would reflect badly on the experimenter.

METHOD

Experimenters

Nineteen male graduate students served as paid volunteer experimenters. All were in their first 2 years of work at Harvard's Division of Engineering and Applied Physics.

Subjects

The experimenters ran a total of 60 paid volunteer subjects, all of them female students at a Boston secretarial school. The experimental task was explained to the subjects as a test of verbal facility.

Experimental Task

The experimental task was a modified Taffel (1955) procedure. The experimenters presented their subjects with four sets of 20 verbs, each of which was to be used in a sentence constructed by the subject. Each sentence was to begin with any of the following pronouns: I, WE, YOU, HE, SHE, and THEY. In order to reduce any errors of observation or recording, subjects wrote down each sentence and then read it aloud to the experimenter who checked to be sure that the subject had read the same pronoun she had recorded. On the last 60 trials (three blocks of 20), the experimenters said "good" whenever I or WE was the pronoun selected. The dependent variable was a measure of the increase in the use of I or WE from the operant level to the subsequent blocks of trials.

Procedure

The experiment was conducted in one day at two different hours. All experimental conditions were represented in each session. The experimenters in each session were trained as a group. They were given factual material about the phenomenon of verbal conditioning. Two reasons were advanced for their participation in this experiment. The first stressed the need for replication by researchers who were not behavioral scientists in order to extend the generality of the findings in the verbal conditioning literature. The second stressed our interest in learning more of the relationship between the experimenters' personality and their subjects' conditioning scores. All experimenters were then administered the Marlowe-Crowne Social Desirability scale, the Taylor Manifest Anxiety scale, a form for establishing birth order, and the first set of 20 verbs they would present to their subjects. This was done to obtain the experimenters' operant level for using I and WE and was obtained of course before the experimenters knew which pronouns they would be reinforcing. The experimenters were told that their subjects would be assigned them on the basis of the subjects' similarity to the experimenters in personality as measured by the tests the experimenters had taken. The same tests were in fact administered to the subjects, but assignment of subjects to experimenters was essentially random.

After each subject finished her experimental task and left her experimenter's research room she filled out two questionnaires designed to define the degree of her awareness that she had undergone a verbal conditioning procedure. The first questionnaire (Q_1) simply asked the subject to state the purpose of the experiment (Matarazzo, Saslow, & Pareis, 1960). The second questionnaire (Q_2) repeated the substance of the first but asked more specific and more leading questions (Levin, 1961). Both questionnaires had been modified for use in an earlier study (Rosenthal et al., 1963). Each subject also filled out a series of 28 rating scales designed to assess her perception of her experimenter. Each scale had 20 points running from +10 (e.g., extremely businesslike) to −10 (e.g., extremely unbusinesslike) with intermediate labeled points. This same questionnaire had been employed in earlier experiments (Rosenthal, Fode, Friedman, & Vikan-Kline, 1960).

Experimental Conditions

The experimental treatments were administered in the form of "last-minute instructions" placed on each experimenter's desk. For half the experimenters the instructions claimed that their subjects had personality characteristics such that they would condition well. The remaining experimenters were led to expect their subjects to condition poorly. The desirability of these two outcomes was implemented by telling half the experimenters that conditionability was highly correlated with general learning ability and by telling the others that it was highly correlated with susceptibility to deliberate manipulation. Since the experimenters believed themselves to be similar to their subjects in personality, the first group of experimenters should find good conditioning data a desirable outcome since it would imply that the experimenter, like his subjects, had good general learning ability. The remaining experimenters should find good conditioning data an undesirable outcome since it would imply that the experimenter, like his subjects, was highly manipulatable.

Those portions of the instructions used to implement data desirability were as follows:

[Desirable]: There are a few things we now know about subjects who are more and less conditionable. Our hope, of course, is to learn a good deal more about that. What we know so far suggests that highly conditionable people tend to have high general learning ability. They pick up new concepts and ideas quickly and have skill in analyzing and solving problems. Poor conditioners, in contrast, tend to have lesser abilities in these areas.

[Undesirable]: There are a few things we now know about subjects who are more and less conditionable. Our hope, of course, is to learn a great deal more about that. What we know so far suggests that highly conditionable people tend to be manipulatable. They are often like putty in the hands of advertisers and salesmen. Poor conditioners, in contrast, tend to be very resistant to such manipulation; in other words, they seem to have minds of their own.

Within each of the two above conditions of data desirability, half the experimenters received one of the following two additional instructions specifying expectancy:

[Expect]: The particular subjects assigned to you, on the whole, tend to be good conditioners. That is, they will tend to show a significant increase in the number of "I" and "WE" pronouns from the first set of 20 sentences to the later sets.

[Don't expect]: The particular subjects assigned to you will, on the whole, tend to be poor conditioners. That is, they will not tend to show a significant increase in the number of "I" and "WE" pronouns from the first set of 20 sentences to the later sets.

The method described above of implementing our outcome-desirability variable was selected on the basis of an instruction pretest with Harvard undergraduates from a course in motivation. These subjects received eight characterizations of the personality correlates of conditionability. Of these, four were designed to be desirable and four undesirable. The subjects were instructed to imagine themselves to be experimenters running an experiment on the personality correlates of verbal conditioning. Further, they were asked to imagine that their "subjects" were assigned to them on the basis of similarity (to themselves) on important personality dimensions "so that any interpretation of experimental results should apply to [them] . . . as well as to [the] subjects." Under these role-playing conditions subjects were asked to rate the eight characterizations on five scales: the desirability of having highly

conditionable subjects, assuming the characterizations to be correct; the desirability of having subjects who were highly resistant to conditioning, assuming the characterizations to be correct; the probability that a competent psychologist would be right if he predicted their subjects to be highly conditionable; the probability that a competent psychologist would be right if he predicted their subjects to be highly resistant to conditioning; the believability of the characterization if made by a competent psychologist.

The two characterizations used in the present experiment were selected because the patterns of ratings assigned them on our five scales were generally superior to those of the other characterizations. That is, our pretest subjects rated these two characterizations as relatively believable, and relatively desirable, in one case and undesirable in the other. Moreover, they expressed considerable readiness to concur with either of the two opposite predictions by a competent psychologist.

Precautions against Authors' Expectancy Effects

We took a number of precautions to prevent our own outcome expectancies and outcome desires from having major effects on the data collected by the experimenters. These included: randomly assigning rooms to conditions; assigning experimenters to rooms in order of departure from the experimenter reception room; implementing the independent variables in a way involving no contact with the experimenters by persons who were aware of the experimenters' treatment conditions; assigning subjects to experimenters on the basis of (a) order of subjects' departure from the subject reception room, (b) the experimenter's immediate availability to run a new subject, and (c) the number of subjects run by each experimenter up to that point.

The above procedures left all the major investigators except one blind to each experimenter's treatment condition. The lone exception was the author who was in charge of assigning rooms to conditions and ensuring that approximately equal numbers of experimenters and subjects were assigned to each treatment condition. He had no contact with either experimenters or subjects during the course of the experiment. With the foregoing precautions, the likelihood that the major investigators' own expectancies and desires substantially affected the data seems small.

RESULTS

Conditioning

Initially four alternative definitions of conditioning were employed: increase in I-WE usage from the operant level to Block 4; increase in I-WE usage from the operant level to the mean of the subsequent three blocks; increase in I-WE usage from the operant level to Block 4 plus one-third the increase from Block 2 to Block 3; monotonicity of increase

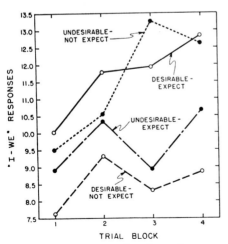

FIG. 1. Frequency of choice of I and WE as a function of experimenter expectancy, outcome desirability, and trial block.

of I-WE usage from Blocks 1 to 4 as measured by rank correlation between number of I-WE responses and block number. The median intercorrelation of these dependent variables was .79. Because the first of these definitions was both the simplest and most highly correlated with the other definitions, it was accepted as the definition of magnitude of conditioning.

Figure 1 shows the mean of the mean number of I-WE responses obtained by experimenters in each of the four experimental groups for each of the four blocks. Table 1 shows the mean conditioning scores (Block 4 − Block 1) and Table 2 the results of the analysis of variance. Only the interaction was significant. Apparently, then, neither experimenter's expectancy nor the desirability of conditioning data alone affect the magnitude of conditioning scores reliably but the *congruence* between expectancy and data desirability does make a substantial difference. Under the congruent conditions 100% of the experimenters showed a mean increase in their subjects' use of I and WE ($p = .001$). Under the incongruent conditions only 56% of the experimenters showed a mean increase ($p = 1.00$).

Awareness

The awareness questionnaires were independently and blindly scored by two of the authors on a 3-point scale: clearly unaware, 1; vaguely aware, 2; and clearly aware of the response-reinforcement contingency, 3. The reliabilities of Q_1 and Q_2 were .95 and .97, respectively.

Of all subjects 17% were classed as clearly aware,[2] 8% as vaguely aware, and 75% as clearly unaware (Q_2).

Experimenters who expected conditioning tended to obtain a lower rate of clear awareness (7%) than did experimenters who did not expect conditioning (25%). Because the bulk of subjects in both experimenter expectancy conditions were "clearly unaware," the difference in rates of clear awareness approached significance ($p = .10$) only when

[2] Among subjects judged as clearly aware a few specifically mentioned their decision to go along or not go along with their experimenters' attempts to influence them.

TABLE 1

EXPERIMENTERS' MEAN CONDITIONING SCORES FOR FOUR EXPERIMENTAL GROUPS

Outcome desirability	Expectancy	
	Expect	Don't expect
Desirable	3.0	1.3
Undesirable	0.8	3.1

the analysis was limited to subjects who were either vaguely or clearly aware.

Aside from her experimenter's treatment condition, two factors proved to be related to the subject's subsequent awareness: the subject's personality and the order in which she was run by the experimenter. Subjects who scored as more anxious ($r = -.22$, $p = .10$) and as higher in need for social approval ($r = -.30$, $p = .02$) were less likely to become aware subsequently. Subjects run later by a given experimenter were more likely to become aware ($r = .26$, $p = .05$). In addition, all the subjects run in the second experimental session were more likely to become aware than subjects run in the first session ($p = .08$).

Subjects' Perceptions of Experimenters

Subjects had rated their experimenters on 28 variables immediately after the experiment. Those experimenters who had been in the congruent experimental treatment groups were rated by their subjects as more casual ($r = .33$, $p = .01$), more courteous ($r = .27$, $p = .05$), more pleasant ($r = .24$, $p = .08$), more expressive-voiced ($r = .24$, $p = .08$), and as less given to the use of movements of the trunk region ($r = -.26$, $p = .05$). Because of the intercorrelations among these particular variables and among the total set

TABLE 2

ANALYSIS OF VARIANCE OF EXPERIMENTERS' MEAN CONDITIONING SCORES

Source	df	MS	p
Expectancy (A)	1	0.18	
Desirability (B)	1	0.06	
A × B	1	22.26	10.55*
Within	15	2.11	

* $p = .006$.

TABLE 3

SUBJECTS' CONDITIONING SCORES AND THEIR
PERCEPTION OF EXPERIMENTERS

Variable	r	p
Interested	.43	.001
Businesslike	.43	.001
Professional	.33	.01
Quiet (nonloud)	.31	.02
Enthusiastic	.28	.04
Behaved consistently	.26	.05
Expressive-voiced	.24	.08

of 28 variables, no simple statement is possible of how many of these particular correlations might be attributed to chance. It seems likely, however, that the experimenters' behavior during the experiment, as defined by their subjects' ratings was at least in part determined by the experimental treatment conditions.

Table 3 shows the correlations between the magnitude of the subjects' conditioning scores and their perceptions of their experimenters. We cannot be sure, of course, that these ratings of experimenters actually do reflect differences in experimenter behavior. It is also possible that those subjects who are more susceptible to the interpersonal influence of a reinforcing experimenter simply describe experimenter behavior differently. Or, having been influenced by a reinforcing experimenter, these subjects may have rated that experimenter according to their preconceptions of the sort of person by whom they would permit themselves to be influenced. Assuming for the moment that these ratings accurately described experimenter behavior, subjects were more influenced by experimenters showing a general enthusiastic interest in them; conveying a consistent, professional, businesslike manner; and speaking in a quiet but expressive tone of voice. If these experimenters did *not* in fact behave in this way, at least it seems warranted to believe that more influencible subjects ascribe such characteristics to the experimenters by whom they are influenced.

Experimenter Characteristics

Experimenters' birth order, operant level of I and WE, and need for social approval were

not related to their subjects' conditioning scores. Experimenters' anxiety scores were related to their subjects' conditioning in a nonlinear manner. Both high- and low-anxious experimenters obtained greater conditioning than did medium-anxious experimenters ($F = 3.08$, $df = 2/13$, $p = .08$).

While not related to subjects' conditioning, experimenters' birth order appeared to be a significant predictor of experimenters' behavior in the experiment as defined by subjects' ratings. Table 4 shows the correlations between experimenters' birth order and a number of behavioral variables. First-born experimenters were generally rated as fast but reluctant speakers who used fewer body and facial movements and expressions.

Experimenters who used more I and WE pronouns in their pretesting were rated by their subjects as more casual ($r = .34$, $p = .01$), more enthusiastic ($r = .22$, $p = .10$), and more pleasant-voiced ($r = .22$, $p = .10$).

Experimenters scoring higher in need for social approval were rated by their subjects as less personal ($r = -.32$, $p = .02$), less loud ($r = .27$, $p = .05$), less talkative ($r = .22$, $p = .10$), more enthusiastic ($r = .27$, $p = .05$), but less well-liked ($r = -.22$, $p = .10$). None of the subjects' ratings of experimenters' behavior during the experiment showed a correlation with experimenter anxiety which was significant at the .05 level.

Subject Characteristics

Subjects' birth order, anxiety, and need for social approval were found to be unrelated to subjects' conditioning scores. Subjects high in need for social approval were found to be later born more often than first born ($r = -.24$, $p = .08$) and, interestingly enough,

TABLE 4

RELATIONSHIPS BETWEEN EXPERIMENTERS' BEING
FIRST BORN AND RATINGS BY THEIR SUBJECTS

Variable	r	p
Less talkative	.37	.006
Fast speaking	.32	.02
Body use	-.32	.02
Trunk use	-.27	.05
Hand gestures	-.26	.05
Expressive face	-.24	.08

to have arrived earlier at the site of the experiment ($r = .40$, $p = .003$).

Subjects' operant levels of I and WE responses were not significantly related to their conditioning scores ($r = -.10$). Subjects' operant levels, however, tended to be a function of experimenters' treatment conditions. Those experimenters for whom data desirability and expectancy operated conjointly obtained higher rates of operant level responding from their subjects ($F = 3.22$, $df = 1/15$, $p = .10$). Thus while congruence of data desirability and experimenter expectancy was associated both with high operant levels and high conditioning scores, it is clear that the conditioning scores cannot be attributed to the operant levels.

Model Bias

The extent to which a given experimenter's own performance of a task determines his subjects' performance of the same task is the extent to which the experimenter "models" his subjects. A recent summary of experiments testing the hypothesis of modeling effects suggested that in different experiments there might be different orders of magnitude of experimenter modeling effects (Rosenthal, 1964).

In the present study, modeling effects were defined by the correlation between experimenters' own operant levels of I and WE and the mean operant levels of their subsequently run subjects.

Table 5 shows these correlations for each of the four experimental conditions. Two of the four correlations were significant at the .05 level, and the four r's were significantly different from one another ($\chi^2 = 17.68$, $df = 3$, $p < .001$). It appears then, that whether the experimenter expects and/or desires a certain outcome may significantly affect the direction and magnitude of experimenter modeling effects.

Qualitative Analysis of Awareness Questionnaires

Most of the subjects (88%) felt the purpose of the experiment was to assess their personality. Since the subjects had filled out personality questionnaires, this ascription of purpose was natural enough. Many of the

TABLE 5

CORRELATION BETWEEN EXPERIMENTERS' AND SUBJECTS' OPERANT LEVELS FOR FOUR EXPERIMENTAL CONDITIONS

Outcome desirability	Expectancy	
	Expect	Don't expect
Desirable	−.88*	+.997**
Undesirable	+.03	−.74

* $p < .05$, two-tailed.
** $p < .005$, two-tailed.

subjects, however, saw the "test of verbal facility" as a personality test akin to word-association or sentence-completion techniques. More specifically, several subjects saw it as a test of their egocentricity, as measured by the frequency of their use of I.

Only 30% of all subjects believed their experimenters when they told them their verbal abilities were being assessed. Among subjects run by experimenters in the congruent conditions, only 18% believed their abilities were being assessed. In the incongruent conditions, 46% of the subjects believed their abilities were being assessed. The differences in belief rates were significant ($\chi^2 = 5.68$, $p = .02$) suggesting that the behavior of the experimenters in the congruent conditions made it seem more unlikely to their subjects that their verbal abilities were being assessed.

It has been suggested elsewhere (Rosenthal et al., 1963) that subjects may be interested in their experimenters as people rather than simply as "scientists." Evidence of a "transference reaction" was presented. In the present study, 20% of all subjects made some reference to one or more physical characteristics of their experimenter which were irrelevant to the experimenter's role performance. These included mention of the experimenter's posture, clothing, facial blemishes, wearing of glasses, condition of teeth, and relative attractiveness.

DISCUSSION

The results of the present experiment were both unequivocal and surprising, and their interpretation can at best be only tentative. This was the first experiment in our research program in which the experimenters' expec-

PAUL G. SWINGLE

tancies were varied independently of the desirabilities of the outcomes. In most of the earlier research experimenters who expected a given outcome probably also desired it while those who did not expect that outcome also did not desire it. There have, however, been a few studies in which it could be argued that all experimenters desired a given outcome while differing in their expectancy of it. Such would be the case in experiments employing animal subjects in which all experimenters wanted their subjects to perform well since their course grades might depend on it (Rosenthal, 1964). Those experimenters who expected better performance from their subjects obtained better performance than did those who expected poorer performance. For these experiments it could be argued from the results of the present study that if there had been a group of experimenters who neither expected nor desired good performance from their subjects they would have obtained performance as good as that obtained by experimenters who both wanted and expected good performance. Only another experiment can answer this question for us.

But, from one point of view, the present study seems to contradict the bulk of the earlier research in which *opposite* expectancies (coupled with presumably congruent motives) were associated with correspondingly *opposite* results (Rosenthal, 1964). In the present study, on the other hand, opposite expectancies combined with congruent motives produced *identical* results. The present study differed from earlier ones in a number of ways any of which alone or in interaction with one another could account, even if not simply, for the differences. The present study was the first to: employ expectancies about verbal conditioning performances, employ as experimenters graduate students in the physical sciences, and create expectancies about verbal behavior in which experimenters were explicitly taught how such behavior could be intentionally manipulated thereby confounding the unintentional biasing process with the intentional reinforcement process.

Perhaps the simplest tentative explanation is based on a reexamination of the phenomenology of the experimenters in the various experimental conditions. Those experimenters who both expected and wanted conditioning or neither expected nor wanted conditioning were told by us essentially that we thought they were particularly clever in the one case and that they had minds of their own in the other. Thus the congruent experimenters were complimented by the investigators. On the other hand, experimenters in the incongruent conditions were told essentially we thought them to be either not too bright or like putty in the hands of manipulators. The experimenters in the incongruent condition then were anything but complimented by their employers. These experimenters could have been emotionally affected to the point where their verbal "reinforcements" lacked sufficient conviction to be positive reinforcers for their subjects. Experimenters in the noncongruent condition were in fact rated by their subjects as less expressive-voiced than experimenters in the congruent condition ($p = .08$) and expressiveness of voice was positively correlated with successful conditioning ($r = + .24$, $p = .08$).

If the interpretation offered to account for our surprising results is correct, then the present experiment in no way contradicts earlier findings, although the relation between the two sets of results requires further clarification. In the bulk of the previous work, affect was not experimentally manipulated, while in this study we must conclude that the experimenter's affect or mood is a more important determinant of his effectiveness as a reinforcer than either his expectancy or the desirability of the outcome in studies of verbal conditioning.

Among those subjects showing some indication of awareness, more clear awareness was shown by subjects whose experimenters had had been led to expect no conditioning. It seems possible, therefore, that some of the ambiguity surrounding the question of awareness rates in studies of verbal conditioning may be associated with the experimenter's expectancy regarding subjects' conditionability as well as his expectancy about subsequent awareness (Rosenthal et al., 1963).

Studies by Crowne and Strickland (1961) and by Marlowe (1962) found that subjects with a greater need for social approval showed greater verbal conditioning effects. The present study, like that by Spielberger, Berger, and Howard (1963) found no such relationship. However, those of our subjects with a greater need for approval showed significantly less awareness of the "response-reinforcement" contingency. Quite possibly these subjects recognized that the socially desirable thing to do when a psychological investigator inquires after awareness in a conditioning experiment is to "not see through" the experimental situation. This interpretation is quite consistent with the position that the need for approval is a tendency to respond appropriately to perceived situational demands (Crowne & Marlowe, 1964). Further construct validation of the Marlowe-Crowne scale comes from our finding that subjects higher in need for approval were more likely to arrive earlier at the site of the experiment than subjects lower in need for approval. However, why subjects higher in need for approval should more often be later born than first born is by no means obvious.

The finding that subjects run later by a given experimenter were more likely to be aware is most parsimoniously interpreted as due to later-run subjects having a lower need for social approval. The finding that subjects run in the second experimental session were more likely to be aware is less clearly explained. One likely interpretation involves the possibility of feedback from Session I subjects to Session II subjects. This is not a trivial problem. We may wonder about the effects of feedback from earlier- to later-run subjects in a good deal of behavioral research. Needed are some hard data on the efficacy of the optimistically solicited loyalty oath wherein we swear our earlier-run subjects to secrecy "until the experiment is over."

Asking subjects to describe their experimenter's behavior during the experiment seems to be a useful technique. On the basis of these descriptions we were able to differentiate experimenters under the various experimental conditions. These descriptions suggest how the preexperimental manipulations of experimenter variables (as well as the experimenter's more enduring personal characteristics) might be translated into unprogramed experimenter behavior during the experiment. Our data suggest that it is this unprogramed behavior which is responsible for the experimenter's unintentional effect upon the results of his experiment.

REFERENCES

CROWNE, D. P., & MARLOWE, D. *The approval motive.* New York: Wiley, 1964.

CROWNE, D. P., & STRICKLAND, BONNIE R. The conditioning of verbal behavior as a function of the need for social approval. *Journal of Abnormal and Social Psychology,* 1961, *63,* 395–401.

LEVIN, S. M. The effects of awareness of verbal conditioning. *Journal of Experimental Psychology,* 1961, *61,* 67–75.

MARLOWE, D. Need for social approval and the operant conditioning of meaningful verbal behavior. *Journal of Consulting Psychology,* 1962, *26,* 79–83.

MATARAZZO, J. D., SASLOW, G., & PAREIS, E. N. Verbal conditioning of two response classes: Some methodological considerations. *Journal of Abnormal and Social Psychology,* 1960, *61,* 190–206.

MILGRAM, S. Behavioral study of obedience. *Journal of Abnormal and Social Psychology,* 1963, *67,* 371–378.

ROSENTHAL, R. The effect of the experimenter on the results of psychological research. In B. A. Maher (Ed.), *Progress in experimental personality research.* New York: Academic Press, 1964. Pp. 79–114.

ROSENTHAL, R., FODE, K. L., FRIEDMAN, C. J., & VIKAN-KLINE, LINDA L. Subjects' perception of their experimenter under conditions of experimenter bias. *Perceptual & Motor Skills,* 1960, *11,* 325–331.

ROSENTHAL, R., PERSINGER, G. W., VIKAN-KLINE, LINDA L., & FODE, K. L. The effect of experimenter outcome-bias and subject set on awareness in verbal conditioning experiments. *Journal of Verbal Learning and Verbal Behavior,* 1963, *2,* 275–283.

SPIELBERGER, C. D., BERGER, A., & HOWARD, KAY. Conditioning of verbal behavior as a function of awareness, need for social approval, and motivation to receive reinforcement. *Journal of Abnormal and Social Psychology,* 1963, *67,* 241–246.

TAFFEL, C. Anxiety and the conditioning of verbal behavior. *Journal of Abnormal and Social Psychology,* 1955, *51,* 496–501.

(Received July 10, 1964)

Brainstorming

Whether to work individually or in groups is a question which almost always arises whenever an organization must solve a problem or produce products. To answer this question one must ask several others about the nature of the task. If the task is the production of a complex product such as an automobile, then it would seem reasonable to work in "groups" and have each person responsible for only one small part of the completed product. Thus, one worker may be responsible for mounting the wheels, another for installing the windshield, etc., with the result that each individual becomes highly proficient at his assigned task.

If the task were less complex, so that every worker could reasonably become quite proficient at all aspects of the task, two questions then become obvious. First, whether or not the presence of others influences one's productivity. Second, given the presence of others and a task that can be divided into subtasks, are there any differences in producitivity when the task is divided among several workers as opposed to each worker completing an entire product?

In general, the research to date seems to suggest that for repetitive physical tasks, the presence of others and an interdependent task both operate to enhance productivity. This effect is most pronounced in the short run and is limited to situations in which the group goals or norms are not antagonistic to increased production.

When the task is not of a repetitive physical nature but rather an intellectual one such as problem solving, the question of group effect becomes somewhat more difficult to deal with. The reason for this, of course, is that there are many different factors which must be considered. Does the group increase the productivity of a given member in terms of the number of different ideas produced? Is the individual's "creativity" hampered or enhanced by the presence of an interaction with others? What about the quality of ideas — are ideas produced independently superior or inferior to those produced in the group situation? What about the variety of different ideas produced?

When one thinks about the best way to come up with solutions to a problem, several advantages and disadvantages of the group situation suggest themselves. First, if the solution of the problem requires special abilities, for example, it would seem reasonable to expect the group to be superior to the individual simply because the probability of obtaining the necessary combination of talents is far greater in the group situation than is the probability of finding a single individual with the required combination of skills. Second, individuals may be motivated to contribute more in the group situation either because of competition or obligation to contribute. Third, hearing one member's idea may bring a different idea to another member's mind. Finally, the necessity to communicate one's thoughts in the group situation may sharpen a member's ideas and thereby make errors in reasoning subject to more rapid correction.

On the individual side, it seems reasonable to wonder whether the presence of others might make a member reluctant to suggest an idea of which he is uncertain or one which is at variance with that suggested by a powerful group member. It is also possible that an authoritarian group member may dominate the conversation to such an extent that other members' ideas tend not to be voiced. Finally, it is possible that the group may develop a "one-track mind" or stereotypy of thought in that the expression of ideas of a certain nature may generate ideas of the same nature in other group members, with the result that the variety, quality, or number of ideas may be adversely affected.

The experiment for the laboratory session is a test of the "group-think" or "brainstorming" notions. Subjects will be asked to think of as many different ways to deal with a given problem as they can. Some subjects will work alone, others in groups of three or five. Idea production will be recorded and analyzed to determine the effects of group interaction upon the number and quality of ideas produced, on the average, by a subject over a given period of time.

All subjects will be given the brainstorming instructions which are supposed to reduce the restraints against creative thought. It should be noted that groups given brainstorming instructions may behave quite differently from groups which are not so instructed.

INSTRUCTIONS

Experimental Team Size: Class project.
Subjects: This experiment will use classmates for subjects.
Apparatus: Pencils; file cards; stopwatch; tape recorder.
Experimental Situation: Groups of three and five subjects think of solutions to various problems. Some of the subjects work alone,

simply tape-recording their ideas. Other groups of subjects work together in a group situation in which each person calls out his thoughts
hoping to generate ideas in his group members. All of the discussion
in the latter groups is also recorded.

Procedure

1. Divide the class into the following brainstorm (BS) and individual (I) groups (draw subjects randomly):

    a. One group of three subjects (3 BS).

    b. One group of five subjects (5 BS).

    c. One group of three to five subjects (I).

    d. A group of at least two experimenters.

2. The instructor and the group of experimenters should make up
two problems to be presented to the subjects for brainstorming. The
problems should be of a nature which facilitates many possible ideas
or partial solutions. Such topics as "How to increase the number of
European tourists coming to this country" and "What may be done to
reduce the incidence of juvenile crime?" would be suitable. It is
important, of course, that the subjects be kept unaware of the actual
problem prior to the experiment.

3. Each experimental group is to be run in private. As many groups
may be run simultaneously as there are tape recorders available.

4. For group I, seat each subject, singly, in a private room with
the tape recorder.

5. For groups 3 BS and 5 BS, seat the entire group of three or five
members in a private room with the tape recorder.

6. Read the rules of brainstorming to the subject:

    a. "Quantity of ideas is important; the more ideas, the greater
       the possibility of a good one."

    b. "No ideas should be held back; none should be criticized."

    c. "The wilder the idea the better."

    d. "Combining and enlarging upon ideas is encouraged."

7. After reviewing the brainstorming rules, present the individual
subject in group I or the entire group in 3 BS and 5 3S with the first
problem (present the problems in the same order in every condition).

8. Turn on the tape recorder. Experimenter says: "Call out as many
ideas as you can. Go."

9. During each session, the experimenter takes a footage reading
from the tape recorder exactly every 3 minutes to permit sorting the
ideas into the time periods for analysis. If the tape recorder has no
footage meter or an unreliable one, the experimenter may audibly

mark the tape with a clap of the hands or a short drumming of the fingers on the microphone, etc.

10. After exactly 12 minutes, stop the group (or individual in condition I) and allow a 5-minute rest period.

11. Present the second problem following the above procedure.

Data Analysis

A. *Transcribing and Coding*

1. Transcribe the tape-recorded ideas onto individual file cards. To qualify as an idea a statement must be of the form: do a specified thing *(X)* to produce Y effect. For example, replies to the tourist problem such as "increase the amount of advertizing abroad," "legalize prostitution in this country," and "provide tourists with free one-way air fare to this country" would qualify as ideas. Comments such as "do something to increase their interest," "why do we want tourists?" and "what would the Germans want to see?" would not qualify as ideas. (Although the latter comments do not qualify as ideas, people involved in brainstorming should not hesitate to make such comments since they may stimulate ideas in other group members or in themselves.)

2. Identify the problem to which the idea applies by writing 1 or 2 on the front of each file card.

3. Code the file cards by placing the following symbols on the back of the appropriate card in the upper left corner (see Table 4.1 and Fig. 4.1). It will now be possible to identify each data card by the symbol on the back. A card with I 6 on it, for example, is an idea produced by an individual working alone during the second 3-minute period.

TABLE 4.1
CONDITION

Elapsed time (minutes)	I	Group 3 BS	5 BS
3	I 3	3 BS 3	5 BS 3
6	I 6	3 BS 6	5 BS 6
9	I 9	3 BS 9	5 BS 9
12	I 12	3 BS 12	5 BS 12

4. Eliminate duplicated ideas in each condition. Condition I will probably have the most duplication since the subjects do not com-

municate while producing ideas. Thus, the same idea may contribute to the total score of each condition but will not contribute to the score of any particular condition more than once.

B. *Quantity of ideas produced*

1. Record the number of ideas each group produced in a table such as Table 4.2 (where T stands for total).

2. Compute the mean number of ideas per individual as in Table 4.3 (where N_1 stands for the number of subjects in group I).

3. Compute the mean number of ideas per subject during each 3-minute period and record in a table such as Table 4.4.

TABLE 4.2
NUMBER OF IDEAS

Group	Problem I Time unit					Problem II Time unit				
	1	2	3	4	T_1	1	2	3	4	T_2
I	(I_{11})	(I_{21})				(I_{12})	(I_{22})			
3 BS	$(3\ BS_{11})$					$(3\ BS_{12})$				
5 BS		$(5\ BS_{21})$					$(5\ BS_{22})$			

TABLE 4.3
MEAN NUMBER OF IDEAS

Group	Mean formula
I	$T_1 + T_2 / N_1 \times 2$
3 BS	$T_1 + T_2 / 3 \times 2$
5 BS	$T_1 + T_2 / 5 \times 2$

TABLE 4.4
MEAN NUMBER OF IDEAS

Group	Time unit			
	1	2	3	4
I	$I_{11} + I_{12} / N_1 \times 2$	$I_{21} + I_{22} / N_1 \times 2$		
3 BS	$3\ BS_{11} + 3\ BS_{12} / 3 \times 2$			
5 BS		$5\ BS_{21} + 5\ BS_{22} / 5 \times 2$		

C. *Quality of ideas*
1. Obtaining quality ratings.
   a. After the ideas have been transcribed, coded, and tallied
      prepare the back of each card with the format shown in Fig.
      4.1.

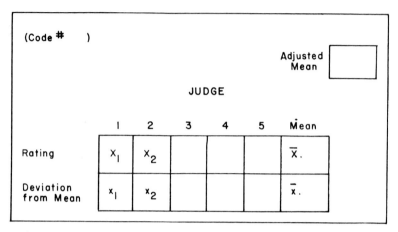

FIG. 4.1. Format for the back of each data card:
$x = |X_1 - \bar{X}.|$ and $\bar{x}. = \Sigma x/5$.

   b. Keeping the ideas for each problem separate, shuffle the cards
      and divide them into five equal packs.
   c. Randomly select one of the five packs of cards, to be called
      the "intrajudge reliability" (IJR) pack, and prepare the back
      of each card with the data-recording format shown in Fig. 4.2.
      (*Note:* The first half of the format shown in Fig. 4.2 will al-
      ready be on each card in the IJR pack as a result of the prep-
      aration called for in item a.)
   d. Select five individuals at random (unless there are five persons
      who did not participate as subjects, in which case use these
      as judges) from the laboratory class to serve as judges.
   e. Seat the judges at separate tables and give them each one
      of the five packs of cards for the first problem and have each
      judge sort the cards into four *equal* piles, numbered 1 through
      4. (*Note:* Judges must never look at the back of the cards.) In
      pile 1, the judges should place that 25% of the ideas which are
      the poorest; in pile 2, that 25% of the ideas which are not very
      good; in pile 3, that 25% of the ideas which are fairly good;
      and in pile 4, that 25% of the ideas which are best.

		JUDGE				
(Code #)					Adjusted Mean	

	1	2	3	4	5	Mean
First Rating (A)	X_{1A}	X_{2A}				$\bar{X}._A$
Deviation from Mean	x_{1A}	x_{2A}				$\bar{x}._A$
Second Rating (B)	X_{1B}	X_{2B}				$\bar{X}._B$
A-B	d_1	d_2				$\bar{d}.$

FIG. 4.2. Format for the back of each data card in the intrajudge reliability pack of cards:

$$x_{1a} = |X_{1A} - \bar{X}._A|$$
$$\bar{x}._A = \Sigma x/5$$
$$d_1 = |X_{1A} - X_{1B}|$$
$$\bar{d}. = \Sigma\ d/5.$$

The judges should assign quality rankings to the ideas according to the following three criteria:

(i) What is the probability of the suggested action having the desired effect?

(ii) Could the suggestion be put into practice (i.e., is it realistic)?

(iii) Is there a favorable cost-to-gain ratio (i.e., is the cost (effort) of putting the program into effect too great relative to probable returns from the program)?

f. Once the judges have completed sorting, the experimenter will record the judgments on the back of each card on the tally format shown in Figs. 4.1 and 4.2. The experimenter simply records the number of the pile in which the card was placed. If the card was placed in pile 1 (poorest ideas) the experimenter records a 1 on the back of the card under the particular judge's column. Thus, the rankings will vary from 1 (poorest) to 4 (best).

g. After the cards have been tallied, reshuffle each individual pack and give it to a different judge for sorting. Continue this process until all packs have been sorted once by each judge.

h. The IJR pack should be rated twice by each judge. The first rating is recorded in row A on the back of the card; the second, in row B.

i. Once the judges have sorted the problem I file cards, allow a 5-minute rest then repeat the process for the problem II file cards.

2. Inter- and intrajudge reliability. Whenever one must depend upon judges' ratings for the basic data in an experiment, the reliability of the data should be determined. In the present study, two questions may be asked about the ratings. First, do the judges tend to agree as to what constitutes good and poor ideas? Second, do the individual judges' standards of good and poor remain constant over time?

There are, as previously stated, several statistical approaches to determining reliability of ratings. For the purpose of the present experiment, however, graphic analyses will again be used so that the student can see what is meant by inconsistency of judgments, both between and within judges.

a. *Interjudge reliability*

The value for $\bar{x}$. ($\bar{x}_A$ on the IJR pack) on the back of each idea card gives the average deviation of the ratings for that idea, that is, the average amount by which each judge deviates from the mean of all judges' ratings. The reader will probably note

TABLE 4.5
MEAN DEVIATION OF JUDGES' RATINGS OF IDEA QUALITY

Problem		JUDGE 1	2	3	4	5	Total mean
I	Sum	Σx_{11}	Σx_{21}				
	Mean	$\bar{x}_{11}$					$\bar{x}.1$
II	Sum	Σx_{12}	Σx_{22}				
	Mean	$\bar{x}_{12}$					$\bar{x}.2$
Average mean deviation		$\bar{x}_{1.}$	$\bar{x}_{2.}$				$\bar{x}..$

that some ideas or classes of ideas result in greater diversity of rating than others.

(i) Sum the x_n values for each judge for problem I and problem II and record in a table similar in form to Table 4.5.

$\bar{x}_{11} = \Sigma x_{11}$/total number of ideas rated for problem one
$\bar{x}_{12} = \Sigma x_{12}$/total number of ideas rated for problem two
$\bar{x}_{1.} = (\bar{x}_{11} + \bar{x}_{12})/2$
$\bar{x}_{.1} = (\bar{x}_{11} + \bar{x}_{21} + \ldots + \bar{x}_{51})/5$
$\bar{x}_{.2} = (\bar{x}_{12} + \bar{x}_{22} + \ldots + \bar{x}_{52})/5$
$\bar{x}_{..} = (\bar{x}_{.1} + \bar{x}_{.2})/2$

(ii) Plot the above mean values $\bar{x}_{n1}$, $\bar{x}_{n2}$, and $\bar{x}_{n.}$ in the form of the accompanying graph.

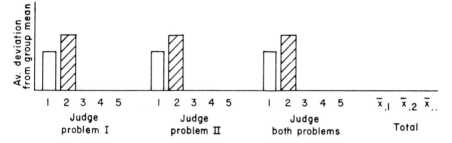

b. *Intrajudge reliability*

(i) From the IJR pack of cards, sum the d values and record in a form similar to Table 4.6.

TABLE 4.6

MEAN OF THE DIFFERENCE BETWEEN FIRST AND SECOND
RATINGS OF THE IJR PACK FOR EACH JUDGE

Problem		1	2	Judge 3	4	5	Total mean
I	Sum d_{n1}	Σd_{11}	Σd_{21}				
	Mean	$\bar{d}_{11}$	$\bar{d}_{21}$				$\bar{d}.1$
II	Sum d_{n2}	Σd_{12}	Σd_{22}				
	Mean	$\bar{d}_{12}$	$\bar{d}_{22}$				$\bar{d}.2$
		1	2	Judge 3	4	5	Total mean
Total Deviation		$\bar{d}_{1.}$	$\bar{d}_{2.}$				$\bar{d}_{..}$

$\bar{d}_{11} = \Sigma \, d_{11}/(\text{number of IJR pack cards for problem one})$

$\bar{d}_{.1} = (\bar{d}_{11} + \bar{d}_{21} + \cdots + \bar{d}_{51})/5$

$\bar{d}_{1.} = (\bar{d}_{11} + \bar{d}_{12})/2$

$\bar{d}_{..} = (\bar{d}_{.1} + \bar{d}_{.2})/2$

(ii) Plot the above mean values $\bar{d}_{n1}$, $\bar{d}_{n2}$, and $\bar{d}_{n.}$ in the form of the accompanying graph.

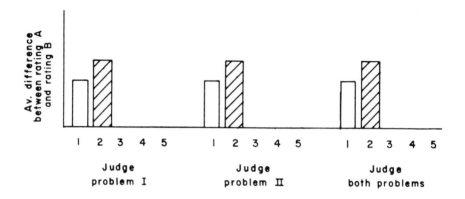

c. *Selecting judges*

In actual practice, problems of low intra- and interjudge reliability are handled by rigorous training of the judges since most variability of the ratings is usually a matter of shifting standards, boredom, disinterest, misunderstanding of the criteria, etc. By requiring the judges to practice the task of rating and then reviewing the results of every rating trial one can, in almost all instances, train judges to evaluate the items against a relatively stable and uniform set of standards such that the ratings are highly consistent between judges and within any particular judge over time.

It should be obvious that the above calculations are just the first step in developing stringent rating procedures. Further training and recalculation would undoubtedly be necessary.

For the purposes of the present study, disregard the ratings of the judge with the greatest total intrajudge variability [$\bar{d}_{n.}$ from graph in item b(ii)] and the ratings of the judge with the greatest total group mean deviation [$\bar{x}_{n.}$ from graph in item a(ii)]. This may, incidentally, be the same judge, in which case only one judge's ratings will be discarded. Enter the adjusted mean quality rating score on the back of each card (i.e., the new mean disregarding the ratings of the disqualified judges).

BRAINSTORMING

As a final note, remember the calculations indicate only the degree of consistency, not validity. The group may be in 100% agreement that an idea is very good when in fact is is completely wrong, unrealistic, or stupid.

3. *Analysis of idea quality*
   a. Compute the mean quality of ideas per person per time unit in each of the three groups and enter in a table such as Table 4.7.

TABLE 4.7
MEAN QUALITY OF IDEAS PER INDIVIDUAL IN EACH EXPERIMENTAL CONDITION

	\multicolumn{16}{c}{Condition}
	\multicolumn{5}{c}{I}		\multicolumn{5}{c}{3BS}		\multicolumn{5}{c}{5BS}
	\multicolumn{5}{c}{Time unit}		\multicolumn{5}{c}{Time unit}		\multicolumn{5}{c}{Time unit}
	1	2	3	4	T	1	2	3	4	T	1	2	3	4	T
Mean	X_{I_1}					X_{3BS}									

X_{I_1} = total I_1 adjusted means divided by the number of ideas (cards)

D. *Summarizing the Data*
1. Prepare a summary table of means such as Table 4.8.

TABLE 4.8
SUMMARY TABLE OF MEANS

Subjects	\multicolumn{5}{c}{Mean number of ideas}	\multicolumn{5}{c}{Mean quality of ideas}
	\multicolumn{5}{c}{Time unit}	\multicolumn{5}{c}{Time unit}
	1	2	3	4	Total	1	2	3	4	Total
Working alone										
Working in groups of 3										
Working in groups of 5										

2. Plot a curve of the mean number of ideas per individual over the course of the 12-minute session for each group. Place all three curves in one graph using different types of lines (i.e., solid lines or dashes) to distinguish between the groups, as shown in the accompanying graph.

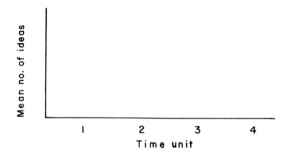

3. Plot a curve of the mean quality of the subjects' ideas over the course of the 12-minute session for each group, as shown in the accompanying graph.

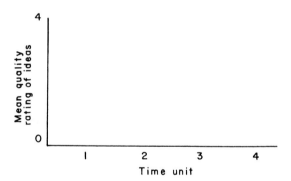

Experimental Report

1. Do subjects produce more ideas when working alone or in groups?

2. Which condition (i.e., alone or in groups) produces the ideas of highest quality?

3. Does the size of the group (i.e., three *vs.* five members) affect either the number or quality of ideas produced?

4. Are there any interactions with time? That is, does the number and/or quality of ideas produced increase or decrease over time in the session? Do some conditions give many good ideas early in the session but few later on?

5. a. Which measure of consistency of ratings results in greatest variability? Why?

   b. Which measure do you think is best?

    c. What causes intrajudge inconsistency in ratings?

    d. What causes interjudge inconsistency in ratings?

  6. Are the quality ratings data sufficiently reliable to allow one to have confidence in the experimental results? [Look at the percent difference in rated idea quality between conditions *vs.* the percent difference in ratings between (and within) judges.]

Reprinted from Journal of Applied Psychology, 1963, Vol. 47, pp. 30–37 by permission of the authors and the publisher.

THE EFFECT OF GROUP PARTICIPATION ON BRAIN-STORMING EFFECTIVENESS FOR TWO INDUSTRIAL SAMPLES [1]

MARVIN D. DUNNETTE, JOHN CAMPBELL, AND KAY JAASTAD [2]

Problems were presented for brainstorming to 48 research scientists and 48 advertising personnel employed with the Minnesota Mining and Manufacturing Co. Within a counterbalanced experimental design, each S brainstormed certain problems individually and other equated problems as a member of a 4-man team. Individuals produced not only more ideas than groups, but they accomplished this without sacrificing quality. The net superiority of individual performance over group participation is highlighted by the fact that 23 of 24 groups produced a larger number of different ideas under the individual condition. The superiority of individual brainstorming over group brainstorming was relatively greater when it was preceded by group participation. Apparently, group participation is accompanied by certain inhibitory influences even under conditions (e.g., brainstorming) which place a moratorium on all criticism.

Proponents of brainstorming, as an idea eliciting or problem solving technique, emphasize the value of group participation as a facilitating factor in producing ideas. For example, Osborn (1957) concludes on the basis of experiments conducted at the University of Buffalo, that "the average person can think up twice as many ideas when working with a group than when working alone" pp. 228–229). He adds that a combination of group and individual effort is probably best, but he fails to specify the exact nature of the optimal combination. A widely cited study by Taylor, Berry, and Block (1957) suggested that group participation actually inhibits the potential ideational output of individuals. Taylor et al. presented three different problems to 96 Yale juniors and seniors who had previously worked together in small group discussion sections. Forty-eight of the subjects were divided into 12 real groups of 4 men each; the other 48 brainstormed the problems alone. The number of

different ideas produced by the real groups was compared with the number produced by so-called "nominal" groups formed after the experiment by randomly dividing the 48 individual subjects into 12 groups of 4 each. Scores of nominal groups represented, therefore, the expected level of achievement if actual group participation neither inhibits nor facilitates creativeness during brainstorming. For each of the three problems presented, the nominal groups produced an average of nearly twice as many different ideas as the real group. Taylor et al. concluded, therefore, that group participation actually has an inhibiting influence on creative thinking during brainstorming—a conclusion radically different from the one by Osborn cited earlier.

Our purpose has been to repeat the Taylor et al. study among two different occupational groups: research scientists and advertising men. Further, we have modified the design of the Taylor study in order to allow subjects to participate in *both* individual and group brainstorming sessions. We believe our results lend support to the conclusions reached by Taylor and his associates and that they also help to define the conditions for the optimal combination of group and individual effort mentioned by Osborn.

[1] Research reported here was supported by grant from the Graduate School Research Fund of the University of Minnesota.

Appreciation is extended to Raymond O. Collier of the University of Minnesota who helped greatly in planning the statistical analyses of the experimental data.

[2] Now employed with McKinsey and Company, Chicago, Illinois.

GROUP PARTICIPATION AND BRAINSTORMING EFFECTIVENESS

METHOD

The subjects of the experiment were 48 research personnel from one of the larger laboratories of Minnesota Mining and Manufacturing Co. (3M) and 48 persons employed with 3M's central staff Advertising Department. Our choice of research and advertising personnel was based on our hypothesis that advertising personnel would more likely profit from any facilitating influence of group interaction and that research persons would more likely be inhibited by group participation; thus, we hypothesized opposite effects of group interaction in the two groups. Each of the two sets of subjects was divided into 12 groups of 4 men each. The assignment was not random. Instead, persons were placed together who had worked together and who were well acquainted with one another. In no case, however, were persons of differing job levels placed in the same group; among the researchers no one with supervisory responsibilities participated in the study. Among the advertisers, different supervisory levels were represented but never in the same group, thereby reducing any possible inhibiting effects due to differing status levels within a group. In addition, no persons with advanced degrees participated in the study; the researchers included only persons with BA or equivalent degrees. The range of education represented in the advertising group was from high school through college.

Each subject in Taylor's study participated in only one of the two experimental conditions. Such an experimental design does not allow a test of possible effects of prior group experience on individual brainstorming behavior or vice versa, and it also, of course, depends on randomization to effect an equating of any individual differences in brainstorming ability between subjects in the two experimental conditions. Because of these factors, our experiment allowed each subject to take part in *both* group and individual brainstorming sessions. The experimental design shown in Table 1 was used separately for the researchers and the advertisers. It will be noted that individual and group performance, the two problem sets, and order of participation are counterbalanced.

The problems used in our study were the same as those used by Taylor et al. with the addition of a fourth, the People problem. The four problems are stated below:

Thumbs problem. We do not think this is likely to happen, but imagine for a moment what would happen if everyone after 1960 had an extra thumb on each hand. This extra thumb will be built just as the present one is, but located on the other side of the hand. It faces inward, so that it can press against the fingers, just as the regular thumb does now. Here is the question: What practical benefits or difficulties will arise when people start having this extra thumb?

Education problem. Because of the rapidly increasing birthrate beginning in the 1940s, it is now clear that by 1970 public school enrollment will be

TABLE 1

DESIGN OF THE EXPERIMENT

Group	Individuals	First	Second
A	1, 2, 3, 4		
B	5, 6, 7, 8	I,1	G,2
C	9, 10, 11, 12		
D	13, 14, 15, 16		
E	17, 18, 19, 20	G,1	I,2
F	21, 22, 23, 24		
G	25, 26, 27, 28		
H	29, 30, 31, 32	I,2	G,1
I	33, 34, 35, 36		
J	37, 38, 39, 40		
K	41, 42, 43, 44	G,2	I,1
L	45, 46, 47, 48		

Note.—1 = Problem Set 1, Thumbs and Education; 2 = Problem Set 2, People and Tourists; G = Group; I = Individual.

very much greater than it is today. In fact, it has been estimated that if the student-teacher ratio were to be maintained at what it is today, 50% of all individuals graduating from college would have to be induced to enter teaching. What different steps might be taken to insure that schools will continue to provide instruction at least equal in effectiveness to that now provided?

People problem. Suppose that discoveries in physiology and nutrition have so affected the diet of American children over a period of 20 years that the average height of Americans at age 20 has increased to 80 inches and the average weight has about doubled. Comparative studies of the growth of children during the last 5 years indicate that the phenomenal change in stature is stabilized so that further increase is not expected. What would be the consequences? What adjustments would this situation require?

Tourists problem. Each year a great many American tourists go to visit Europe. But now suppose that our country wished to get many more European tourists to come to visit America during their vacations. What steps can you suggest that would get more European tourists to come to this country?

The problems were pretested along with several others among University of Minnesota engineering and business administration students in order to select those problems which elicited a large volume and diversity of responses and to equate approximately the idea eliciting qualities of the two problem sets. The pretest problems were presented in counterbalanced order to each subject, and he was allowed 10 minutes for each problem to write his responses. The mean number of responses given by the pretest subjects was not significantly different for Thumbs and People (10.70 and 10.08) or for Education and Tourists (9.62 and 9.80); Thumbs and Education were, therefore, used for Problem Set 1 and People and Tourists for Problem Set 2.

About a week prior to the experiment, the senior author met with the subjects "over coffee" and discussed creative thinking with particular emphasis on brainstorming. The nature and purpose of the forthcoming experiment were explained and questions concerning scheduling and procedural details were answered. The importance of applying the "principles" [3] of brainstorming was heavily emphasized, and participants were urged to refrain from discussing their experimental sessions (particularly the problems used) with any of their coworkers who may not yet have participated in the experiment.

The same graduate student (Kay Jaastad) served as experimenter for *all* subjects. She began each experimental session by reading aloud the instructions which emphasized the importance of research study and which restated the techniques and principles of brainstorming. She then presented each problem by first reading it aloud and then distributing dittoed copies to each of the subjects. She allowed time for questions, if any, and then instructed the subjects to "begin brainstorming." Responses were recorded on a DeJur-Grundig *Stenorette* with conference microphone. Subjects were allowed to spend 15 minutes on each of the problems; in every session, nearly all ideas and solutions had been expressed at the end of 10–12 minutes. The time limit did not in any instance result in cutting off a flow of ideas. On the other hand, it did serve as a stimulus to the rapid and free wheeling expression of ideas and solutions. Each subject participated in both experimental conditions on the same afternoon.[4] The individual brain-

[3] The following principles have been suggested by Osborn and were emphasized by Taylor in his study: the more ideas the better, the wilder the ideas the better, improve or combine ideas already suggested, and do not be critical.

[4] For example, members of Groups A, B, and C participated first as individuals using Problem Set 1 followed immediately by group brainstorming using Problem Set 2. Those in Groups D, E, and F participated first in the group situation using Prob-

storming condition was carried out by placing subjects in four widely separated offices where each would be free to brainstorm without interruption.[5]

RESULTS

After completing the experimental sessions, the responses of the 96 subjects in both individual and group situations were transcribed. Each idea or solution was placed on one side of a 3×5 card, and appropriate identifying information (e.g., problem set, condition, order) was entered on the opposite side. Using the cards, it was an easy (albeit voluminous and time consuming) task to sort responses, delete duplications, rate the quality of ideas, etc. The first step in the analysis of results was simply to compare the number of different ideas or solutions produced by group participation with the number of different ideas or solutions produced by the same group members during the individual brainstorming condition. It should be emphasized that the "score" (number of ideas) under the individual condition includes only *different* ideas. Thus, if two or more members of a group, during their individual sessions, suggested the same idea or solution to a problem, it was counted as only a single contribution to the total score of the nominal group. Comparisons were made between individual and group brain-

lem Set 1 followed immediately by individual brainstorming using Problem Set 2—and so on.

[5] Unfortunately the individual sessions were not *entirely* free from interruption. In at least one instance, a man answered a phone in the middle of his session. At other times, men were interrupted briefly by passers-by who looked in to ask, "What the heck are you doing?" or to make similar comments. Of course, all such slip-ups worked to the disadvantage of individuals' achievements in comparison with groups.

TABLE 2

MEAN TOTAL NUMBER OF DIFFERENT IDEAS AND/OR SOLUTIONS TO PROBLEMS BY SUBJECTS UNDER CONDITIONS OF INDIVIDUAL AND GROUP BRAINSTORMING

Problem	Research personnel		Advertising personnel	
	Individual	Group	Individual	Group
Thumbs and People	78.3	60.9	82.9	59.8
Education and Tourists	62.2	49.3	58.5	37.3
Total	140.5	110.2	141.4	97.1

TABLE 3

ANALYSIS OF VARIANCE: TOTAL NUMBER OF DIFFERENT IDEAS AND/OR SOLUTIONS
TO PROBLEMS BY RESEARCH PERSONNEL UNDER CONDITIONS OF INDIVIDUAL
AND GROUP BRAINSTORMING

Source	df	Total (both problems of each set)		Thumbs and People problems		Education and Tourists problems	
		MS	F	MS	F	MS	F
Between individuals							
Order	1	1001	6.37*	585	9.39*	56	1.57
S × C	1	1291	8.21*	277	4.44	372	10.54*
S × O × C	1	30	0.19	3	0.05	14	0.40
Error (b)	8	157.1		62.3		35.3	
Within individuals							
Condition	1	1380	23.71**	455	15.12**	250	31.64**
C × O	1	40	0.69	10	0.33	10	1.26
Set	1	96	1.65	32	1.05	19	2.40
S × O	1	135	2.33	53	1.74	19	2.40
Error (w)	8	58.3		30.1		7.9	

Note.—S = Set, C = Condition, O = Order, (b) = between, (w) = within.
* $p < .05$.
** $p < .01$.

storming for the total of both problems in each set, for the Thumbs-People problems of each set, and for the Education-Tourists problems of each set. Results are shown in Tables 2, 3, and 4. For all comparisons, the condition effect is highly significant, the indi-

vidual condition yielding a markedly greater number of ideas than group participation. Of the 24 groups, only one failed to produce more ideas under the individual condition than under the group condition, and the difference in this one instance was only 163–162

TABLE 4

ANALYSIS OF VARIANCE: TOTAL NUMBER OF DIFFERENT IDEAS AND/OR SOLUTIONS TO PROBLEMS
BY ADVERTISING PERSONNEL UNDER CONDITIONS OF INDIVIDUAL
AND GROUP BRAINSTORMING

Source	df	Total (both problems of each set)		Thumbs and People problems		Education and Tourists problems	
		MS	F	MS	F	MS	F
Between individuals							
Order	1	274	0.96	153	1.63	18	0.31
S × C	1	293	1.03	78	0.83	69	1.17
S × O × C	1	73	0.29	2	0.02	82	1.39
Error (b)	8	285.1		93.6		58.8	
Within individuals							
Condition	1	2949	93.61**	800	27.78**	677	34.02**
C × O	1	170	5.40*	101	3.51	9	0.45
Set	1	316	10.03*	196	6.81*	14	0.70
S × O	1	125	3.97	24	0.83	39	1.96
Error (w)	8	31.5		28.8		19.9	

Note.—See note in Table 3.
* $p < .05$.
** $p < .01$.

in favor of group participation. Only 5 of the 48 research subjects failed to produce more ideas when working individually than when participating in a group. Clearly, individual brainstorming achieves more ideas than group brainstorming. Our hypothesis that group interaction would facilitate the output of advertising personnel and inhibit the output of research personnel failed to be sustained. Apparently, the inhibiting influence of group participation cuts across the kinds of personal and occupational differences investigated in this study.

It will be noted from Tables 3 and 4 that certain other effects also showed significance. The significant Order effect shown by researchers was most pronounced on the Thumbs and People problems. A larger number of ideas or solutions was produced when subjects experienced the individual brainstorming *after* having experienced the group session than when they "went in cold" to the individual session. Although the Order effect was not significant for the advertisers, the Order × Condition interaction was. A plot of Individual versus Group scores for each of the two orders shows that the relative superiority of individual brainstorming was greatest when it was preceded by the group session. For example, the mean number of ideas for Individual and Group sessions was 143 and 109, respectively, under Order A (Individual session followed by Group session); the corresponding means under Order B (Individual session preceded by Group session) were 140 and 95. These results help to specify the conditions for combining group and individual effort. Apparently, a brainstorming session (either group or individual) can serve the important function of a "warm up" for subsequent brainstorming. In this study,

the net superiority of individual brainstorming over group brainstorming seems to have been enhanced by such a warm-up session.

Two other statistically significant effects are shown in Tables 3 and 4. The Set effect is significant for the advertising group. Problem Set 1 (Thumbs and Education) gave a higher yield than Problem Set 2 (People and Tourists). The major source of the difference was between the Thumbs and People problems, probably reflecting the fact that they were somewhat less perfectly matched on the basis of the pretests than were the Education and Tourists problems. For the researchers, the interaction effect Set × Condition is significant. A plot of Individual versus Group scores for each of the two problem sets shows that the superiority of individual brainstorming was greatest (151–91) for Problem Set 1 and that it actually was negligible for Problem Set 2 (130–129). We are at a loss to explain this outcome, particularly in view of the consistent results obtained for *both* problem sets in the advertising group.

Although the total number of ideas and solutions was greater for individual than for group participation, it could be argued that this may have been accompanied by a corresponding decrease in the quality of ideas produced. Two of the scales used by Taylor et al. for rating the quality of ideas were employed in this study. The first two authors used Taylor's Effectiveness scale [6] to rate

---

[6] Effectiveness scale: $0 =$ no conceivable contribution to solution of problem. Suggestion impossible of attainment; $1 =$ very little, if any, contribution to solution of problem; $2 =$ probably some contribution to solution of problem; $3 =$ definite minor contribution to solution of problem; and $4 =$ clearly a major contribution to solution of problem.

TABLE 5

MEAN TOTAL QUALITY SCORES OBTAINED BY SUBJECTS UNDER CONDITIONS OF INDIVIDUAL AND GROUP BRAINSTORMING

Problem	Research personnel		Advertising personnel	
	Individual	Group	Individual	Group
Thumbs and People	171	131	192	131
Education and Tourists	128	94	116	65
Total	299	225	308	196

TABLE 6

ANALYSIS OF VARIANCE: TOTAL QUALITY SCORES FOR IDEAS AND/OR SOLUTIONS TO PROBLEMS BY RESEARCH PERSONNEL UNDER CONDITIONS OF INDIVIDUAL AND GROUP BRAINSTORMING

Source	df	Total (both problems of each set)		Thumbs and People problems		Education and Tourists problems	
		MS	F	MS	F	MS	F
Between individuals							
Order	1	6225	8.18*	3385	9.45*	429	3.92
S × C	1	4916	6.46*	1734	4.84	811	7.41*
S × O × C	1	45	.06	0	.00	50	.46
Error (b)	8	761		358		109.5	
Within individuals							
Condition	1	8049	20.17**	2361	11.86**	1691	20.37**
C × O	1	340	.85	103	.52	69	.83
Set	1	995	2.49	425	2.14	119	1.43
S × O	1	172	.43	12	.06	94	1.13
Error (w)	8	399		199		83	

Note.—See note in Table 3.
* $p < .05$.
** $p < .01$.

solutions to the Education and Tourists problems and his Probability scale [7] to rate responses to the Thumbs and People problems. Although not *all* responses were rated

[7] Probability scale: 0 = very highly improbable or clearly impossible; 1 = conceivable, but improbable; 2 = possible; 3 = probable; and 4 = highly probable.

by both investigators, the interrater reliabilities were estimated on the basis of sampling randomly the ideas from each group of subjects for each of the four problems. The resulting coefficients ranged between .54 and .77 with a median value of .66. These reliabilities are *not* impressively high; even so,

TABLE 7

ANALYSIS OF VARIANCE: TOTAL QUALITY SCORES FOR IDEAS AND/OR SOLUTIONS TO PROBLEMS BY ADVERTISING PERSONNEL UNDER CONDITIONS OF INDIVIDUAL AND GROUP BRAINSTORMING

Source	df	Total (both problems of each set)		Thumbs and People problems		Education and Tourists problems	
		MS	F	MS	F	MS	F
Between individuals							
Order	1	2063	1.67	1162	2.56	133	.63
S × C	1	2959	2.40	1162	2.56	404	1.92
S × O × C	1	1528	1.24	92	.20	883	4.20
Error (b)	8	1235		453		210	
Within individuals							
Condition	1	18676	54.44*	5460	16.25**	3966	60.00**
C × O	1	595	1.73	504	1.50	4	.06
Set	1	115	.34	140	.42	1	.02
S × O	1	10	.03	8	.02	0	.00
Error (w)	8	343		336		66	

Note.—See note in Table 3.
* $p < .05$.
** $p < .01$.

TABLE 8

Mean Quality Ratings for Ideas and/or Solutions Produced by Subjects
under Conditions of Individual and Group Brainstorming

	Research personnel			Advertising personnel		
Problem	Individual	Group	Significance level[a]	Individual	Group	Significance level[a]
Total (both problems of each set)	2.12	2.04	ns	2.18	2.02	$p < .05$
Thumbs and People	2.18	2.15	ns	2.32	2.19	ns
Education and Tourists	2.06	1.91	ns	1.96	1.74	$p < .01$

[a] The significance tests were made using the same analysis of variance design shown in Tables 3, 4, 6, and 7. Copies of additional analysis of variance tables may be obtained upon request from the senior author.

the ratings of the second author (which were done for *all* problems in *all* groups) were used to provide a rough index of the quality of each solution proposed. The ratings were summed for all the different ideas produced under each of the conditions. Comparisons of means and statistical tests of significance are shown in Tables 5, 6, and 7. It is apparent that quality was *not* sacrificed for quantity under the condition of individual brainstorming. It is noteworthy that the Set and Condition × Order effects are not significant among the advertisers for the quality score comparisons. For the advertisers, the Thumbs problem elicited a significantly larger number of responses than the People problem, but the total quality of output did not differ for the two problems.

A remaining question has to do with the mean quality of ideas and solutions produced under the two experimental conditions. Table 8 summarizes the mean quality ratings and the significance levels of the mean differences between individual and group conditions. The values in Table 8 were obtained by dividing the mean total quality score (Table 5) by the mean total number of different ideas (Table 2). It is evident that individuals produce responses of quality equal to or greater than that of the ideas produced in groups. The evidence is clear-cut: brainstorming is most effective when undertaken by individuals working *alone* in an atmosphere free from the apparently inhibiting influences of group interaction.

Discussion

Our results confirm those of Taylor et al. and tend to refute Osborn's argument that

individuals are stimulated by group brainstorming to produce more ideas than when brainstorming alone. Of special interest is our finding that group interaction has an inhibiting influence for advertising people (that area in which brainstorming was developed and where it first came into widespread use) as well as for technical research personnel and for college students at Yale University (Taylor's study). Individuals not only produce *more* ideas when working alone, but they do this without sacrificing quality; indeed our results show that advertising personnel, working as individuals, produced ideas on the Tourists and Education problems of significantly higher mean quality than when they worked in groups. The net superiority of individual performance over group participation for these two sets of industrially employed subjects is highlighted by the fact that 23 of the 24 groups produced a larger number of different ideas under the individual condition. To the extent that we may generalize these findings to future situations, we can state that four persons, attacking a problem individually, and then pooling their efforts will, on the average, produce about 30% more ideas than if they attempted to solve the problem in a group session or meeting.

Our findings also suggest that group participation may be useful in "warming up" for individual brainstorming sessions. Research personnel produced more ideas when individual brainstorming followed group participation than when it preceded it. Advertising men also exhibited relatively greater superiority in the individual sessions when they had been preceded by a group session.

PAUL G. SWINGLE

Neither the Taylor study nor our study has identified the exact nature of the inhibiting influence which apparently acts to reduce the productivity of group brainstorming. Taylor et al. suggested, and we concur, on the basis of our observations during these experiments, that a group tends to "fall in a rut" and to pursue the same train of thought. The effect of this is to limit the diversity of approaches to a problem, thereby leading to the production of fewer different ideas. It was also apparent that the output of many individuals who were highly productive when working alone was considerably less in the group situation. In spite of the stimulus of group brainstorming and our specific directive to avoid all criticism, it was apparent that these persons were inhibited simply by the presence of other group members. The central idea underlying brainstorming of placing a moratorium on all criticism is a good one. It appears, however, that group participation still contains certain inhibitory influences which are not easily dissipated. The "best bet" for creative thinking in attacking problems seems, therefore, to be the pooled individual efforts of many people with perhaps an initial group session to serve simply as a warm up to their efforts.

REFERENCES

OSBORN, A. F. *Applied imagination.* (Rev. ed.) New York: Scribner, 1957.

TAYLOR, D. W., BERRY, P. C., & BLOCK, C. H. Does group participation when using brainstorming facilitate or inhibit creative thinking? Technical Report No. 1, 1957, Yale University, Department of Psychology, Office of Naval Research.

(Received February 2, 1962)

Coalition Formation

There are many situations which require that two or more persons combine their resources to guarantee, or at least increase the probability of, the procurement of some object or condition of value — the payoff. Two children who have been pillow fighting might, when an approaching parent is heard, both pretend to be asleep to escape an unpleasant situation. The children have, in essence, formed a coalition against the parent.

A group of businessmen, each with a large portion of a company's stock but not enough singly to control the company, may decide to combine by voting in a block so that between them they will have a majority vote and thus control of the company. These businessmen, we would say, have formed a coalition against the other stockholders.

A coalition then is the forming of an alliance by two or more persons to bring about some action or result. A coalition differs from collusion only in terms of the action or object desired. In collusion, the persons are attempting to obtain an illegal object or to obtain the object illegally. This basic difference results in some other differences between the two types of agreements. Because of the illegal aspect of collusion, the agreement will most likely be kept secret, whereas secrecy in the coalition situation is a question of strategy, i.e., the disadvantage, if any, of making an agreement known to others. In short, collusion is simply a type of coalition under certain conditions. Card games form a natural setting for collusive behavior in that the payoff or "pot" is a legitimate object, but obtaining it by "cooperating" with another player is usually regarded as illegitimate so that successful coalitions are kept secret.

The research to date on coalition formation has, with a few exceptions, been done in laboratory situations. Groups of three or more subjects compete for a prize. The situations are such that coalitions between two or more players are usually necessary to guarantee winning the prize, and characteristically each player has a different amount of control over reward attainment; i.e., if no coalition were formed some players would win more than others. The game situation also usually includes a bargaining period in which the members of the winning coalition must decide upon the division of the payoff.

There are several theories of coalition formation, each of which, at the present state of our knowledge, has some supporting evidence and some discomfirming evidence.

The "Lion's Share" Notion

Assume that three men are seeking a prize of $100, which will be won as soon as 51% or more of a group of 100 persons vote in favor of any one or combination of two of the men. Each man has control over a certain portion of the vote: A has 49% of the votes, B has 26%, and C has 25% of the votes. Now, at first glance, A might feel that, since he was just short of a simple majority, he would be willing to pool his votes with either B or C and give them, say, $20 of the prize in return for the use of 2% of their votes (i.e., what A needs to win). Now, if B or C has been offered this deal (or if they surmise that A would want a large proportion of the prize) their best move would be to form a coalition between themselves and split the prize more or less evenly. In short, expectations of A's desiring a "lion's share" enhance the attractiveness and hence the probability of the BC coalition.

Any Two Can Win

If one looks closely at the above situation, it is apparent that A's initial power is illusory; that is, without enough vote control to prevent his own loss, he has, in actuality, no more power than his competitors. Actually, the situation is one in which a coalition between any two of the three men will guarantee winning the prize. The power structure is identical to that of each man controlling one-third of the votes. Strategically, therefore, A, realizing the possibility of B and C misperceiving the situation, should initiate the first offer of coalition to either B or C with an even payoff split. This strategy might convince B or C that A correctly perceives the situation. If B or C misperceives the situation, on the other hand, A's offer might be received as generous. Thus, A's even split offer would, at worst, make his inclusion in a coalition as attractive as a BC coalition.

Conflict Reduction

Research has suggested that at times coalitions tend to form along paths of least conflict. In the example offered above, B and C may be attracted to alliance because the expectation of difficulty over dividing the payoff would be minimal. That is, because they both have about equal control over votes, an even split of the payoff might appear to be the obvious division and therefore very little bargaining would be necessary. If an alliance is formed with A, on the other hand, B or C may feel that A will drive a hard bargain by demanding an unequal division of the rewards.

If the situation were slightly changed, one could make the BC coalition bargaining session the most conflict laden. Assume that the number of votes controlled by each man is the same as in the previous example but the payoff or prize is that of administrative offices. Let us say that the winning coalition will be awarded the presidency and vice-presidency of the organization and that the two coalition members must by negotiation decide who shall be president and who shall be vice-president. If coalitions are formed along paths of least resistance one would expect A to be included most often in the coalitions and that because of the almost two-to-one ratio of controlled votes, A would be the obvious person to be president. If B and C were to form an alliance, the payoff division would not be as obvious and therefore more bargaining conflict might be anticipated.

The experiment for this laboratory session will be a test of the conflict notion of coalition formation. The study will be conducted in the laboratory with three-person groups.

INSTRUCTIONS

Experimental Team Size: Two.

Subjects: Arrange for exactly three subjects per experimental team. Follow the same procedure for obtaining subjects as used in Experiment 2. All three subjects in each group must be of the same sex. Try to obtain an equal number of groups of males and females.

Apparatus: Standard deck of 52 playing cards; watch with a second hand; pencils; paper; communication sheets; nine identification place cards: three with the letter "A" printed on them, three with the letter "B," and three with the letter "C."

Experimental Situation: Groups of three subjects each play a card game with provision for forming coalitions. Each subject's power (chance of winning the game) is varied from trial to trial. The nature of the payoff (pot) is either evenly divisible or unequally divided so that for some trials of the game equal power coalitions will be exposed to greater bargaining conflict than coalitions between players with unequal power. Three power distributions will be included in the study. First, a condition of "all different" in which no two players have the same power, but one in which a coalition between any two players will practically guarantee a win (denoted as condition 2, 3, 4). Second, a "two equally weak, one strong" condition in which a coalition between the two weak will result in an almost sure win over the strong member (2, 2, 3). Finally, a "two equally weak, one very strong" condition in which a coalition between the two weak members will just equal the power of the stronger member and therefore result in a 50% probability of winning the game (2, 2, 4).

Procedure

1. Prepare the materials required for the experiment. Type and duplicate a sufficient number of communication sheets so that each team has one for the divisible reward condition (Fig. 5.1) and one for the indivisible reward condition (Fig. 5.2).

	Offer		Reply
	I Receive	You Receive	
	Cents	Cents	
⟶	0	24	
⟶	4	20	
⟶	8	16	⟶ AGREED
⟶	12	12	⟶ NO
⟶	16	8	
⟶	20	4	
⟶	24	0	

FIG. 5.1. Communication sheet for the divisible payoff condition.

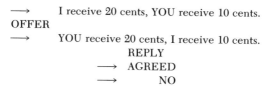

⟶   I receive 20 cents, YOU receive 10 cents.
OFFER
⟶   YOU receive 20 cents, I receive 10 cents.
REPLY
⟶   AGREED
⟶   NO

FIG. 5.2. Communication sheet for the indivisible payoff condition.

2. Seat the three subjects around a table and place one of the place cards in front of each person identifying him as player A, B, or C. Give each player a pencil and a sheet of lined paper for recording his payoff winnings.

3. Give each subject one of each of the remaining two sets of place cards. That is, player A receives place cards B and C, player B receives cards A and C, and player C receives cards A and B.

4. From the deck of cards remove one 3, one 4, and two 2's. Thus,

48 cards will be left in the deck. Place the four removed cards to one side to be used later.

5. Shuffle and deal the 48 cards to the three players, 16 cards to each player, face down, with instructions not to turn over the cards.

6. Read the following instructions to the subjects while demonstrating the game.

"We are interested in how people form partnerships in bargaining situations. You are going to play a special type of card game for the next half-hour or so in which you may form an alliance with one of the other two players, but not both, on each trial of the game to try to guarantee winning the payoff on that trial.

"Each trial of the game begins with my dealing 16 cards to each player as I have just done. I will then shuffle and deal out, face up, one of these [experimenter points to pack of four cards placed aside (item 4)] cards to each of you. The cards have three values: 2, 3, or 4. These values will determine your strength in that trial of the game.

"The game is played as follows: I will announce the payoff for each game which will be either 24 cents, which the winning team may divide any way they choose, or 30 cents, which may only be divided as 20 cents and 10 cents if the team wins. That is, one player receives 20 cents, the other 10 cents. Which player receives the 20 cents is up to the team, but it must be divided 20–10. If the single player wins, he receives exactly one-half of the payoff—no one receives the second half of the payoff.

"After I have announced the payoff and have dealt out your power cards I will say, 'Get ready to choose your partner,' at which time you should decide which of the other two players you want as your partner and prepare to hold up the card with that player's letter on it. Keep the card out of sight under the table. I will then say, 'One, two, three— choose,' at which time you will rapidly hold up your choice card. The two persons who choose each other will be considered as a team for that trial and will pool their power against the third player. If there are no mutual choices we will go through the choosing procedure again until a team is formed.

"After the team is formed, I will remove one of the team's two packs of 16 cards—the team may choose the pack they wish to play with, but without looking at the faces of the cards—so that the team and the third player each have one deck of 16 cards. The team also adds the value of their power cards to obtain a single power factor. For example, if one player with a power card of 3 forms an alliance with a player with a 2 power factor the team has a power factor of 5.

"The game is played in 'tricks.' That is, the team and the third player each turn over one of their cards and multiply the face value of the card by their power factor. The highest obtained number wins and removes those two cards, scoring the win as one trick. There are, of course, 16 tricks and the team or player who wins the most tricks wins that game. In case of a draw (each wins eight tricks) no one wins the prize and a new trial of the game is played for the same payoff. The values of the cards are aces, 15 points; all picture cards, 10 points; all other cards are at face value.

"If the game is won by the single player he receives one-half of the total payoff (that is, either 12 cents or 15 cents), the remaining one-half goes back to me. If the team wins they decide upon the prize division by negotiation. To save time we have made up communication sheets (experimenter shows sheets) which contain the necessary statements for you to communicate silently right at the table by simply pointing to the statement you wish to make to your partner. You will have 30 seconds to agree upon a prize division. Once you have both agreed raise your hands, and I will then record your decision. You are to keep your own score on the paper provided for you. If you fail to agree within 30 seconds neither of you wins anything for that game.

"Now you may find that after a coalition is formed the team's power factor is so large relative to the single player's power factor that the single player has no chance of winning the game. When the single player feels he has no chance of winning he may forfeit that game to the team. The team, after a forfeiture, proceeds immediately to the bargaining phase of the trial to determine the payoff division.

"There must be absolutely no talking during any part of the game.

"Now, since we cannot afford to give you all that money, it will have to be imaginary money, but we want you to play the game as though real money were at stake.

"Any questions?"

7. Have subjects play the game twice for practice.
   a. First practice game (use playing decks dealt out during the instructions).
      (i) Remove a 2 card from the power card deck so that three cards having face values 2, 3, and 4 remain. Shuffle the three cards and deal out one card to each subject, face up.
      (ii) Experimenter says:
         "This game is worth 30 cents; teams must split 20 cents and 10 cents."
         "Get ready to choose your partner."
         "One, two, three—choose."

(iii) If the single player forfeits the game, proceed to instruction (vi).

(iv) If no forfeiture, remove one of the team's playing decks.

(v) Experimenter says "Begin." The players turn over one card at a time until one side has won more than one-half of the tricks (i.e., the first side winning nine tricks wins the game).

(vi) If the team wins, as it usually will, give the team the appropriate communication sheet (Fig. 5.2) and allow 30 seconds for them to decide upon the payoff division. Announce the time every 10 seconds and at the last 5 seconds; i.e., after 10 seconds, experimenter says "20 seconds left"; after 20 seconds, experimenter says "10 seconds left"; then, after 25 seconds, experimenter says "5 seconds left." If the team does not arrive at a decision collect the cards immediately and start a new game.

(vii) Tell the subjects to record their winnings. Make sure that the subjects actually do keep a running total of their winnings. If the single player wins, tell him to record one-half of the payoff as his winnings (15 cents in the present case).

b. Practice game two.

(i) Collect and shuffle the 48 playing cards and deal out three packs of 16 cards each. (If the previous game was forfeited the three unused decks of 16 cards may be used again without reshuffling and redealing.)

(ii) Remove the 4 card from the power card deck so that the 2, 2, and 3 cards remain. Shuffle and deal one card to each player, face up.

(iii) Experimenter says:

"This game is worth 24 cents. Teams may split the payoff as they wish."

"Get ready to choose your partner."

"One, two, three – choose."

(iv) Follow the same procedure as in practice game one. Be sure to give the team, if it wins, the correct communication sheet (Fig. 5.1).

8. The experiment will require at least 60 trials – 10 repetitions of each of the three power conditions times the two payoff conditions. Do not count any trial which ends in a draw (eight tricks for each side), or in which the coalition team does not win. Also, do not count any trial in which the coalition does not agree on a payoff division within the time limit. Run a repeat trial for any trial not counted.

Power Condition

TRIAL	223 Coalition Formed (a)	223 Payoff Division (b)	224 Coalition Formed	224 Payoff Division	234 Coalition Formed (c)	234 Payoff Division (d)
1		22_____ 2___3___		22_____ 2___4___		2___3___ 2___4___ 3___4___
2		22_____ 2___3___		22_____ 2___4___		2___3___ 2___4___ 3___4___
3		22_____ 2___3___		22_____ 2___4___		2___3___ 2___4___ 3___4___
4		22_____ 2___3___		22_____ 2___4___		2___3___ 2___4___ 3___4___
Equal Payoff 5 Possible		22_____ 2___3___		22_____ 2___4___		2___3___ 2___4___ 3___4___
6		22_____ 2___3___		22_____ 2___4___		2___3___ 2___4___ 3___4___
7		22_____ 2___3___		22_____ 2___4___		2___3___ 2___4___ 3___4___
8		22_____ 2___3___		22_____ 2___4___		2___3___ 2___4___ 3___4___
9		22_____ 2___3___		22_____ 2___4___		2___3___ 2___4___ 3___4___
10		22_____ 2___3___		22_____ 2___4___		2___3___ 2___4___ 3___4___

COALITION FORMATION

TRIAL	Coalition Formed	Payoff Division 2 3	Coalition Formed	Payoff Division 2 4	Coalition Formed	Payoff Division 2 3 4
1						
2						
3						
4						
Un- 5						
equal 6						
Payoff 7						
8						
9						
10						

FIG. 5.3. Experimenter's tally sheet.

9. Have one experimenter run the game while the second experimenter assists and records the data on a tally sheet such as that shown in Fig. 5.3.

10. Run the experiment in a balanced order, that is, one trial of the equal payoff 2, 2, 3, condition first, followed by equal payoff 2, 2, 4 and 2, 3, 4, then unequal payoff 2, 2, 3, followed by 2, 2, 4, then 2, 3, 4. After all trial one lines are filled start the sequence over again until all ten lines are completed.

11. To run any particular power condition the one power card not required must be removed from the pack before the shuffling and dealing (e.g., for 2, 2, 4, remove the 3 card; for 2, 3, 4, remove a 2 card, etc.).

Instructions for Tally Sheet Entries: The entries on the tally sheet should include the coalition formed on a particular trial and the payoff division. For example, in the equal payoff condition under the 223 power condition the coalition formed would be entered in column (a) either as 22 or 23.

The payoff entries [column (b)] would either be on the 22____ line, giving the actual division (e.g., 12:12, 24:0, 8:16, etc.) or on the 2____ 3____ line giving the actual payoff agreed upon (e.g., 2(12), 3(12); 2(24), 3(0); 2(8), 3(16), etc.).

For the 234 condition, coalition entries in column (c) would be 23, 24, or 34, while the payoff entries [column (d)] would give the precise division of the payoff as agreed upon by the particular coalition (e.g., if a 34 coalition had been formed, the payoff division would be entered on the 3____ 4____ line).

In the unequal payoff condition, the recording of coalitions formed is the same as described above. Since the payoff ratio is fixed, no entry is required for 22 coalitions. All other coalition payoff agreements are to be recorded by simply entering the payoff obtained by each player in the appropriate column.

If no agreement is reached by the coalition members in the required time, all payoff entry spaces are left blank.

Data Analysis

A. Individual data

1. Sum the number of coalitions in each condition which included the powerful member and record in a table similar to Table 5.1.

TABLE 5.1

NUMBER OF COALITIONS IN WHICH THE POWERFUL PLAYER WAS INCLUDED

Payoff Condition	Condition		
	2 2 3	2 2 4	2 3 4
Divisible	$C_{e\,223}$		
Indivisible			$C_{\bar{e}234}$

C_{e223} = all 23 coalitions in the divisible payoff condition
$C_{\bar{e}234}$ = all 24 and 34 coalitions in the indivisible payoff condition

B. Group data

1.   a. Sum all the totals from each team's Table 5.1 and record in a table such as Table 5.2.

ΣC_{e223M} = sum of the C_{e223} totals (from Table 5.1) for all male triads
$\bar{C}_{e223M}$ = ΣC_{e223M}/number of male triads
$\Sigma C_{\bar{e}234F}$ = sum of the $C_{\bar{e}234}$ totals for all female triads
$\bar{C}_{\bar{e}234F}$ = $\Sigma C_{\bar{e}234F}$/number of female triads

  b. Plot the mean values in Table 5.2 in a form similar to Fig. 5.4 (where D stands for divisible payoff; and I stands for indivisible payoff).

  c. Payoff division: Sum the total number of equal (=) and unequal (≠) payoff divisions in the divisible payoff condition and record in a form such as Table 5.3.

TABLE 5.2
TOTAL AND MEAN NUMBER OF COALITIONS FORMED
WHICH INCLUDED THE POWERFUL PLAYER

			Condition		
			2 2 3	2 2 4	2 3 4
Males Payoff	Divisible	Sum	$\Sigma C_{e_{223M}}$		
		Mean	$\overline{C}_{e_{223M}}$		
	Indivisible	Sum			
		Mean			
Females Payoff	Divisible	Sum			
		Mean			
	Indivisible	Sum			$\Sigma C_{\overline{e}_{234F}}$
		Mean			$\overline{C}_{\overline{e}_{234F}}$

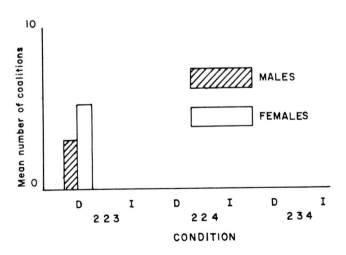

FIG. 5.4. Form for plotting mean values of Table 5.2.

TABLE 5.3
PAYOFF DIVISION WHEN EQUAL PAYOFF WAS POSSIBLE

	Condition					
	2 2 3		2 2 4		2 3 4	
	22	23	22	24	23	$\overline{23}$
	= ≠	= ≠	= ≠	= ≠	= ≠	= ≠
	Males					
Sum						
Mean	X					
	Females					
Sum						
Mean						

X = number of 22 coalitions in which the payoff was divided evenly/number of 22 coalitions
$\overline{23}$ = coalitions 24 and 34 (i.e., "not 23")

    d. Plot the means of the unequal (≠) payoff column in a form similar to Fig. 5.5.

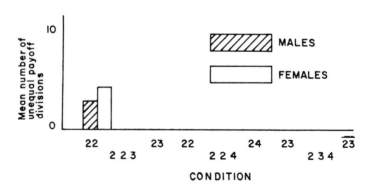

FIG. 5.5. Mean number of unequal payoff divisions.

e. Sum the total payoff obtained by the powerful member when included in a coalition and record in a table such as Table 5.4.

ΣP_{3e} = total amount obtained by the powerful member (3) when included in a coalition

$\bar{P}_{3e}$ = ΣP_{3e}/number of 23 coalitions formed

$\%\bar{P}_{3e} = [\bar{P}_{3e}/24] \times 100$

$\%\bar{P}_{3\bar{e}} = [\bar{P}_{3\bar{e}}/30] \times 100$

TABLE 5.4

TABLE OF MEANS AND MEAN PERCENT OF THE TOTAL PAYOFF OBTAINED BY THE POWERFUL PLAYER WHEN INCLUDED IN A COALITION

		Condition		
		2 2 3	2 2 4	2 3 4
		Males		
Divisible Payoff	Sum	ΣP_{3e}		ΣP_{4e}
	Mean	$\bar{P}_{3e}$		
	% of total	$\%\bar{P}_{3e}$		
Indivisible Payoff	Sum	$\Sigma P_{3\bar{e}}$		
	Mean	$\bar{P}_{3\bar{e}}$		
	% of total	$\%\bar{P}_{3\bar{e}}$		
		Females		
Divisible Payoff	Sum			
	Mean			
	% of total			
Indivisible Payoff	Sum			
	Mean			
	% of total			

f. Plot the mean percent of total from item e. in a graph similar to Fig. 5.6.

EXPERIMENT 5

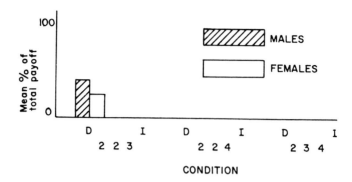

FIG. 5.6. Form for plotting mean percent from item e.

Experimental Report

1. Do the "weak" form coalitions against the "strong" in the divisible payoff condition but not in the indivisible payoff condition?

2. Does the powerful person tend to receive the "lion's share" under conditions of divisible payoff?

3. Who tends to receive the larger part of the payoff in the in- divisible payoff condition?

4. Do males form different coalitions or divide the payoffs differ- ently from females? Have you any idea as to what principle is creating the difference?

PAUL G. SWINGLE

Reprinted from Sociometry, 1960, Vol. 23, pp. 231–244, by permission of the authors and the publisher.

Coalitions in the Triad: Critique and Experiment

HAROLD H. KELLEY AND A. JOHN ARROWOOD,
Laboratory for Research in Social Relations, University of Minnesota [1]

Vinacke and Arkoff (4) have presented an experiment which tests some of Caplow's hypotheses (2) about how the relative power of three persons affects the formation of pair coalitions. The situation studied is one in which each person is trying to obtain for himself as much of some valuable but scarce commodity as he can. The three individuals differ in ways relevant to their ability to gain a share of the rewards (referred to as "power"). This work has been especially interesting because of the paradoxical result that with certain distributions of power among the three individuals, in Caplow's words, "the triadic situation often favors the weaker over the strong." Under certain conditions the stronger of the three is at a disadvantage and actually receives the smallest share of the available rewards.

The purpose of the present research is to state with greater precision than heretofore the conditions under which this phenomenon prevails and to test experimentally some of the limits of these conditions. In order to do so, it is necessary to clarify certain ambiguities in the concept of power as used in the Vinacke and Arkoff experiment. This clarification is accomplished through use of the analysis of power provided by Thibaut and Kelley (3).

The problem can best be illustrated by a brief description of the Vinacke and Arkoff procedure. Three subjects play a game in which each moves his counter along the spaces of a game board. The first one to reach the goal receives a prize of 100 points. On successive trials, the experimenter rolls a single die and each player advances a number of spaces determined by the product of two numbers: (a) the number of pips turned up on the die and (b) a "weight," ranging from 1 to 4, which was randomly assigned him at the beginning of the game. For example, in one game player A may have weight 4, player B, weight 2, and player C, weight 1. Since all players start at the same point on the board and move each time the die is cast, the person assigned the largest weight automatically wins. A further rule, however, enables any pair of players to form a coalition by combining their weights at any time during the game. When they do so, they are given a single counter placed at a position equal to the sum of the distances the two have attained at that time. On subsequent rolls, they advance according to the sum of

[1] This research was supported by grant G-5553 to the senior author from the National Science Foundation.

their two weights. The formation of a coalition is acknowledged by the experimenter only when the two players have agreed upon how they will divide the 100 point prize, should they receive it; and, once formed, a coalition is indissoluble for the remainder of that game. Thus, the individual or coalition that can mobilize the largest weight automatically wins that game and there is really no need for going through the motions of rolling the die.

The weight each player receives is said to constitute his *power,* but consider this point more closely. In what sense does a player with a weight of 4 have more power than a player with a weight of 2? In the game where the three weights are 4, 2 and 1, the player with the 4 weight has power in the sense that he is able, regardless of the actions of the other two players, to induce his "environment" (the game) to give him the prize. However, in the game with weights 4, 3 and 2, the player with 4 weight can exercise this control over the environment only if the other two players fail to form a coalition. Since any pair can mobilize more weight than the remaining person, each pair has the same amount of power over the third person as does any other pair. The variability in 4's outcomes is as much under the control of the joint actions of the other two players as is the variability in either 2 or 3's outcomes. Hence, as Vinacke and Arkoff point out, the initial weights in the 4–3–2 game are irrelevant with respect to the power a person has in the three-way bargaining situation.

In view of this logical analysis of the objective interdependency relations among the three players, Vinacke and Arkoff's results from the 4–3–2 and similar games are unexpected: The three players treat the weight 4 as if it does yield greater power. As his price for entering a coalition, player 4 apparently asks for a lion's share of the prize, because he typically receives more than 50 of the 100 points when he is in a coalition. Furthermore, players 2 and 3 tend to form the majority of the coalitions, presumably because each one can make a better deal with the other than he can with 4. From the point of view of rational analysis, then, the subjects act inappropriately, attributing to 4 a power that he does not in fact possess. The irony of the situation is that this erroneous belief about 4's advantage, which he usually shares, works to his disadvantage in the long run because of his exclusion from coalitions.

The first of the experiments reported below has the purpose of showing that Vinacke and Arkoff's data are, in a sense, spurious. They reflect a misunderstanding of the experimental situation that is not intrinsic to it, but results from the complexity of their total procedure. Confronted with the complexity, subjects erroneously equate initial weights with real power. (Our reasons for believing this erroneous assumption to be a reasonable one, considering the circumstances, are given in the Discussion.) The experimental hypothesis is that with a simpler procedure, subjects will acquire an adequate understanding of the true power relations and act more in accord with a rational analysis of the situation than the Vinacke and Arkoff data would suggest.

The second experiment has the purpose of testing Caplow's hypothesis under conditions where the power differences among the three persons are real rather than illusory. We expect the resulting bias in coalition formation (predominantly between the weaker members) to persist even though subjects are permitted thoroughly to familiarize themselves with the situation. (The limiting conditions under which the Caplow effect can be expected to appear are also described.)

In the Vinacke and Arkoff procedure, the relationship between weights and power is quite complicated. Each trio of subjects is required to play a series of games in which six different sets of weights are used. In the games played with a given set of values, a player need not have the same weight twice. With some sets of weights (such as 4–2–1) initial weight is relevant to power, and with others (such as 4–3–2) it is not.

In the present experiment, in order to simplify the subjects' task, only one set of weights was used (4–3–2) and each triad was given a lengthy series of trials, each player keeping the same weight throughout. It was expected that, with repeated experience in the single situation, the subjects' analyses of it would come to correspond with the analysis presented above, and their coalition formation and bargaining behavior would be increasingly consistent with an understanding that all players in the game have the same power.

Procedure

Ninety male students, volunteers from an introductory (sophomore) psychology class, served as subjects in thirty experimental triads. There is no reason to believe that the subjects were notably different from Vinacke and Arkoff's. Data were gathered first from 20 triads and, later, from ten additional triads. The first series were given a variable number of trials (10 to 70 trials, 26 on the average), and in the second series all groups completed 20 trials.

With the exceptions noted above, the experimental procedure followed that of Vinacke and Arkoff as closely as was possible from the available statements of their procedure. A major difference is that, whereas they gave very brief introductory instructions and relied on informal answers to questions to clarify the procedure, we gave rather full formal instructions and tried to minimize the necessity for subjects to ask questions. The subjects were given an individualistic orientation, it being emphasized that each was to accumulate as many points for himself as possible, attempting to maximize his outcomes without regard to those of any other players.

Results

In Table 1 are presented the frequencies of occurrence of the various coalitions. Data from our first and last three trials are presented for comparison

TABLE 1

Frequency of Occurrence of Various Coalitions in the Three Experiments

| | Vinacke and Arkoff's Three Trials | | Experiment I | | | | | Experiment II | | | |
| | | | First 3 Trials | | Last 3 Trials | | | First 3 Trials | | Last 3 Trials | |
Coalitions	N	%	N	%	N	%	(Coalitions)	N	%	N	%
2–3	59	66	41	46	37	41	(0–2)	24	53	29	64
2–4	20	22	24	27	26	29	(0–4)	12	27	13	29
3–4	9	10	21	23	27	30	(2–4)	9	20	3	7
No coalition	2	2	4	4	0	..		0	..	0	..
Totals	90	100	90	100	90	100		45	100	45	100

$$X^2 n=88 \atop 2df = 47.07$$
$$p<.001$$

$$X^2 n=90 \atop 2df = 2.47$$
$$.20<p<.30$$

$$X^2 n=45 \atop 2df = 22.93$$
$$p<.001$$

$$X^2 n=86 \atop 2df = 8.12$$
$$.01<p<.02$$

$$X^2 n=45 \atop 2df = 8.40$$
$$.01<p<.02$$

with those from Vinacke and Arkoff's three trials in the 4–3–2 condition. They calculated a Chi-square for the 88 instances of coalition formation (excluding the two instances of "no coalition") to determine the likelihood of the departure of the observed distribution from a theoretical distribution in which the three possible coalitions occur equally often. This procedure is not strictly justified, inasmuch as each group of subjects provides three instances of coalition formation, hence the various entries are not independent. However, we present similar Chi-squares in order to provide some basis for comparing the two sets of results.

It appears that the present procedure yields a distribution of coalitions which, although biassed in a manner similar to Vinacke and Arkoff's, is closer to the chance distribution than is theirs. The divergence from the earlier experiment appears even on the first three trials. A comparison of our first three with theirs yields a Chi-square of 8.48, p = .02. (The distribution of first coalitions formed in each triad resembles their distribution most

PAUL G. SWINGLE

closely, the percentages, in order, being 63, 20 and 17.) These results suggest that, either because of the concentrated experience with the single situation, or perhaps because of greater clarity in the experimental instructions, a number of subjects became aware of the objective power relationships rather early in the game.

From the first to the last trials there is not a significant change in the incidence of the three coalitions, hence we cannot be sure that further experience increased their understanding of the situation. However, this result must be interpreted in the light of the rather limited degree to which the occurrence of the early coalitions departed from chance. To the extent that subjects achieved an understanding of their relationships very early, further improvement in this respect was limited. Upon examination of the data on a trial-by-trial basis, it is clear that the learning is very rapid, so that after the first three or four trials there is little more than chance exclusion of 4 from coalitions.

In Vinacke and Arkoff's experiment, associated with the tendency for 2 and 3 to be reluctant about forming coalitions with 4, was the tendency for him to receive more than half of the 100 point prize when he did manage to enter a coalition. This effect appears in the early trials of the present experiment and declines, though not significantly so, during its course. During the first three trials, player 4 was a member of a coalition in 26 triads and in 17 of these he managed to come out with more than 50 per cent of the rewards. During the last three trials of the experiment, this was true in only 10 of 29 possible instances. Of the 25 groups in which person 4 was in coalitions during both the first and last three trials, his share of the coalition reward declined in 13 instances, increased in six instances and did not change in the remaining six. Omitting the last six, the difference between the number of decreases and increases yields a p-value of .168 by the Sign test.

There are, then, two behavioral manifestations of the players' perception that 4 has the most power: (a) He is excluded from coalitions and, (b) when he is included in coalitions, he receives more than half the points. When early and later trials are compared, the extent to which 4's frequency of being included increases and the extent to which his percentage winnings per trial decrease provide two indicators of downgrading in the perception of his power. A comparison of the first and last three trials of the experiment reveals that in 18 triads the 4 man was downgraded on both of these indicators or downgraded on one with no change on the other; in six triads, he was upgraded on both indicators or upgraded on one with no change on the other; and in six triads, he did not change on either indicator or was upgraded on one and downgraded on the other. When the last six are omitted from the analysis, the Sign test indicates there was significantly more downgrading than upgrading ($p = .026$).

On the questionnaire at the end of the experiment all subjects were asked the following open-ended question: "Many subjects believe that 4 is more to be feared, has greater potential, etc. Did you at any time think that this was the case?" All but 14 of the 90 subjects admitted that they at some time had held this belief. This estimate of the extent of the belief, if it errs at all, is probably an underestimate because of the general realization at the end of the experiment of the incorrectness of this view. Most of those admitting to this belief reported having it "at first" or on the first one or two trials. Subjects with the three different weights were equally susceptible to this belief.

The next question asked when the subject realized that no position has any more power than any other and that nobody is justified in asking for more than half the 100 points. Forty-three of the 90 claimed to have realized this before or during the first three trials. Another 33 did not localize their insight so sharply in time. Only 13 admitted they had never realized this. On the basis of their answers to other questions about power relations, preferred position, position likely to win, and ease of bargaining with various positions, another nine subjects were added to the latter category of those who had failed to attain a correct understanding of the situation by the end of the experiment.

In brief, the self-report data suggest that, while some 85 per cent of our subjects believed at some time during the experiment (largely, in the early stages) that the 4 weight carries greatest power, only 25 per cent held this belief at the end of the experiment. As far as we could judge from their answers to questions asked after the experiment, the other 75 per cent had achieved a correct understanding of the power relations and apparently most of them did so during the actual trials of the experiment.

One may ask to what extent this change in belief about power relations reflects the subjects' direct experience with the game, as opposed to their being taught by the small number of their colleagues who had analyzed the situation correctly from the start. To answer this question, a comparison was made between those groups in which, from the sound recordings of the discussion, there appeared to have been some possibility of "teaching," and the remaining groups. There were no differences between the two sets of data either in the amount of learning that took place or in the coalitions formed. Hence, explicit teaching seems not to account for the observed effects.

A final open-ended question asked: "Why do you think that many subjects would believe that 4 is more to be feared, has greater potential, etc.? What is there in the situation that leads to this belief?" The most frequent response, given by 34 of the 90 subjects, dealt with the fact that 4 would win invariably if no coalitions were formed. Another 13 merely stated, without further amplification, that 4 was the largest number. Nine subjects mentioned the multiplicative aspect of the game, pointing out that multiples of 4 are larger than multiples of 2 or 3. Apparently, the 56 responses in these three categories either discount or overlook the possibility of coalition formation. A fourth category of response deals with 4's "psychological" or "cultural" power. Seventeen of the 90 suggested that it was natural to react to 4's higher weight in the light of their previous experience in games that higher numbers are generally better ones and in everyday life that quantity often has the upper hand. This answer is silent concerning the possibility of coalitions but highlights the stereotype that "more" is "better."

It is difficult to evaluate the validity of these post-experiment explanations for the earlier misinterpretation. Because the misperception of 4's power is largely corrected by the end of the experiment, subjects may be somewhat reluctant or even unable to discuss the real basis for their mistaken views. Hence the reasons given by the 22 players who seem never to have realized the true nature of the power situation may be especially valuable indications of the source of the error. Seven of the 22 seemed to believe that coalitions including 4 were somehow more sure of obtaining the prize than were other coalitions or that 4 was the only player capable of bargaining and that the other players had either to accept his terms or receive nothing. We believe it noteworthy that it is only among these 22 players that we find the assertion (made by another seven of them) that a high-weight player is justified in demanding a majority share of the coalition reward because he *contributes more* to the coalition. One might guess that this interpretation figures more prominently in the early reaction to the situation than the overall figures would indicate. The comments about 4's larger number and the multiplicative aspects of the game may well be oblique references to earlier beliefs (which now appear to the subjects as totally unjustified) that the higher weight player makes a greater contribution to coalition success.

EXPERIMENT II

Under the Vinacke and Arkoff procedure, the alternative to being in a coalition on any given trial has the same value (zero) for each player regardless of his weight. Hence, 4's outcomes are as much subject to control through the joint actions of the other two players as are either 2 or 3's outcomes. It is in this sense that 4 has no more power than they. In the present experiment, real power differences are created by giving the three subjects differential ability to obtain rewards from the game, an ability that can not be attenuated by the actions of the other two persons. This is done by giving each person a specific alternative level of outcomes which he receives if he fails to gain membership in a coalition or if, once in a coalition, he and his partner fail to reach agreement on a division of the spoils. (The bargaining involved in the division of the prize *follows* rather than precedes the choice of coalition partners.) The person with a higher alternative value has high power in the sense that (a) he is less dependent upon getting into a coalition, and (b), during the bargaining following coalition formation, he can hold out for a larger share because he has less to lose if no agreement is reached. The long run effects of the latter, demanding a preponderant share of the reward, are of rather little concern to him because of the first fact. At the same time, factor (b) makes him less desirable than a weaker person as a coalition partner. Hence, we would expect that the poorer a player's alternative, the greater the likelihood of his being included in a pair coalition. Of course, this will be true only when the size of prize given a coalition does *not* increase in proportion to the power of its members. (In the present case, as in the Vinacke and Arkoff procedure, the prize is the same for all coalitions.) It is under these circumstances that Caplow's statement is relevant—that "the weakest member of the triad has a definite advantage, being sure to be included in whatever coalition is formed."

Procedure

Forty-five male students, volunteers from an introductory (sophomore) psychology class, served as subjects in 15 experimental triads. The task was presented as a simple business game in which each player was a corporation chairman, controlling a certain share of the market each month. Each player's object was to accumulate as many points for himself as possible, not to compete but to attempt to maximize his own outcomes without regard to how this might affect the outcomes of the other players. Each subject was randomly assigned a weight—either 4, 2, or 0—which represented the number of points he could earn on each trial if he chose to play the game independently. Any pair of subjects, however, had the option of forming a coalition which was then given one minute to decide in what manner to divide a ten-point prize between them. Coalitions were formed by a series of written choices. At the beginning of each trial, each subject privately indicated the number of the other player with whom he would most like to form a coalition. Reciprocated choices became coalition partners, thereby having the opportunity to attempt to decide how they wanted to divide the ten points between them. The third man, the player *not* in the coalition, was paid off immediately with the number of points equal to his weight or alternative and did not enter into the bargaining for that trial. (If there happened to be no reciprocated choices on a given trial, the subjects were requested to consider the problem again and indicate their choices once more. This procedure was continued until a reciprocated choice appeared. This was necessary on only 43 of the 300 trials. Most of the instances of non-reciprocation were found early in the game.) If the two members of the coalition reached some mutually satisfactory division of the ten points during the minute allotted for bargaining, they then received that number of points as their scores for that trial. If, however, they did not agree before the time limit, they forfeited the ten points and each received the number of points equal to their weights or alternatives. A time limit was placed on the bargaining so that the weaker player could not gain power by stalling and controlling time. Each subject retained the same weight throughout the game, and each triad completed 20 trials.

Although the weights employed in the present study differ from those used in the Vinacke-Arkoff experiment, they are comparable in at least two ways: first, if no coalitions are formed, or if no agreement is reached in the coalitions which are formed, the high-weight man will always win; and, second, the coalition is always assured a chance at a larger number of points than is any independent player. For certain analyses, then, we shall consider the present 0–2, 0–4, and 2–4 coalitions as equivalent, respectively, to the 2–3, 2–4, and 3–4 coalitions in the previous experiment.

Results

Table 1 presents the frequencies of occurrence of the various coalitions. Data from the first and last three trials of Experiment II may be compared with those from Vinacke and Arkoff and Experiment I. The relative incidence of the various coalitions for the first three trials of Experiment II does not differ significantly from that of Experiment I. The difference between the two distributions for the last three trials of each experiment is significant at the .01 level with a Chi-square of 10.72. The difference between the two distributions for Experiment II is not significant (Chi-square $= 3.48$, $p < .20$).

It appears, then, that the present procedure yields a distribution of coalitions which, although departing initially from the Vinacke-Arkoff distribution, does not do so as markedly as does the distribution from Experiment I and comes to approximate the Vinacke-Arkoff distribution far more closely as the trials progress.

The data also suggest that this is not merely an illusory effect which disappears with repeated experience in the situation. Table 2 presents the mean frequencies per triad of the various coalitions, and the significance levels for these differences. The 0–2 coalition occurs significantly more frequently than do either of the other possible pairs, both over the whole series of 20 trials and in both the first and second halves of the experiment; but only over the entire series of trials does the difference between the relative incidence of the 0–4 and 0–2 coalitions approach significance. Moreover, the average frequency of 0–2 coalitions tends to increase from the first to the second half of the experiment, while that of the 2–4 coalitions tends to decrease during the same period (in both instances $.05 < p < .10$, using the ordinary t-test for differences).

TABLE 2

*Mean Frequency of Occurrence of Various Coalitions Overall and by Halves of Experiment II with Comparisons**

Mean Frequency per Triad	Overall	First Half of Trials	Second Half of Trials
0–2	12.33	5.67	6.67
0–4	5.20	2.80	2.40
2–4	2.47	1.53	.93
	20 trials	10 trials	10 trials

Mean Difference per Triad			
0–2 > 0–4	7.13	2.87	4.27
	t = 10.62	t = 8.28	t = 9.19
	p < .02	p < .02	p < .02
0–2 > 2–4	9.87	4.13	5.73
	t = 14.68	t = 11.94	t = 12.35
	p < .02	p < .02	p < .02
0–4 > 2–4	2.73	1.27	1.47
	t = 4.07	t = 3.66	t = 3.16
	.02 < p < .10	p = NS	p = NS

* The t values in this table were calculated using the Tukey method for multiple comparisons.

Another way of looking at the evidence is in terms of partnership choice data. Each of the positions predominantly chose the lower alternative man as a partner—i.e., 0 chose 2 66 per cent of the time, 2 chose 0 77 per cent of the time, and 4 chose 0 60 per cent of the time. Sign tests show that the results differ significantly from those expected by chance (equally frequent choice of the other two players) at beyond the .05 level in all three cases.

The previous experiments revealed an initial tendency for the 4 man to ask for and receive the majority of points from those coalitions which he did manage to enter. Over the entire series of 20 trials in the present experiment, there was a similar tendency for both 4 and 2 to receive more points than 0 in the 4–0 and 2–0 coalitions respectively (significant at better than the .02

level by the Tukey method for multiple comparisons). The slight tendency for 4 to receive more points than 2 from 2–4 coalitions proved non-significant. The over-all results are duplicated in the first half of the trials for each triad, but largely disappear during the second half—the only significant result remaining in the 4–0 coalition. As expected, on the average 4 received significantly more points per coalition from 0 than he did from 2, as did 2 from 0 over 4. The 0 man was slightly better rewarded by 2 than by 4, and especially during the second half of the game ($.05 < p < .10$). A comparison of first and second half scores reveals that 0's scores per coalition increase significantly ($p < .01$) while 4's scores per coalition decrease slightly ($.05 < p < .10$).

In a questionnaire administered at the end of the experiment the subjects were asked to indicate the following: which weight they would choose as a permanent partner; in general, which weight they believed each of the players should form coalitions with; which weight had the most power; which are the easiest and hardest weights with which to bargain; which weight would win in the long run; and which member, if either, of any coalition is justified in asking for a majority of the points. Their answers reflect the coalition formation and bargaining behavior discussed above. Only five of the 45 subjects, for example, failed to pick the available lower alternative player as a permanent coalition partner. The question: "Which of the three players has the most power?" was asked twice—once early in the questionnaire and once again at the end. At the first asking, four subjects responded that 0 had the most power, three picked 2, 36 chose 4, and two said that there were no power differences. At the later asking, 13 of the subjects who had previously singled out 4 as having power changed their answers to 2. The open-ended explanations accompanying these changes indicate a growing awareness of 2's ability to entice 0 into a coalition although still noting that, *if selected,* 4's higher weight becomes important. In general, however, subjects continue to view power as residing in a higher alternative.

DISCUSSION AND SUMMARY

It appears that Vinacke and Arkoff's procedure does initially give player 4 an illusory kind of power. In Experiment I, most of the subjects are initially subject to this misperception but apparently achieve a more correct understanding in a few trials. These results are in accord with our general contention that the phenomenon reported by Vinacke and Arkoff is limited to instances where the complexity of the learning task is so great in relation to the amount of contact and experience subjects have with it that they are not able properly to analyze it. In consequence, we witness actions that are "irrational" with respect to the analysis the experimenter makes at his leisure. However, these actions are not necessarily irrational when viewed in the light of the understanding subjects are able to achieve under the pressures of time and task complexity. Incomplete understanding is not to be confused with irrationality.

There are at least two possible interpretations of the initial erroneous attribution of power to player 4. The first is that the initial attribution of power to 4 reflects a general pessimism about the dependability of cooperative action. Logically, player 4 is more powerful *unless* the others join forces against him. Until one knows that joint action will be instituted dependably, attributing superior power to him is not wholly unwarranted. This interpretation is suggested by the most commonly given explanation for the attribution: 4 has more power because he would win if no coalitions were formed. The declining tendency to attribute power to 4 may reflect a growing confidence that in this situation, at least, cooperative action against him is to be taken for granted.

Another possible interpretation is that our subjects have learned to use a person's potentialities in a field of independent actors as an indication of his ability to contribute to cooperative efforts. This is explicitly suggested by the comments that he makes a larger contribution to any coalition he enters and is consistent with other more general explanations provided by the subjects. In view of their likely experiences with these matters, this conclusion is a highly reasonable one. It is probably true that in everyday situations a person's effectiveness, when everyone is acting for himself, is rather closely related to how much he can add to any joint effort. Thus, the common misperception in the Vinacke and Arkoff situation may reflect a positive correlation in the social environment of the typical subject. The reader may note the similarity of this interpretation to Brunswik's explanation (1) of, for example, the size-weight illusion as reflecting a correlation between size and weight over the universe of objects the person has experienced in his physical environment. In Brunswik's terms, we are suggesting that a person's effectiveness as an individual has "ecological validity" as a cue from which to predict his ability to contribute to joint efforts, and thus enjoys considerable "impression value" or "response-eliciting power." This is the case in the Vinacke and Arkoff situation. In Experiment I, subjects initially utilize this cue extensively, but later learn that it is inappropriate in this situation and, hence, its subsequent degree of utilization declines.

The procedure of Experiment II, in contrast to that of Vinacke and Arkoff, appears to create large and lasting power differences among the members of the triad. Given differentially good alternatives to being in a coalition or, more important, to acquiescing to a coalition partner's demands, the predicted pattern of coalition formation emerges, and the weakest member of the triad is in the most favored position when it comes to joining pair coalitions. The score and self-report data, however, suggest certain minor trends worth brief consideration. We have noted a tendency for 0's average score per coalition to increase and 4's to decrease. This finding may be taken as an indication that during the course of the trials some 0's are beginning to capitalize on their status as preferred coalition partners by asking for a larger share of the prize and some 4's are recognizing that they must be more generous in dividing the prize if they are to be allowed to enter further coalitions. We have also noted some changes in subjects' perceptions of the most powerful player and in the reasons accompanying their answers. Mention of 2's greater ability to entice 0 into coalitions suggests that some subjects are becoming aware of the truth of Caplow's hypothesis. These findings raise the interesting side problem of how a high-power individual in a situation with limited communication possibilities would go about establishing trust. Once excluded from coalitions, the high-weight man would probably tend to remain excluded, since unless he could enter a coalition there would be no way for him to demonstrate to the others that he would not use his power against them.

It must be noted that in general 4 tends to accumulate the most points during the game—93 on the average as compared with 86 for 2 and 66 for 0. However, this is probably an artifact of the relative sizes of the alternatives and the prize to be divided. By making the coalition reward larger in relation to the largest weight, one could create a situation in which the highest alternative player would, by reason of his exclusion from coalitions, end up with the smallest accumulated score. However, as the coalition prize becomes larger, the differential power implications of any given set of weights becomes less important.

One might also manipulate the weights and coalition prize in such a manner that the highest alternative player would emerge as the most preferred partner. This is an important point because it indicates the boundary conditions for the phenomena observed in Experiment II. For example, different sizes of rewards might be given to different coalitions. If the various rewards were proportional to the weights of the persons comprising the various coalitions, one would expect no difference in the relative incidence of the three possible types of coalition or even a bias in favor of coalitions including the high-power person. The latter effect would be expected, for example, if the 2–4 coalition received a prize of 12 points, the 0–4 coalition, 8 points, and the 0–2 coalition, 4 points. This would reproduce the situation where the more effective a person is as an independent actor, the more effective is the joint effort to which he contributes. It is not unreasonable to believe that, in many natural situations, joint effectiveness is a direct function (and perhaps even a multiplicative one) of individual effectiveness. In these cases, if the above analysis is correct, coalitions would appear largely among persons of high power. On the other hand, the Caplow effect will appear when coalition effectiveness bears no relation (or a negative one) to the effectiveness of the component members.

Manuscript received: October 9, 1959
Revised Manuscript received: January 28, 1960
   Harold H. Kelley
   Laboratory for Research in Social Relations
   University of Minnesota
   Minneapolis 14, Minnesota

REFERENCES

1. Brunswik, E., *Systematic and Representative Designs of Psychological Experiments*, Berkeley: University of California Press, 1949.
2. Caplow, T., "A Theory of Coalitions in the Triad," *American Sociological Review*, 1956, 21, 489–493.
3. Thibaut, J. W., and H. H. Kelley, *The Social Psychology of Groups*, New York: Wiley and Sons, Inc., 1959, Chapters 7 and 11.
4. Vinacke, W. E., and A. Arkoff, "An Experimental Study of Coalitions in the Triad," *American Sociological Review*, 1957, 22, 406–414.

Reprinted from Behavioral Science, 1966, Vol. 11, pp. 180–189, by permission of the authors and the publisher.

When a game of strategy is played by three or more players and coalitions are allowed, the outcome of the game depends on how the players will form coalitions. In the simplest case, the coalition which includes the majority of the players wins the same prize regardless of who is in the winning coalition. In a somewhat more general situation, different "weights" are assigned to different players and a coalition with the preponderant total weight wins. One hypothesis on the formation of coalitions states that if two weaker players can combine their weights to defeat the third stronger player, they will do so. To what extent is this so and under what conditions?

THE EFFECT OF INFORMATION ABOUT STRATEGY ON A THREE-PERSON GAME[1]

by W. Edgar Vinacke, Doris C. Crowell, Dora Dien, and Vera Young

IN 1956, Theodore Caplow presented a series of hypotheses pertaining to the coalitions to be expected when three persons interact under conditions of varying intragroup power (Caplow, 1956). He took his point of departure from Simmel (1955), who suggested that there is a strong tendency for triads to subdivide into a pair and an odd person. Caplow showed that power relationships between the members of such a group could well determine which pair would establish alliances. The points with which this study is concerned can best be understood by examining the several possible power patterns, as presented in Figure 1.

At the right are indicated the results to be expected under competitive conditions according, on the one hand, to Caplow's analysis and, on the other hand, to derivations from the theory of games (these implications have been set forth in some detail in previous reports, e.g., Vinacke and Arkoff, 1957). It is evident that Caplow's argument is based upon the principle of perceived

strength. When the three members of a triad are equal (Type I), no one perceives any special advantage; as a consequence there would be no special preference for partner. In situations in which members vary in power, but any pair in combination is stronger than the odd man (Types II, III, and V), the weaker members would see an advantage in joining forces as a means to overcome the greater apparent strength of their rival, leading to the prediction of weak coalitions. Finally, if one member is stronger than the other two in combination, no alliance would be expected, since the strongest need not join forces with either of the others, and a coalition of the weaker members would be perceived as futile.

Under the simple conditions formulated, game theory offers an alternative set of predictions, based on the premise that the members of the triad would act in a completely "rational"[2] manner. They would accordingly analyze all the facts and relate this information to the final outcome of their behavior. In the case of Types II, III, and V this means that no one can possibly win without entering into a coalition (assuming that coalitions are possible and, therefore,

[1] This research was conducted under contract with the Office of Naval Research (Nonr 4370 (00)), and has been issued in Technical Report No. 6, April 2, 1964. Reproduction in whole or part is permitted for any purpose of the United States Government. A pilot study leading to the present investigation was supported by a grant from the Social Science Research Council.

[2] "Rational" throughout this report means an attitude corresponding to the objective, quantitatively defined facts; of course, behavior based on other considerations (those perceived by the subjects) may have its own rationality.

Type[3]	Players			Description	Predicted Coalitions	
	A	B	C		By Caplow	By Game Theory
I	1	1	1	All-Equal: A = B = C	Any pair	Any
II	3	2	2	One-Stronger: A > B; B = C A < (B + C)	BC	Any
III	1	2	2	One Weaker: A < B; B = C	AB or AC	Any
IV	3	1	1	All-Powerful: A > B; B = C; A > (B + C)	None	None
V	4	3	2	All-Different: A > B > C; A < (B + C)	BC	Any
VI	4	2	1	All-Powerful: A > B > C; A > (B + C)	None	None

[3] We omit still other versions in which a tie is possible, not because they may not be important but because they have not been used in our experiments.

Fig. 1. Types of Power Pattern and Predicted Coalitions.

that players would form them); furthermore, no one can hope for any special advantage because, were he to seek it, the other two would simply ally against him. In this manner, the three members are logically equal to each other, and reduce to more complicated cases of Type I. It is easy, of course, to formulate other conditions under which the power relationships have a more solid foundation in fact than under conditions so far mentioned. For example, if rewards accrue as the outcome of competition in accordance with strength, then the weaker players must, in fact, join forces to compensate for the real advantage of the stronger player. (This situation has been studied by Kelley and Arrowood, 1960.)

Vinacke and Arkoff (1957) conducted an experiment to test these alternative predictions. They had triads play a simple game in which counters were moved around a board. The strength was represented by a weight inscribed on the counter, and this weight determined the distance a player could move following the casting of a die. An arbitrary prize of 100 points was awarded for winning, and players in alliance had to arrive at deals in dividing the prize. Their results confirmed Caplow's argument, in opposition to game

theory, leading to the conclusion that regardless of sheer logic, people tend to operate on the basis of perceived strength. An extensive series of experiments has continued to support this conclusion (Vinacke, 1963). An important additional dimension has been added in experiments with female triads, who play this game in ways that depart even more widely from game theory than do those of male triads. In fact we have regularly been able to differentiate an exploitative strategy, more characteristic of males, from an accommodative strategy, more typical of females (see Bond and Vinacke, 1961; Vinacke, 1959; Vinacke, 1963). In both strategies, the tendency of the weaker to ally against the stronger is clearly apparent, but this is less frequent in exploitative strategy. There are many other differences which will not be discussed here. In general, exploitative strategy is marked by active and ruthless bargaining and efforts to make favorable deals, with an orientation towards winning; accommodative strategy is characterized by emphasis on fairness, avoidance of "hard bargaining," and orientation towards the socially interactive aspects of the situation.

The immediate purpose of the present experiment was to determine the influence of information about opposing views of the power pattern on the behavior of triads. That is, we wished to determine whether knowledge of the true power relationships would produce the rational strategy predicted by game theory. Kelley and Arrowood (1960) advanced a number of criticisms of the Vinacke and Arkoff procedure which might have been responsible for their results. In particular Kelley and Arrowood contended that the procedure of the earlier experiment was so complicated as to interfere with proper analysis of the power situation, and that the players had undue difficulty in learning what the most logical or rational outcome really was.

There can be no doubt that the original procedure was complicated in certain respects. Each triad played a total of 18 games, three each of the six power types. These games were played in three series or sets, with the six types randomized within a set. At the outset of each event, the players drew the requisite counters with weights concealed, with the result that the weights varied from player to player. These devices were adopted both to control for position effects and to augment natural interest in the game. It was also expected that these arrangements would tend to equalize learning for any given triad across power patterns and to reduce the likelihood of following a routinized style of play.

Kelley and Arrowood tried to simplify the conditions of play and to extend trials over a long enough period to allow an adequate opportunity to learn. Since Type V (4-3-2) can be judged as an especially critical situation in which to test predictions, they confined play to this pattern.[4] Each triad played 20 or more times, each player keeping the same weight throughout. In addition, they evidently sought to give their subjects more detailed instructions than did Vinacke and Arkoff, who offered their Ss written instructions which could be consulted ad libitum.

Two experiments were reported by Kelley and Arrowood. In the first, the incidence of the weak BC coalition was markedly less than in the Vinacke and Arkoff experiment, thus suggesting the possibility that the Ss may have come to appreciate the true conditions of the game. A postsession questionnaire confirmed the fact that a majority of players came to realize the illusory character of "4's" power (85% reported that they believed at some point in the superior strength of "4," whereas only 25% still held this conviction at the end of play).

In their second experiment, Kelley and Arrowood used somewhat different weights, with a payoff according to weight and the additional opportunity to win a bonus by coalition. This procedure gives real power to the strongest member, and makes it possible for the weaker players to counterbalance his advantage by winning the bonus. Under these conditions, results very similar to Vinacke and Arkoff's were found. The pres-

ent report is really concerned with the first Kelley and Arrowood experiment.

There are several aspects of the Kelley and Arrowood procedure which raise questions about the degree to which their results actually disagree with Vinacke and Arkoff.

In the first place, their decision that each player should keep the same weight throughout probably changes the character of the game. Certainly this procedure maximizes the probability that fixed routines could develop, with a consequent loss of interest. Players might then simply mix up their alliances to alleviate boredom. A more basic consideration concerns a striking phenomenon observed in experiments when a cumulative score has been maintained (Vinacke, 1963). That is, each player's acquired points are accumulated so that each can assess his success relative to the other two. Under these circumstances, there is a significant tendency for alliances to occur between the two players who are behind at the time—and this tendency reduces the incidence of coalitions between the weaker players (indeed, it approximates closely the findings of Kelley and Arrowood). Frequent comments by players reveal the fact that they often maintain a kind of informal record of this sort, even under the game by game conditions of the experiments here under discussion. The Kelley and Arrowood procedure is ideally designed to promote the operation of this principle. If one player keeps the same weight throughout and there is any tendency for the others to ally against him, he is bound to fall behind. He is thus in an excellent position to appeal for help on any of several grounds, including a complaint about being "fair," proposing that equalizing the score will make the game more interesting, and merely addressing the self-interest of the other players who can more effectively compete against each other by including him in coalitions.

There is, then, some reason to suppose that the Kelley and Arrowood method did not fully establish the supposition that players will follow the most rational procedure (at least as it is viewed in game theory) if only they know enough to do so.

The present experiment was intended to follow up the Kelley and Arrowood experi-

[4] It is worth noting, in passing, however, that any of the power-patterns can be used to test game theory, since in each of them "irrational" results occur. For example, a considerable number of alliances occur in the All Powerful types, even when players know, and openly state, that none is necessary or fruitful; and deals reached between partners in the All Equal type are by no means always on a 50/50 basis, and so on.

ment under conditions of freer choice, so to speak, between the alternative strategies that lead to the contrasting predictions indicated above. At the same time, it was hoped that various other findings might be cast into fuller perspective, notably the difference between the sexes which might change with variation in the amount of information available to the participants.

We wanted to allow players an opportunity to learn about the conditions of play, and then to have at their command the option of choosing alliances according to the perception of strength principle or according to the strictly rational analysis of outcome principle.

PROCEDURE

Sixty-nine triads provided the data, 35 composed of males, and 34 of females (207 Ss). They were recruited from introductory psychology classes and rewarded for their services with laboratory credits.

Game situation. The board game described above was employed, following conditions identical to the Vinacke and Arkoff experiment. In particular this means, in contrast to Kelley and Arrowood, that the weights for a particular game were drawn in turn by the players, leaving to chance who would possess each weight. Four power patterns were selected: All Equal[(1-1-1)], One Stronger[(3-2-2)], All Different[(4 3 2)], and All Powerful[(4-2-1)] (types I, II, V, and IV). In each session six successive games of each of the four power patterns were played, randomizing order of patterns. In the interests of brevity, we shall ignore the All Equal and All Powerful types.

Information conditions. The games were played in two sessions. The triads first engaged in a "learning" period, during which games were played merely with the original instructions. After that, the experimenter took aside randomly designated Ss and gave them special information about the two alternative strategies. It was necessary to avoid as carefully as possible any suggestion that one of these was to be preferred over the other, for the obvious reason that Ss might pick up the hint that they were supposed to act in accordance. The instructions were therefore couched neutrally, with the two explanations as nicely balanced as possible. With these points in mind, the experimenter gave the following information to the Ss chosen:

You people have just played a simple game and thus have had a chance to learn about its characteristics. I should like to make certain that you understand how the problem of winning can be settled. There are really two general principles that you can follow. By now you can see that the weights of the three players must be taken into account. In one combination, a single player can win no matter what the other two do. This was the combination of 4–2–1 weights. Of course this does not mean that two people *cannot* join forces—that is, form a coalition—if they want to. But it does mean that the person who draws the "4" could win all by himself (herself) if he (she) chooses. In the other combinations, however, any pair could win if they wished to do so. I want to be sure that you see the two principles that could be used to decide who should form a coalition. Let us use as examples the combinations in which the numbers differ in strength. As you remember, these were the patterns 3–2–2 and 4–3–2. One principle is that the two weaker players could join forces to defeat the third player. For example, those holding the two weights of 2 could ally, and thus defeat the stronger person, who holds the weight of 3.

The other principle is that it doesn't matter who holds which weight, because any pair can win. The three players might add up pairs of weights and thus see that each pair is equal, insofar as being able to win is concerned. For example, the combination 3 and 2 can win just as much as the combination 2 and 2. To repeat, then, according to one principle, it makes no difference who enters into a coalition, since any pair can win the prize. According to the other principle, the two weaker players try to defeat the stronger man by forming an alliance against him.

In one set of triads, these explanations were given to one member, in a second set to two members, and in a third set to all three members. At the conclusion of the information session, a questionnaire was administered to assess degree of understanding and motivation. Ten triads of each sex were assigned to the "One Informed" condition, ten male triads and nine female triads to the "Two Informed" condition, and fifteen of each sex to the "Three Informed" condition. As mentioned above, 24 games were played by each triad in both the Learning and Informed sessions.

W. Edgar Vinacke, Doris C. Crowell, Dora Dien, and Vera Young

RESULTS

In previous experiments, many different characteristics of play have been revealed in this game situation, including the kind of outcome (coalition) reached, the deals agreed upon by allies, and the amount of bargaining that occurs preceding final coalition. For the purpose of this report, however, we shall focus upon those data that pertain to the crucial point at issue, namely, the kinds of coalition that are established under contrasting information conditions. (For other aspects of the data, see Vinacke, Crowell, Dien, and Young, 1964.)

TABLE 1

INCIDENCE OF WEAK ALLIANCES IN THE ONE STRONGER (3-2-2) AND ALL DIFFERENT (4-3-2) PATTERNS UNDER THREE INFORMATION CONDITIONS

	Male Triads						Female Triads					
	1-Inf.		2-Inf.		3-Inf.		1-Inf.		2-Inf.		3-Inf.	
	L*	I*	L	I	L	I	L	I	L	I	L	I
Above Chance	9	9	7	7	10	10	10	10	8	9	14	11
Chance, or Below	1	1	3	3	4	4	0	0	1	0	1	4
	—	—	—	—	—	—	—	—	—	—	—	—
	10	10	10	10	14	14	10	10	9	9	15	15

No difference is significant for any comparison.
* L refers to Learning session, I to Information session.

TABLE 2

WEAK COALITIONS EARLY AND LATE IN PLAY

% of 2-Person Alliances	In Patterns 3–2–2 and 4–3–2				% of 2-Person Alliances	In Pattern 4–3–2			
	First 2 Games of Each (Learn)		Last 2 Games of Each (Inform)			First 3 Games (Learning)		Last 3 Games (Information)	
	M	F	M	F		M	F	M	F
One-Informed									
100	4	8	4	7	100	5	9	5	6
51–99	3	1	1	1	67	3	0	1	2
34–50	2	1	3	0	50	1	0	0	0
33 or Less	1	8	2	0	33 or Less	1	0	3	0
	—	—	—	—		—	—	—	—
	10	10	10	8†		10	9†	9†	8†
Mean %	73.4	92.5	68.3	96.9		78.4	100	74.0	91.8
Two-Informed									
100	3	5	5	4	100	2	6	2	5
51–99	1	0	1	2	67	3	1	6	1
34–50	4	3	2	2	50	0	0	0	0
33 or Less	2	1	2	1	33 or Less	5	1	2	2
	—	—	—	—		—	—	—	—
	10	9	10	9		10	8†	10	8†
Mean %	62.5	75.0	72.5	75.0		43.4	83.4	63.5	75.0
Three-Informed									
100	4	9	0	6	100	4	9	2	6
51–99	7	4	3	1	67	5	3	6	2
34–50	3	1	8	4	50	0	1	0	1
33 or Less	1	1	4	4	33 or Less	6	2	7	6
	—	—	—	—		—	—	—	—
	15	15	15‡	15		15	15	15	15
Mean %	72.8	84.5	45.0	62.2		60.0	78.9	46.7	58.9

† Difference from 10 (9, or 15) shows number of triads which did not establish any two-person alliances in these games.
‡ Vs. first 2 games, $X^2 = 8.58$, $P < .01$.

TABLE 3

FATE OF INFORMED PLAYERS UNDER THREE-INFORMATION CONDITIONS, ALL PATTERNS (% TWO-PERSON)

Triad	One Informed				Two Informed			
	Male		Female		Male		Female	
	IU*	UU	IU*	UU	IU*	II	IU*	II
1	27	47	34	33	38	25	38	25
2	32	38	28	44	34	33	33	35
3	25	50	46	9	29	42	34	33
4	35	31	29	43	36	28	37	27
5	34	32	29	43	34	33	25	50
6	45	11	32	36	38	24	36	29
7	34	33	34	33	36	27	19	63
8	19	63	36	28	32	38	39	22
9	32	35	24	53	38	24	37	27
10	25	50	50	0				
Mean	31	39	34	32	35	30	33	35

* Average of two pairs.

TABLE 4

INCIDENCE OF WEAK ALLIANCES IN TRIADS DISPLAYING MORE UNDERSTANDING AND LESS UNDERSTANDING OF POWER RELATIONS.[†]

Degree of Understanding	Weak Alliances		Mean Incidence		
	0–50%	51–100%	Groups at Left	5 Best	6 Worst
Male Triads More	11	7	51.4	51.2	
Less	7	9	64.1		66.3
$X^2 = 1.04$, n.s.				4	4
	0–99%	100%		Best	Worst
Female Triads More	12	7	69.2	40.3	
Less	7	8	79.7		87.5[‡]
$X^2 = .93$, n.s.					

† This distinction was made by analyzing patterns of answers on the Questionnaire.

‡ By one-tail "t-test", $P < .05$

The primary question concerns the preferred partner when players differ in relative strength, but any two can win. Therefore, we should look at the two patterns, 3-2-2 and 4-3-2 (Types II and V in Figure 1). Any alliance involving the apparently strongest player will be called a "strong" alliance; the remaining alliance, between the weaker players, will be called a "weak" alliance. It will be remembered that a strictly rational approach would predict that both kinds of coalition will occur (under the conditions of our experiment) in accordance with chance. This means, then, that weak alliances ought to be reached about 33% of the time. Further, if information about the true power situation leads to a more rational strategy, then weak alliances should more nearly approximate chance under our information conditions. Table 1 sets forth the result. It is quite apparent that special information did not result in chance occurrence of weak coalitions. They are preferred to a high degree under both the initial learning and subsequent information conditions. The result is similar for both sexes.

To allow more fully for the effect of learning, the earliest and latest games over the two sessions were compared. Table 2 gives the results in two different ways. It can be seen that there is very little change, except

for the male triads when all three players are informed. In this instance, there is a significant tendency for there to be fewer weak alliances towards the end of the information session.

It could be that full understanding of the power situation is reflected less in the sorts of alliance entered into than in the success of the informed player—that is, his ability to secure an alliance of some kind. Although aware of the fact that differences in power have no bearing upon who wins (a coalition is the only important consideration), he might find it expedient to "go along" with the other players. Were this the case, he might well have a considerable advantage. Of several analyses conducted to examine this point, that shown in Table 3 is typical. Clearly, in neither sex did the informed players enter more often, on the average, into coalitions.

The question naturally arises of whether our subjects understood the power relationships as well as did those of Kelley and Arrowood. To answer it, we can look at the results of the questionnaire, which included three items about the relative strengths of the weights in the 4-3-2 pattern. Responses indicate clearly that the informed subjects had a better understanding than the uninformed members of the fact that "4" was not really the strongest with respect to his

PAUL G. SWINGLE

ability to win. However, the great majority of the uninformed members also arrived at this view (ranging from 70% to 100% in the four relevant conditions, i.e., the two sexes with one or two uninformed members). These latter figures are closely similar to those reported by Kelley and Arrowood. Thus, there does not seem to be a difference between the two experiments in the degree to which the players understood the true character of the power relationships.

Pursuing the matter of understanding a little farther, we might expect that it is not so much a question of which subjects arrived at a correct interpretation of the weights as of how adequate the total triad is in this respect (in effect, how many of the three players reached full understanding.) As a precautionary measure, the questionnaire included three items about the 4-3-2 pattern. Thus, in addition to the index mentioned above, it is possible to look more fully at how players perceived the situation. We therefore used answers to all three questions to determine the level of understanding in each triad. Table 4 shows the relation between understanding, from this standpoint, and the incidence of weak alliances. It can be seen, in the case of the total number of samples pooling across information conditions, that there is a nonsignificant tendency for the better informed groups to arrive at a smaller proportion of weak alliances. As a

more stringent test, a comparison is shown at the right between the groups with the "best" understanding and those with the "worst" understanding. The former include triads in which all three members met the criterion of understanding on all three questionnaire items; the latter include triads in which none of the three members met any of these criteria. It is apparent that this distinction makes no difference whatever in the case of the male triads; however, there is now evident a striking difference in the case of the female triads. The tendency to prefer weak coalitions is significantly greater for the groups with poor understanding of the relative importance of the weights. Thus information has an important effect for females but apparently not for males.

Fortunately, a fourth question casts additional light on the experimental conditions. This item had to do with attitudes towards winning the game, based upon the concepts of exploitative and accommodative strategy advanced in previous reports. There is evidence that desire to win is a central component of the exploitative strategy typical of male groups, whereas indifference towards winning or a desire to make the game come out even ("everybody wins," so to speak) characterizes the accommodative strategy typical of female triads. In the present experiment, this difference was also marked; (for the several conditions, from 40% to

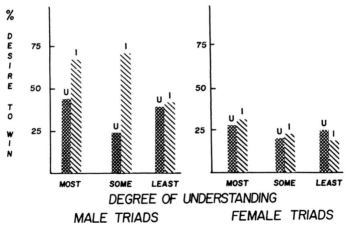

Fig. 2.

78% of the males marked the alternative, "I tried to win," but only 11% to 25% of the females marked it. We can therefore consider the relation of this variable to the formation of coalitions.

Consider, first, the relationship between degree of understanding, just mentioned, and motivation to win. The result is presented in Figure 2. There is clearly a tendency—especially in the male triads—for the informed Ss, who displayed partial or good understanding of the power-situation, to express more frequently a desire to win. This means, then, that the procedure whereby one or more members of the group were provided with special information led to an expression of stronger motivation to win, as well as accomplishing our original aim to instruct players in the two alternative strategies.

TABLE 5
INCIDENCE OF WEAK COALITIONS IN RELATION TO MOTIVATION TO WIN

	Male Triads				Female Triads		
	Incidence of Win				Incidence of Win		
	None	1	2	3	None	1	2
N	4	9	14	7	18	10	6
Mean %	79	73	50	48	85	80	52

It will be recalled that for the male groups the incidence of weak coalitions is not significantly associated either with special information (learning vs. information sessions) or with level of final understanding. For the female triads, however, degree of understanding does show a relation to weak coalitions. What is the picture, now, for degree of motivation?

We can separate triads by the number of members who indicated a desire to win, as a rough measure of the motivation level of the group. Table 5 presents the result (in no female triad did all three members check the "win" alternative). A very clear progression emerges, as shown in Figure 3. The greater the number of members in the triad who express motivation to win, the smaller the proportion of weak alliances. Thus, we are forced to conclude that the formation of weak alliances (as an aspect of strategy) is a function not of understanding the true character of the power situation but of desire to win. It appears that, in the male groups, special information increases motivation, and that this is the crucial factor in strategy. Even so, of course, weak alliances still occur at greater-than-chance levels.

DISCUSSION

In general, understanding of the true power situation has had little effect on play

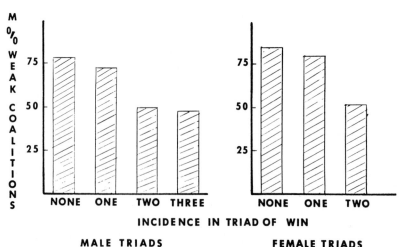

FIG. 3.

in this game. Under all conditions, in both sexes, the tendency for weak coalitions to be preferred in the critical 4-3-2 pattern continues to be present at beyond-chance levels in the informed sessions. When the players are differentiated by degree of understanding, the better informed groups reach fewer weak coalitions, but not significantly so in the case of the males. It is possible that our method of providing pertinent information failed to supply adequate knowledge. It appears to us, however, that it would be difficult to do any better without prejudicing players in favor of one alternative or the other. Any hint that one is more rational or superior to the other would probably result in its adoption by many, if not all, players.

There is, as a matter of fact, a variety of reasons why players might prefer the weak alliance, no matter what their knowledge of the power relationships. They are faced with the problem of winning. Short of taking turns in forming coalitions—a tactic which defeats the competitive character of the game, at least for the males—players must decide with whom to establish alliances. The differences in strength, corresponding to expectations established in everyday life, offer a way out. At least symbolically, the man with a weight of "4" becomes the person to beat. The two weak men are thus in a position to decide between them who will ally. If an impasse develops by competitive bargaining, there might well be a tendency to fall back upon the weights as a means to settle it. Considerations like this make it entirely possible that even under conditions in which power is "unreal," the perception of power operates in accordance with the principle formulated by Caplow and Vinacke and Arkoff. (There is no issue, here, concerning the "real" power investigated by Kelley and Arrowood.)

An alternative interpretation arises from the hypothesis that supplying special knowledge might have had a motivating effect on the players. To test it we have compared degree of understanding, as previously described, with desire to win, as reported on the questionnaire. There is evidence that the informed players who indicated the highest degree of understanding tend to express more frequently a desire to win. Our information

instructions, then, had at least some motivating effect. With respect to the critical weak coalitions, there is a very regular decrease as a function of the number of players in the triad who indicated a desire to win.

These suggestive findings are what might be expected from the standpoint of exploitative strategy. If the special information provided served primarily to increase competitive involvement in the game, then changes in behavior during the informed session were brought about by an increase in exploitative strategy, rather than by understanding of the strictly rational treatment of the power situation. In fact, both exploitative strategy and complete understanding may tend towards the same result. Viewed from the former standpoint, players compete actively, entering into whatever coalitions and deals best serve their interest; as a consequence, both strong and weak players bargain actively and there is a tendency, found in all of our experiments, toward fewer weak coalitions in the male triads, in which exploitative strategy is most pronounced. From the standpoint of understanding there is, of course, no reason why either possible partner would be preferred over the other, with a consequent reduction in weak coalitions. The data of this experiment strongly support the exploitative, rather than the understanding, interpretation. According to strictly rational analysis, any attempt to gain special advantage, short of being alert to opportunity, would be entirely futile. In effect, if all three players are in this fashion equivalent in their treatment of the game, the only solution would be an impasse which could only be resolved by taking turns, by employing a lottery device to choose partners, or by abandoning the game. In point of fact, these solutions have been adopted sometimes in our experiments. However, they are much more frequent in female groups; they serve an accommodative function, and certainly cannot be interpreted solely as evidence of understanding of the power relationships.

Because of all these considerations, we do not believe that people necessarily act in accordance with the "real" characteristics of a situation, once those features are learned. In this game, rational analysis turns out to be more that of the investigator than that of the player. In the first place, little evidence has been found that good understanding of the power relationships, given by special information and assessed by a questionnaire, had much effect on play in the fashion demanded by derivations from game theory. In the second place, there is evidence that the special information served more to motivate players to win than to make them adopt the rational approach to the game. Finally, players who expressed desire to win displayed marked differences from players who expressed other attitudes. In general, exploitative strategy appears to explain behavior in this situation much better than any reference to degree of understanding.

CONCLUSIONS

An experiment was conducted to determine whether or not information about alternative strategies in a competitive game would result in a shift from outcomes determined by perception of strength to outcomes in line with strictly rational analysis of power conditions. In the board game investigated, previous research has supported the proposition that players tend to establish alliances between weaker members of the triad, in contrast to the proposition that thorough understanding of the power relationships (as created in this situation) would result in approximately chance occurrence of the three possible coalitions. The experiment ran triads first through an extended learning session, consisting of six successive games in each of four power patterns, followed by an identical information session. In one set of triads (ten of each sex), one member was provided with information about both strategies; in a second set (ten male and nine female triads), two members were informed; and in a third set (fifteen of each sex), all three members were informed. Otherwise, conditions were similar to those employed previously. Results may be summarized as follows:

1. In the critical power patterns, when two players were weaker than the third

(but could win in alliance), there was little evidence for a significant shift to an equal incidence of the three possible coalitions (i.e., weak alliances continued to occur at a level above chance under the information conditions). However, triads that displayed the best understanding of the objectively correct power relationships, as assessed from responses on the postsession questionnaire, tended to arrive at fewer weak alliances compared to those triads with least understanding (significant for females).

2. There was no evidence that the specially informed players differed from the uninformed players in their ability to enter into coalitions.

3. There is evidence that the chief effect of the information conditions was to increase motivation to win. An item of the postsession questionnaire permitted a comparison between triads with high motivation to win and those with low motivation to win. The former display a lower incidence of weak coalitions, and therefore a motivational interpretation accounts for the results better than one based on understanding.

REFERENCES

Bond, J. R., & Vinacke, W. E. Coalitions in mixed-sex triads. *Sociometry*, 1961, 24, 61–75.

Caplow, T. A theory of coalitions in the triad. *Amer. Sociol. Rev.*, 1956, 21, 489–493.

Kelley, H. H., & Arrowood, A. J. Coalitions in the triad: Critique and experiments. *Sociometry*, 1960, 23, 231–244.

Simmel, G. The significance of numbers for social life. In E. P. Hare, E. F. Borgatta, & R. F. Bales (Eds.) *Small groups: Studies in social interaction.* New York: Knopf, 1955. Pp. 9–15.

Vinacke, W. E. Sex roles in a three-person game. *Sociometry*, 1959, 22, 343–360.

Vinacke, W. E. Power, strategy, and the formation of coalitions in triads under four incentive conditions. Office of Naval Research Nonr 3748 (02), 1963. Tech. Rep. No. 1.

Vinacke, W. E., & Arkoff, A. An experimental study of coalitions in the triad. *Amer. Sociol. Rev.* 1957, 22, 406–414.

Vinacke, W. E., Crowell, Doris C., Dien, Dora, & Young, Vera. The effect of information about strategy on a three-person game. Nonr 4374 (00), 1964. Tech. Rep. No. 6.

Operant Control of Group Decision Making

When a group of individuals has to arrive at a single decision, the distinction between conformity and the rational use of available information becomes at times quite difficult to make. If an individual simply "goes along with the crowd," as anticipated in the experiment on petition signing, one has a clear example of social pressure affecting a change of opinion in a presumably indifferent subject. When one is a member of a group which is required to arrive at a decision regarding a given situation, taking the advice of an expert, a more experienced or knowledgeable person, may simply reflect the group member's intelligent use of all available information and not, in the strict sense of the word, be indicative of conformity. On the other hand, should the group members simply accept the opinions of the expert without question, one might justifiably refer to this behavior as conformity.

Regardless of whether group members are conforming or making their most rational decision, a question of particular interest is: Can the nature of the decision made by the group be controlled if one gains control over the rewards appropriate to the decision making situation? Stated more simply: Could one create an "expert" by arranging the rewards such that the group is most well off when the members follow the advice of the "expert"?

An "authority" can be created in the laboratory group situation in a variety of different ways. One might, for example, make use of a true expert in a given area, or announce to the other group members that X is most qualified for certain reasons, or one may simply arrange things so that the chosen expert is, in fact, correct most of the time.

The latter technique, which will be used in the present experiment, has a number of advantageous characteristics for the laboratory situation. First, it may be operationally defined; that is, if one assumes that experts are experts because they tend to be correct, then one may simply create an expert who is correct 50%, 80%, or 100% of the time. One may therefore define and measure the degree of expertise of the expert with the same operation, namely, the percentage of occasions on which the expert was correct. If the expert has been defined and created in this manner, anyone else who cares to replicate the experiment may duplicate the extent of expertise to which the other group members were exposed.

Second, the expertise of the expert may be varied at any time during the experiment by simply manipulating the rewards. One may wish to determine the effects of changing the percentage of correct advisements of the expert upon other group members' acceptance of his advice. Suppose the expert had a previous history of being wrong 60% of the time and then the experimenter arranged things so that the expert was correct 80% of the time. Would the acceptance of his opinions be less than that of an expert without such a previous history? Or, one might ask, can we "make and break" the expert? That is, can one increase and then decrease the group's acceptance of the advice of the expert simply by manipulating rewards?

Third, the technique facilitates objectivity and experimental control in that one can choose the expert at random and create a uniform perception of expertise by the other group members almost regardless of the actual abilities of the expert.

The experiment will be that of creating an expert in a small group decision making situation. We will then manipulate the expertise of our unknowing agent by manipulating rewards contingent upon his advice and measuring the degree to which the group's decisions are brought under the experimenter's control.

INSTRUCTIONS

Experimental Team Size: Minimum of three.

Subjects: Arrange for exactly three naive subjects per team. Subjects may be obtained as in Experiment 2.

Apparatus: One table; three chairs; small screen; pencils; paper; die; stopwatch; three place cards colored on one side — one blue, one red, one green.

Experimental Situation: Three subjects are seated around a table and have the task of predicting which of three cards, placed with the white side up in front of the experimenter, will be turned over on each trial. Each subject writes his initial choice and then reads it aloud to the other group members (and the experimenter). After everyone has read his initial prediction, the group discusses the situation and arrives at a single prediction. If the group follows the advice of the expert (his prediction read aloud) the group will be rewarded (feedback of being correct) on a particular reinforcement schedule.

Procedure

1. Form teams of three or more.

2. Before the subjects enter the room, roll the die to determine which subject will be the expert. Assign the number 1 to the subject who *will* sit on the left, 2 to the center, and 3 to the subject on the right. Roll the die until either a 1, 2, or a 3 appears, and the subject with this number will be the expert.

3. Arrange the table and chairs so that experimenter 1 (E_1) and the three subjects are all at the same table.

4. Arrange the three cards, white side up, in front of E_1, but in clear view of the subjects, and place a pencil and some paper in front of each subject.

5. Place the small screen (a medium-sized cardboard box with the top cut off would do) in front of E_1, so that the die may be thrown and read without the subjects being able to see the numbers on the die.

6. Have E_2 and E_3 seated behind the subjects as far away as pos- le. (E_2 must be close enough to hear the predictions of the expert.)

7. Once everyone is seated, E_1 should give the instructions:

"The experiment you are involved in is a study of group decision making. We are interested in how well small groups of about three persons can predict the occurrence of probabilistic events. On each trial, I am going to roll this die (E_1 shows die) behind this screen. Depending upon which number rolls up, I will turn over one of these cards in front of me — either red, blue or green (E_1 turns over cards to show subjects). What we want you to do is to predict which color card will be turned over on a given trial. The prediction will be made as follows: After I roll the die I will say "choose," at which time each of you will write the color you think will come up. After everyone has written his prediction you will each read it aloud to the group. After everyone has read his prediction you will, as a group, discuss the situation and decide upon a single prediction agreed upon by all. After you have all agreed I will turn over the card determined by the die so that you will know whether or not you are correct. We will then repeat the procedure for the next trial, and so on."

8. Experimenter 1 will then roll the die and say "choose." The numbers on the die will actually determine the reinforcement schedule for the group (i.e., performance feedback).

9. Experimenter 2, seated behind the subjects, will record the advice of the expert, the group's decision, and whether the accept- ance of the advice was rewarded. (See Fig. 6.1 for model of tally sheet to be used.)

PREDICTIONS

Trial	Expert	Group	Rewarded (prediction correct)
PHASE ONE			
1			
2			
3			
.			
.			
.			
48			
49			
50			
PHASE TWO			
1			
2			
3			
.			
.			
.			
48			
49			
50			
PHASE THREE			
1			
2			
3			
.			
.			
.			
48			
49			
50			

FIG. 6.1. Tally sheet for experimenter E_2.

Trial	Time-to-Decision Seconds PHASE 1	Trial	Time-to-Decision Seconds PHASE 2	Trial	Time-to-Decision Seconds PHASE 3
1		1		1	
2		2		2	
3		3		3	
.		.		.	
.		.		.	
.		.		.	
48		48		48	
49		49		49	
50		50		50	

FIG. 6.2. Tally sheet for experimenter E_3.

10. Experimenter 3, also seated behind the subjects, will record the group's time-to-decision (see Fig. 6.2). Experimenter 3 will record the time from the last prediction read aloud by the subjects to the moment when all three subjects agree upon a single decision.

Phase 1 – The Making of an Expert

1. Experimenter 1 will reinforce the group's acceptance of the advice of the expert on about an 83% schedule. That is, when the group decision agrees with the prediction of the expert read aloud, E_1 will turn over the card corresponding to the prediction of the expert on all occasions *except* when a six appears on the die. Thus, the group will be rewarded approximately 83.3% of the time, if it accepts the advice of the expert.

2. When the group does not accept the advice of the expert, the group will be rewarded on a 33% schedule. That is, when the group decision is different from the prediction of the expert, E_1 will turn over the blue card whenever the numbers one or two appear on the die, red whenever three or four appear, and green whenever five or six appear.

3. Experimenter 2 will signal to E_1 (i.e., some previously agreed upon signal which can be hidden from the subjects, such as a nod or cleaning eyeglasses) as soon as 50 trials have been completed.

Phase 2 – The Breaking of an Expert

1. After receiving E_2's signal, E_1 will terminate differential reinforcement of the group's decisions which agree with the prediction of the expert. Experimenter 1 will simply turn up blue whenever the numbers one or two appear on the die, red whenever three or four appear, and green whenever five or six appear. Thus, there will be no advantage in the members' accepting the advice of the defunct expert.

2. Experimenter 2 will signal E_1 once the group has completed 50 trials in phase 2.

Phase 3 – An Expert Once Again

1. After receiving E_2's signal, E_1 will return to the phase 1 procedure of rewarding the group's acceptance of the advice of the expert about 83.3% of the time and rewarding all other decisions about 33% of the time.

2. Experimenter 2 will again signal E_1 as soon as the group has completed 50 trials in phase 3.

3. Experimenter 1 will then stop the experiment, thank the sub-

jects for participating, and explain the purpose of the study and all manipulations.

The entire procedure should be practiced in the laboratory, under the instructor's supervision, until the experimenters are able to handle the situation flawlessly before any naive subjects are used. A summary of the procedure is given below.

Summary of the Experimental Procedure

Phase 1

1. If the group *accepts* expert's prediction: turn over card corresponding to expert's prediction at all times except when the number six turns up on the die.
2. If the group *does not accept* expert's prediction:
   Turn over blue card on die number one or two.
   Turn over red card on die number three or four.
   Turn over green card on die number five or six.
(Experimenter 2 signals end of phase 1 after 50 trials.)

Phase 2

   Turn over blue card on die number one or two.
   Turn over red card on die number three or four.
   Turn over green card on die number five or six.
(Experimenter 2 signals end of phase 2 after 50 trials.)

Phase 3

Repeat phase 1 procedure. (Experimenter 2 signals end of the experiment after 50 trials in phase 3.)

Data Analysis

Individual team data

1. From the "rewarded" column of E_2's tally sheet, sum the total number of rewards received by the group:

   a. When the group accepted the expert's prediction.

   b. When the group did not accept the expert's prediction for each of the phases. This will offer a check on the experimental procedure in that the percent reward actually received should be very close to the programed reinforcement schedule.

2. Record the acceptance data as shown below. Trial block one refers to the number of group acceptances of the expert's predictions for trials 1 through 10.

Number of group acceptances of the expert's prediction are to be set up as shown in the accompanying tabulation.

Ten — Trial Blocks

	Phase one						Phase two						Phase three					
	1	2	3	4	5	T	1	2	3	4	5	T	1	2	3	4	5	T
Acceptances																		

3. Plot a curve of the number of acceptances in each 10-trial block such as in Fig. 6.3.

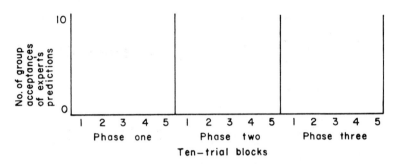

FIG. 6.3. Form for plotting number of acceptances in each 10-trial block.

4. Plot a cumulative record of the above data on a graph such as Fig. 6.4.

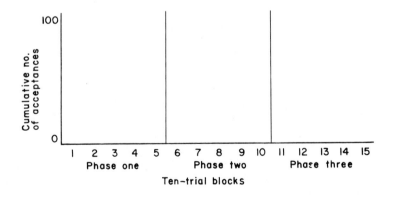

FIG. 6.4. Form for plotting cumulative number of acceptances in each 10-trial block.

A cumulative record is obtained by simply adding the previous number of responses to any particular 10-trial block responses and plotting that value. For example, if we obtained the following data for the first four 10-trial blocks:

Ten–trial block		1	2	3	4
Number of responses		2	8	6	9

The cumulative data to be plotted would be as follows:

Ten–trial block		1	2	3	4
Cumulative number of responses		2	10	16	25

5. Record the time-to-decision, as shown in the accompanying tabulation.

Ten — Trial Blocks

	Phase one						Phase two						Phase three					
	1	2	3	4	5	T	1	2	3	4	5	T	1	2	3	4	5	T
Time to decision																		

6. Plot the *average* time-to-decision curve in each 10-trial block set up as shown in Fig. 6.5.

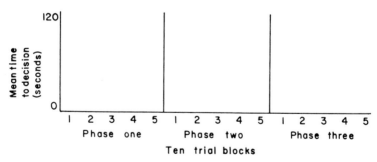

FIG. 6.5. Form for plotting average time-to-decision curve.

Experimental Report

1. Do the curves support predictions?
2. Are the expert's predictions accepted more rapidly in phase 3 than in phase 1 (refer to your cumulative curve)?
3. Are the expert's predictions accepted more or less than chance at the end of phase 2 (chance would, of course, be about one-third)?

4. Does the time-to-decision curve offer any indication of the group's tendency to accept the expert's predictions more rapidly toward the end of phase 1 and phase 3, and less rapidly during phase 2? (The time curve may be expected to show exactly the reverse trends of the acceptance curve.)

Reprinted from Journal of the Experimental Analysis of Behavior, 1962, Vol. 5, pp. 309–316, by permission of the authors and the publisher. Copyright 1962 by the Society for the Experimental Analysis of Behavior, Inc.

THE OPERANT CONDITIONING OF CONVERSATION[1]

GILBERT LEVIN[2] AND DAVID SHAPIRO

Human conversation is a natural place to begin the study of social responses. In a conversation, a number of individuals use one another's responses as cues for their own behavior. So long as a conversation is being held, the speakers must talk in some order. Four experiments were conducted to test whether differentially reinforcing a group of speakers can bring the order of speakers under experimental control. The results are all consistent with the hypothesis. The paper also devises and evaluates different procedures for studying conversational sequences and examines associated statistical problems.

One describable feature of any conversation is the order in which the speakers converse. This order may be an important property of social behavior. These experiments were designed to test whether differentially reinforcing a group of speakers, when the contingency respects the order in which they have spoken, would tend to increase the frequency of speaking in that order.

EXPERIMENTAL PROCEDURE

Several Ss are asked to carry on a conversation in order to reach a series of unanimous decisions on which of several possible solutions to a problem is the correct solution. After each decision, the instructions require that the group stop the conversation and wait silently until it is informed whether or not its solution is correct. Each unanimous decision constitutes one "trial."

Speakers in a three-person group are designated A, B, and C. The record of conversation may look like this:

(a) Trial 1—ABCABCA
(b) Hypothesis X
(c) Silence
(d) Intervention
(e) Trial 2—CBACBA . . .

The first item (a) is a list of the sequence of all speakers during that trial. Next (b), there is an indication of the hypothesis the group chose unanimously which brought an immediate end to (a) and ushered in (c), leading then to (d). The experimenter's intervention consists of telling or signalling the group that its hypothesis is correct or incorrect. What the group is told is determined by some property of (a) which is the response the experiment is designed to bring under control. In no case is the whole of (a) taken into account. Immediately after (d), the group begins (e) and the whole process is repeated without interruption, with the number of trials ranging from 50 to 165. Length of an S's speech or of a group's trial is not fixed and experimental sessions last from 30 min to more than 2 hr.

RESULTS

Experiment I

In the first experiment,[3] four college students were seated at random around a

[1]This research was supported by National Institute of Mental Health Research Grant M-4209, United States Public Health Service, and by a contract between the Office of Naval Research (Group Psychology Branch) and Harvard University, with David Shapiro as Principal Investigator. We wish to thank Eugene Cogan for his part in the early planning and execution of the studies. Prior support was received from National Institute of Mental Health Grant 2M-6378, United States Public Health Service, with Elvin V. Semrad as Principal Investigator.

[2]Now at Carnegie Institute of Technology.

[3]We are indebted to Mrs. Marilyn Glass and Dr. Warren Bennis for their helpful suggestions at this stage of the research. Mrs. Glass helped conduct the first experiment.

table on which there were two stimulus cards. Cards I and X of the standard Rorschach series were used. They were told that they were participating in an experiment in mental telepathy. It was their job to send messages telepathically to a "receiver" (who was a role player) in an adjoining room. They were asked to discuss and decide which of the two messages on the table to try to send to the receiver. They were encouraged to relax and to use their imaginations freely. As soon as they all agreed on a single message, they were asked to stop talking immediately and concentrate on that message as they waited for the receiver to come into the room. The receiver indicated which message had been received by pointing and saying "this."

Two of the four Ss, designated A and B, were selected at random as experimental Ss. The behavior of the remaining Ss was completely disregarded. During each trial, a record was kept of the order in which A and B spoke.

A trial was reinforced; *i.e.*, the receiver claimed to have correctly received the message selected by the group, only if the last utterance of B followed the last utterance of A. Attention was paid to the last few speakers in the trial on the assumption that a group learns a social response more effectively when the delay between the response and its reinforcement is at a minimum. The following is a sample protocol:

Trial	Sequence	Intervention
1	ACBDCBDACBA	not reinforced
2	CBACBCAB	reinforced
3	DBACBACBD	reinforced
4	DCACDBADC	not reinforced

The psychological hyphothesis is sufficiently straightforward: The frequency of AB is expected to increase as a function of the number of reinforced trials. On the other hand, the statistical hypothesis leaves some room for choice. One possibility is to take a sample of the behavior from an early part of the experiment and another from a later part and test the difference between the two observed frequencies. A second possibility is to make some use of a theoretical frequency. Irrespective of the individual frequencies of A and B, they should appear in sequence equally often as AB or BA.

Neither of these approaches is ideal. The first approach is a rather stringent test. Because the experimental conditions have been in effect throughout the 50-trial experiment, a comparison of the early trials with the later ones is really a test of the difference between two levels of the experimental effect. A much longer experiment would minimize this factor. The addition of an initial "emitted behavior" or operant period in which no reinforcement is given would provide a base line for comparison with the achieved level of learning. Both of these solutions make for less economical use of experimental time than in this experiment.

The expected frequency approach is considerably more efficient for these data. It assumes a level of emitted behavior and allows all observations to be reckoned as a measure of the experimental effect. The disadvantage of such an approach is the degree of uncertainty associated with the assumption, namely, that the pre-experimental level of AB=BA= 50%. The assumption is probably accurate for the sampling of a large number of groups, but any conclusion based on the performance of a particular group, or two or three groups, is open to question.

One way to test the assumption for a particular group is to compare that group's performance in a block of early trials with the expected frequencies, accepting the assumption as tenable if the null hypothesis (AB=BA) cannot be rejected. This procedure is not free from defects either; with a small sample size, the probability of accepting the null hypothesis is high if the true difference is not large. On the other hand, the fact that the experimental conditions are in effect during the first block of trials might have the opposite effect on the null hypothesis. Recognizing the difficulties of both the empirical and the theoretical approaches, the latter was arbitrarily chosen in the analysis. In recent studies, as yet unpublished, base-line measures were obtained by using random reinforcement procedures.

The results of Experiment I are given in Table 1. The pattern AB occurred in 35 trials out of a total of 50. This proportion (7/10) is significantly greater than the expected 1/2 ($x^2 = 8.0$; $P < .01$). The results in the first set of 25 trials (14 out of 25) look different enough from the second set (21 out of 25) to cast serious doubt on the possibility that AB would have been the more frequent pattern in the absence of the experimental conditions.

Table 1
Frequency of Two-Person Verbal Sequences
in Experiment I

Trials		Sequence	
		AB	BA
1-5		1	4
6-10		3	2
11-15		3	2
16-20		4	1
21-25		3	2
	Total	14	11
26-30		5	0
31-35		3	2
36-40		4	1
41-45		5	0
46-50		4	1
	Total	21	4
	Grand Total	35	15

Experiment II

A second experiment was designed to permit a test of the hypothesis that a *three-person sequence* can be conditioned. Three Ss took part in this 125-trial experiment, and in each trial the last three speakers were recorded. Because no speaker can precede himself, each trial has 12 possible outcomes: ABC, ACB, BAC, BCA, CAB, CBA, ABA, ACA, BAB, BCB, CAC, or CBC. The last six of these (hereafter called homogeneous patterns)

were expected to occur infrequently because of the nature of the instructions emphasizing *group* decision. And this was the case. In all, these patterns occurred 34 times out of a total of 125. (See Table 2.) For purposes of the analysis to follow, the trials with homogenous outcomes are omitted.

Two of the six heterogeneous patterns, ABC and BAC, are of special interest. The response ABC was chosen as the one to be reinforced. The expectation is that the frequency of ABC will increase as a function of reinforcement. But an increase in ABC is not a guarantee that this specific conversational pattern has been conditioned. Suppose that C alone learns to speak last in every trial. In this case, a critical test is that of the difference between the frequency of ABC and BAC. Because these are the only two three-person outcomes in which C can occur last, a preponderance of ABC over BAC would be evidence that the social response has been conditioned.[4]

Table 2 gives the results of Experiment II. The response ABC occurred a total of 34 times out of 91 heterogeneous trials. This ratio is significantly greater than the 1/6 chance ex-

[4]So far, we have ignored the possible influences upon the results of each individual's overall rate of responding. In a three-person situation in which no person may precede himself, the upper limit for any participant is slightly more than 50% of the total number of speeches. If C learned simply to talk a great deal, to a degree approaching the limit, the frequency of outcomes which include C would increase relative to those outcomes which do not. It would have a still greater effect on those homogeneous outcomes which include C as both ultimate and antipenultimate speaker (*i. e.*, CAC and CBC). However, this effect would not alter the significance of a difference between ABC and BAC.

Table 2
Frequency of Three-Person Verbal Sequences
in Experiment II

Trials	Sequence											
	Heterogeneous						Homogeneous					
	ABC	ACB	BAC	BCA	CAB	CBA	ABA	ACA	BAB	BCB	CAC	CBC
1-25	5	2	4	1	3	3	0	1	1	2	3	0
26-50	7	1	4	3	1	2	1	1	1	1	1	2
51-75	7	1	4	2	2	2	0	0	1	1	1	4
76-100	8	2	3	1	0	2	0	0	1	3	4	1
101-125	7	0	7	2	3	2	0	0	0	1	2	1
Total	34	6	22	9	9	11	1	2	4	8	11	8
Grand Total			91						34			

pectancy ($\chi^2 = 48.0$; $P < .001$). The difference between ABC and BAC is in the predicted direction, but it is not significant ($\chi^2 = 2.6$; $P < .10$).

The frequency of ABC when plotted against trial number lacks some of the properties of a typical acquisition curve. The correct response occurred first at the second trial, and then it did not occur again until the 22nd trial. At this point, it shows an upward spurt which is maintained but does not accelerate further during the remainder of the experiment. (See Table 2.) The Ss exhibited mounting impatience with the experiment, beginning somewhere between trial 50 and 100. This impatience grew to such proportions between the 100th and 125th trial that the experiment which had been planned for 150 trials had to be terminated after 125 trials in a total time of 2 hr and 45 min.

REVISED EXPERIMENTAL PROCEDURE

The work following Experiment II was devoted primarily to increasing the amount of information obtained per unit time, simplifying the instructions, and improving the conditions of observation. To accomplish these goals, a number of innovations were made in (a) the position of the experimenter, (b) the form of reinforcement, (c) the nature of the task, and (d) the method of recording data.

(1) In the first two experiments, the experimenter was in full view of the Ss. This led to difficulties on two counts. First, it was a possible source of contamination. The Ss may have been responding to unintended cues presented by the experimenter. Second, the continued presence of the experimenter made it possible for the group to communicate with him in spite of instructions to the contrary, thus disrupting the flow of conversation. For these reasons, and with the knowledge of the Ss, the experimenter was removed to the other side of a one-way screen.

(2) Reinforcement delivered personally by a serious-looking stranger added interest to the task but was wasteful of experimental time. A tone defined as "correct" and a buzzer defined as "incorrect" replaced the human receiver, with the result of a saving in time greater than 50%.

(3) The task of the Ss was altered in two respects. Instead of looking at several stimulus cards and deciding among them, the Ss are seated around a table on which a bank of different-colored lights is arranged in a circle. The number of lights can be varied from one to six. Each S has before him a small control box with a number of buttons on it corresponding in number and color to the lights in the center of the table. A central light can be turned on only if all three Ss press the appropriate button. The light remains on as long as all three buttons are held down.[5] The Ss are asked to decide unanimously among the colors and to turn on the appropriate light the instant a decision is made and to keep it on while remaining silent until they are signalled right or wrong. This serves to bring a more clear-cut finish to each trial, to inhibit conversation while waiting for reinforcement, and to facilitate recording of hypotheses made by subjects.

Another change in the task was to instruct the Ss that they were to play a guessing game rather than to attempt mental telepathy. They were told that the experimenter has a long list of color names in the next room comprised in the colors before them, and they were to guess the items in this list. The effect of this change seems to depend on the attitudes of the Ss. It may reduce interest in the task, but it also prevents the extremely hostile disruptive reaction observed in one S in the second experiment who was avowedly anti-ESP. The guessing-game procedure may be more nearly free of complications for most Ss.

(4) A persistent difficulty is obtaining an accurate record of the sequence of speakers. This is essential, not only as a means of measuring the experimental effect, but also for deciding, on the spot, whether or not a trial is to receive reinforcement. Incorrect reinforcements may entirely wash out the effect of the independent variable. Sound recordings of the experimental sessions were made, but they offered little help as a post-meeting accuracy check because of the difficulty of identifying voices, particularly in speeches of only one or two words.

In discussing observer reliability, some of the reactions of Ss to the experimental procedure should be described. They have expressed a wide range of attitudes, ranging from a request from members of one group

---

[5]The experimental apparatus was designed and constructed by Bernard Tursky, Instrumentation Engineer.

to "do it again for a hundred trials" to quite negative sentiments in another.

Apart from these group differences, some of the important determiners of behavior seem to be (a) the per cent reinforced trials, (b) the number of hypotheses the group is asked to choose from, and (c) the ratio of (a) to (b). In Experiment I, two stimulus cards (*i. e.*, two possible hypotheses) were presented to the group. This matched very well with the chance probability of the response. The AB sequence would occur about one-half the time by chance; and because the presence of two stimuli led to the same subjective probability estimate, the experiment made sense to the Ss. At the beginning, they were correct in about one-half of the trials, and gradually the ratio changed in the direction they would expect if mental telepathy were taking place.

In Experiment II and in subsequent experiments, the sequential response sometimes had an expectancy different from 50%. When the sequential response is expected to occur in one out of six trials, the choice of one out of two hypotheses would tend to make the group feel that it was not doing well, even after the rate of the response had increased appreciably.

In both Experiments I and II, we were careful to create some sort of correspondence between these two sets of probabilities. In the second experiment, in which the correct sequence response was expected to occur by chance somewhat less often than in 1/6 of the trials, the group was given six hypotheses to choose from. This rather precise matching of the two sets of probabilities proved to be not entirely adequate. The rate of the correct response increased appreciably, and so did the rate of reinforcement. Nevertheless in postmeeting questionaries and interviews, the group felt that the experiment had been a failure.

In some groups, the procedure resulted in so much frustration that the Ss were unwilling to carry out the instructions. A number of solutions were attempted; but, finally, the sequence response itself had to be changed for one with a higher probability. The most successful combination proved to be three stimuli and a sequence response with probability .50. With these values, the groups were compliant, trials were short, and task satisfaction was relatively high.

The variety of these behaviors was reflected in differences in interobserver reliability scores gathered on several groups. Two observers, one experienced and one inexperienced, kept a record of an 80-trial experiment. In this experiment, the group was asked to choose from six hypotheses; the expected frequency of the sequence response was somewhat less than 1/6; and the final three speakers were focussed upon. On 17 of these trials, one or both of the observers were unable to record complete data. Of the remaining 63 observed trials, the two observers were in complete agreement 18 times, or 29% of the time. This result is typical for the groups that worked under conditions of low rate of reinforcement.

When the experimental procedure was less frustrating, observation seemed easier and the data more reliable. In a 165-trial experiment (Experiment IV, discussed below), in which the group was asked to choose from three hypotheses and the expected frequency of the sequence response was 1/2, and in which the last two speakers were focussed upon, two observers produced incomplete data in 43 trials. Of the remaining 122 trials, the observers were in complete agreement in 112 trials, or 92% complete agreement.

RESULTS

In both Experiments III and IV, the revised procedures discussed above were used, and reliable measures were found of the order of conversation. The Ss in each group were three boy scouts of fairly equal rank in their organization who knew one another before the experiment but were not close friends. The colored-light apparatus with three possible hypotheses was used; the instructions were those of the guessing game task. Reinforcement was in the form of a tone signifying "correct" and a buzzer signifying "incorrect."

The last two speakers in each trial were recorded, giving six possible outcomes: AB, BC, CA, BA, CB, and AC. Positive reinforcement was given after every occurrence of AB, BC, and CA (clockwise patterns). The remaining three outcomes (counterclockwise patterns) received negative reinforcement. By chance, the conversational pattern to be reinforced is expected to occur half the time.

We predicted that the reinforced clockwise patterns would occur more frequently than

PAUL G. SWINGLE

Table 3

Frequency of Two-Person Verbal Sequences
per block of 15 trials in Experiment III

Trials	Verbal Sequence						
	AB	BC	CA	BA	CB	AC	One Speaker Only
1-15	3	3	3	1	2	2	1
16-30	1	2	2	3	3	2	2
31-45	3	3	3	1	2	3	0
46-60	2	5	2	0	4	2	0
61-75	3	3	3	1	2	3	0
76-90	6	5	1	1	1	1	0
91-105	2	8	2	0	3	0	0
106-120	3	3	2	1	6	0	0
121-135	0	5	1	3	1	2	3
136-150	2	4	2	2	1	0	4
151-165	0	6	0	4	2	0	3
Total	25	47	21	17	27	15	13
	Clockwise Patterns			Counterclockwise Patterns			
Grand Total	93			59			13

the counterclockwise patterns and that each clockwise pattern would occur more frequently than its counterclockwise mate (matched for individual rates of responding), *i.e.*, AB > BA, BC > CB, and CA > AC.

Tables 3 and 4 summarize the results for Experiments III and IV, respectively.

In Experiment III, both the general predictions (total clockwise > total counterclockwise) and the specific predictions (AB > BA,

Table 4

Frequency of Two-Person Verbal Sequences
per block of 15 trials in Experiment IV

Trials	Verbal Sequence						
	AB	BC	CA	BA	CB	AC	One Speaker Only
1-15	2	5	3	0	1	0	4
16-30	2	1	1	1	6	2	2
31-45	1	3	2	1	3	1	4
46-60	0	4	1	2	3	2	3
61-75	1	5	2	0	5	1	1
76-90	1	3	3	1	2	1	4
91-105	0	5	0	0	2	3	5
106-120	1	7	0	1	1	1	4
121-135	1	3	1	1	2	1	6
136-150	0	5	1	0	1	0	8
151-165	1	7	0	0	0	1	6
Total	10	48	14	7	26	13	47
	Clockwise Patterns			Counterclockwise Patterns			
Grand Total	72			46			47

Table 5
Chi Square Tests
on Frequencies of Verbal-sequence Pairs

Sequence Pair	Clockwise	Counterclockwise	χ^2	Degrees of Freedom	P
		Experiment III			
AB BA	25	17	1.5	1	P < .15
BC CB	47	27	5.4	1	P < .01
CA AC	21	15	1.0	1	P < .20
Total	93	59	7.5	1	P < .005
		Experiment IV			
AB BA	10	7	0.5	1	P < .25
BC CB	48	26	6.5	1	P < .01
CA AC	14	13	0.03	1	P < .45
Total	72	46	5.8	1	P < .01

BC > CB, and CA > AC) are in the expected direction, although the latter differences are significant only for the BC-CB comparison. Table 5 shows the chi square values.

The results of Experiment IV closely resemble those for Experiment III. The total clockwise versus counterclockwise and the three specific pattern differences are all in the expected direction, although two of the latter are very small. Again, the BC-CB comparison yields the only significant difference. (See Table 5).[6]

The results of Experiments III and IV confirm the hypothesis that preselected conversational sequences would occur more frequently than others. The results also indicate that not all of the three possible conversational patterns increased in frequency, but, rather only one of them. In Experiment III, this finding is highlighted in trial blocks 91-105 and 151-165; in Experiment IV, similarly, it is definite by trial block 91-105 and persists until the end of the trial run.

In effect, both groups appeared to learn a more specific social response, namely, of one person talking last, preceded by. a specific other person, and not a general positional response (clockwise or counterclockwise). The next-to-last speaker functions as a discrimi-

native stimulus for a given speaker whose final response brings reinforcement.

Reinforcing a category of two-person sequences may have served to "shape up" a specific conversational sequence. Scrutiny of the results in Tables 3 and 4 indicates the relative fixing of a specific clockwise sequence at about the fourth trial block (46-60). This same sequence is relatively higher than each of the remaining sequences, trial block by trial block, until the end of the runs.

An interesting exception is apparent in trial block 106-120 in Experiment III: CB occurred six times, whereas in the previous block, BC occurred eight times. The reinforcement of conversation between two persons, B and C, in one direction, B to C, seemed to generalize to its reverse sequence, C to B. By the same token, Speaker A learned to be quiet during this particular section of the conversation.

No specific hypothesis was made about increases over time in the frequency of given conversational patterns as a function of the number of reinforced trials. Such a change was observed for the single sequence (BC), as Tables 3 and 4 show. However, the acquisition of this response does not follow an incremental path, but rather seems to become stabilized at some point along the way.

DISCUSSION

We have shown in this paper how the operant conditioning of serial order of con-

[6]The seat positions and clock patterns were not in fact the same for Experiments III and IV; and the specific verbal sequence was clockwise in one instance, and the reverse in the other. The learning was therefore not the same spatially in both groups. Results were expressed in similar terms for simplicity.

PAUL G. SWINGLE

versation may be carried out. In postgroup interviews with subjects, not one noticed a connection between conversational sequence and getting the right answers, although several suspected that the guessing game was rigged in some way. During the experimental sessions themselves, Ss offered a great variety of complex and often inconsistent hypotheses to account for their increasing success in figuring out how the experimenter devised his list of colors.

The results of the studies are all consistent with the hypothesis that the order of speakers in a conversation can be brought under experimental control by manipulating the variable of group reinforcement—success and failure—in a task in which the group has to make a number of unanimous decisions about a number of hypotheses. In each group, a conversational sequence became established at a given level after about 50 to 100 trials, or within a half-hour of conversation.

Further studies are now proceeding on the acquisition and extinction of conversational patterns in three-person groups and on the basic assumptions of the operant techniques used. The procedure is also being adapted to study the course and stability of other kinds of social responses under different conditions of group reinforcement.

Reprinted from Journal of Abnormal and Social Psychology, 1960, Vol. 61, pp. 365–369, by permission of the author and the publisher.

COMPETENCE AND CONFORMITY IN THE ACCEPTANCE OF INFLUENCE[1]

E. P. HOLLANDER

WHEN one member influences others in his group it is often because he is competent in a focal group activity. A member may show such competence by individual actions that further the attainment of group goals (cf. Carter, 1954); more specific situational demands may variously favor the ascent of the expediter, advocate, or what Bales and Slater (1955) have termed the task specialist. An additional condition for the acceptance of influence involves the member's perceived adherence to the normative behaviors and attitudes of his group. His record of conformity to these expectancies serves to sustain eligibility of the sort Brown (1936) calls "membership character."

A person who exhibits both competence and conformity should eventually reach a threshold at which it becomes appropriate in the eyes of others for him to assert influence; and insofar as these assertions are accepted he emerges as a leader. But it is still necessary to account for the "nonconformity" that leaders display as they innovate and alter group norms. Certain shifts must therefore occur in the expectancies applicable to an individual as he proceeds from gaining status to maintaining it.

This process has been considered recently in a theoretical model of status emergence (Hollander, 1958). It features the prospect that behavior perceived to be nonconformity for one member may not be so perceived for another. Such differentiations are seen to be made as a function of status, conceived as an accumulation of positively disposed impressions termed "idiosyncrasy credits." A person gains credits, i.e., rises in status, by showing competence and by conforming to the expectancies applicable to him at the time. Eventually his credits allow him to nonconform with greater impunity.[2] Moreover, he is then subject to a new set of expectancies which direct the assertion of influence. Thus, whether for lack of motivation or misperception, his failure to take innovative action may cause him to lose status.[3]

It is readily predictable that in task oriented groups a member giving evidence of competence on the group task should with time gain in influence. If he simply nonconforms to the procedures agreed upon, the opposite effect should be observed. But the sequential relationship of nonconformity to competence is especially critical.

From the model, it should follow that, with a relatively constant level of manifest competence, the influence of a person who nonconforms *early* in the course of group interaction should be more drastically curtailed than in the case of a person who nonconforms *later*. Indeed, a reversal of effect would be predicted in the latter instance. Once a member has accumulated credits, his nonconformity to general procedure should serve as a confirming or signalizing feature of his status, thereby enhancing his influence. Accordingly, it may be hypothesized that given equivalent degrees of task competence, a member should achieve greater acceptance of his influence when he has conformed in the past and is now nonconforming than he should when nonconformity precedes conformity.

METHOD

Design

Twelve groups, each composed of four male subjects, were engaged in a task involving a sequence of

[1] This paper is based upon a study completed under ONR Contract 1849(00), while the author was at the Carnegie Institute of Technology. The views expressed here are those of the author and do not necessarily reflect those of the Department of the Navy.

The considerable assistance of H. Edwin Titus in this study is gratefully acknowledged.

Parts of the paper were reported at the symposium on "Recent Conceptions in Influence and Authority Process," held under the auspices of Division 8 at the 1959 APA Convention.

[2] This is a newer formulation of an observation long since made regarding the latitude provided leaders (e.g., Homans, 1950, p. 416). It is further elaborated in Hollander (1959).

[3] This proposition is consistent with various findings suggestive of the greater social perceptiveness of leaders (e.g., Chowdhry & Newcomb, 1952).

E. P. HOLLANDER

	Green	Red	Blue	Yellow	Brown	Orange	Black
Able	−1	−12	+5	−1	−2	+15	−4
Baker	+10	−1	−2	−7	+4	−3	−1
Charlie	−5	+5	−3	+3	−11	−1	+12
Dog	+5	−7	+10	−2	−5	+1	−2
Easy	−4	−1	−1	+1	+13	−10	+2
Fox	−6	+15	−5	−1	−3	−1	+1
George	−1	−1	−2	+10	+4	−2	−8

Fig. 1. Matrix used in group task.

15 trials. A group choice was required for each trial from among the row alternatives in a 7 × 7 payoff matrix (see Figure 1). In every group, a fifth member was a confederate whose prearranged response was contrived to be correct on all but four trials, i.e., 2, 3, 6, and 12, thus reflecting considerable competence on the task. All interactions among participants took place through a system of microphones and headsets from partitioned booths. Subjects were assigned numbers from 1 to 5 for communicating with one another. The central manipulation was the confederate's nonconformity to procedures agreed upon by each group in a pretrial discussion. In terms of a division of the 15 trials into three zones—early, middle, and late—of 5 trials each, six treatments were applied: nonconformity throughout, nonconformity for the first two zones, for the first zone alone, for the last two zones, for the last zone alone, and a control with no nonconformity. In one set of treatments the confederate was designated number 5, and in the other number 4, to test possible position effects. Acceptance of the confederate's influence was measured by the number of trials by zone in which his recommended response was accepted as the group's. This was supplemented by post-interaction assessments.

Subjects

The 48 subjects were all juniors in the College of Engineering and Science at the Carnegie Institute of Technology. All had volunteered from introductory psychology sections after being told only that they would be taking part in a study of problem solving in groups. Care was taken in composing the 12 groups so as to avoid either placing acquaintances together or having membership known in advance. Thus, no two subjects from the same class section were used in the same group, and subjects reported at staggered times to different rooms. By the time a subject reached the laboratory room where the experiment was actually conducted, he had been kept apart from the others and was not aware of their identity. The subjects never saw one another during the entire procedure, nor were their names ever used among them.

Instructions and Set

Once seated and assigned a number, every subject was given a sheet of instructions and the matrix used for the task. These instructions fell into two parts, both of which were reviewed aloud with each subject individually, and then with the entire group over the communication network. The first part cautioned the subjects to always identify themselves by number

(e.g., "This is Station 3 ...") before speaking and not to use names or other self-identifying references. The second part acquainted them with the procedures to be used, emphasized the aspect of competition against a "system," and established the basis for evident procedural norms. It read as follows:

1. You will be working with others on a problem involving a matrix of plus and minus values. Everyone has the same matrix before him. The goal is to amass as many plus units as possible, and to avoid minus units. Units are worth 1 cent each to the group; the group begins with a credit of 200 units. You cannot lose your own money, therefore. There will be fifteen trials in all.

2. In any one trial, the task involved is for the group to agree on just *one* row—identified by Able, Baker, Charlie, etc.—which seems to have strategic value. Once the group has determined a row, the experimenter will announce the column color which comes up on that trial. The intersecting cells indicate the payoff. Following this announcement, there will be thirty seconds of silence during which group members can think individually about the best strategy for the next trial, in terms of their notion about the system; note please that there are several approximations to the system, although the equation underlying it is quite complex. But work at it.

3. At the beginning of each trial the group members must report, one at a time, in some order, as to what they think would be the best row choice on the upcoming trial. Members may "pass" until the third time around, but must announce a choice then. Following this, groups will have three minutes on each trial to discuss choices and reach some agreement; this can be a simple majority, or unanimous decision; it is up to the group to decide. If a decision is not reached in three minutes, the group loses 5 units.

4. Before beginning the trials, the group will have five minutes to discuss these points: (a) The order of reporting; (b) How to determine the group choice for a given trial; (c) How to divide up the money at the end. These decisions are always subject to change, if the group has time and can agree. After the 15th trial, group members may have as much as five minutes to settle any outstanding decisions. Then headsets are to be removed, but group members remain seated for further instructions, and the individual payment of funds.

Instruments and Procedure

The matrix was specially constructed for this study to present an ambiguous but plausible task in which alternatives were only marginally discrete from one another.[4] The number of columns and rows was selected to enlarge the range of possibilities beyond the number of group members, while still retaining comprehensibility. The fact that the rows are unequal in algebraic sum appears to be less important as a feature in choice than the number and magnitude of positive and negative values in each; there is moreover the complicating feature of processing the outcome of the last trials in evaluating the choice for the next. All considered, the matrix was admirably suited to the requirements for ambiguity, challenge, conflict, immediate reinforcement, and ready manipulation by the experimenter.

The confederate, operating as either 4 or 5 in the groups, suggested a choice that differed trial by trial from those offered by other members; this was prearranged but subject to modification as required. Since subjects rather typically perceived alternatives differently, his behavior was not unusual, especially during the early trials. For the 11 trials in which the confederate's row choice was "correct," the color that "came up" was contrived to yield a high plus value without at the same time providing a similar value for intersection with another person's row choice. Had his recommendation been followed by the group on these trials, high payoffs would have accrued.

The device of a 5-minute pretrial discussion had special utility for establishing common group expectancies, in the form of procedures, from which the confederate could deviate when called for in the design. Predictable decisions on these matters were reached unfailingly. But their importance lay in having a *public affirmation* of member intent. Thus, on order of reporting, it was quickly agreed to follow the order of the numbers assigned members. Each group, despite minor variants suggested, decided on simple majority rule. Regarding division of funds, equal sharing prevailed, sometimes with the proviso that the issue be taken up again at the end.

In the zones calling for nonconformity, the confederate violated these procedures by speaking out of prescribed turn, by questioning the utility of majority rule, and by unsupported—but not harsh—challenges to the recommendations made by others. He manifested such behaviors on an approximate frequency of at least one of these per trial with a mean of two per trial considered optimum. Thus, he would break in with his choice immediately after an earlier respondent had spoken and before the next in sequence could do so; when there were periods of silence during a trial he would observe aloud that maybe majority rule did not work so well; and he would show a lack of enthusiasm for the choice offered by various others on the matter of basis. Lest he lose credibility and become a caricature, in all instances he chose his moments with care and retained an evident spontaneity of expression.[5]

---

[4] The matrix is an adaptation, at least in spirit, of a smaller one used with success by Moore and Berkowitz (1956).

[5] The same person, H. E. Titus, was the confederate throughout.

RESULTS AND DISCUSSION

The task gave quite satisfactory signs of engrossing the subjects. There was much talk about the "system" and a good deal of delving into its basis, possibly made the more so by the subjects' academic background; the returned matrices were littered with diagrams, notations, and calculations. Though quite meaningless in fact, the confederate's tentative accounts of his "reasoning" were evidently treated with seriousness, perhaps as much because of the contrived time constraint, which prevented probing, as of his jargon regarding "rotations" and "block shifts." In any case, the confederate at no time claimed to have the system completely in hand. He delayed his response from the sixth trial onward to suggest calculation of an optimum choice in the face of conflicting alternatives; and the four trials on which he was "wrong" were spaced to signify progressive improvement, but not total perfection.

Most pertinent, however, is the fact that there were no manifestations of suspicion concerning the confederate's authenticity. The others seemed to believe that he was one of them and that he was "cracking" the system; the post-interaction data were in full agreement.

Since all of the interactions were available on tape, it was possible to derive a number of indices of acceptance of influence. The most broadly revealing of these appeared to be the frequency of trials on which the confederate's recommended solution was followed.

In Table 1 this index is employed to discern the effects of three major variables. The analysis is arranged by zones (Z) of trials, and in terms of the confederate's nonconformity (NC) in the *current* zone and immediate *past* zone.[6] The means given in each cell indicate the number of trials, out of five per zone, on which the confederate's choice was also the group's. In a chi square test, the effect of position upon this measure was found to be nonsignificant, and is therefore omitted as a distinction in the analysis of variance.

---

[6] For Zone I, the "past zone" refers to the discussion period. If he was to nonconform there, the confederate would question majority rule and suggest that the division of funds be left until the end rather than agree then on equal shares.

TABLE 1

MEAN NUMBER OF TRIALS ON WHICH A GROUP ACCEPTS CONFEDERATE'S RECOMMENDED SOLUTION

Confederate's Previous Conformity	Zone I (Trials 1–5)		Zone II (Trials 6–10)		Zone III (Trials 11–15)	
	Nonconforming[a]	Conforming	Nonconforming	Conforming	Nonconforming	Conforming
With Procedural nonconformity in immediate *past* zone	1.67 6[b]	—	3.25 4	3.00 2	4.00 4	5.00 2
Without Procedural nonconformity in immediate *past* zone	—	2.00 6	5.00 2	3.75 4	5.00 2	4.75 4

ANALYSIS OF VARIANCE

Source	SS	df	MS	F
Current Nonconformity	.20	1	.200	—
Zones	47.05	2	23.525	35.01**
Past Nonconformity	3.36	1	3.360	5.00*
Int: Current NC × Z	1.22	2	.610	—
Int: Current NC × Past NC	13.52	1	13.520	20.12**
Int: Z × Past NC	.72	2	.360	—
Int: Current NC × Z × Past NC	4.11	2	2.055	3.06
Residual	16.12	24	.672	
Total	86.30	35		

[a] Confederate showed procedural nonconformity on the trials in this zone.
[b] Indicates number of groups upon which cell is based.
* $p < .05$.
** $p < .001$.

The significant F secured from Zones is in accord with prediction. It reveals the ongoing effect of task competence in increasing the acceptance of the confederate's choice, to be seen in the rising means across zones. While current nonconformity does not yield a significant effect, past nonconformity does. Viewing the table horizontally, one finds that the means for "without" *past* NC exceed the means for "with" *past* NC in all instances but one. Regarding the significant interaction of *current* and *past* NC, the combination "without-without" has a sequence (2.00, 3.75, 4.75) of persistently higher value than has "with-with" (1.67, 3.25, 4.00); this, too, is in line with prediction. Finally, the maximum value of 5.00 in Zone II for the combination "without" *past* NC but "with" *current* NC confirms the key prediction from the model, at least within the context of the relative magnitudes there; the same value is also seen in Zone III for the identical combination; still another reading of 5.00 holds there, however, for the inverse combination, but in a tight range of values quite beyond separation of effects for interpretation.

Considerable consistency was found too in the post-interaction data. On the item "overall contribution to the group activity," 44 of the 48 subjects ranked the confederate first; on the item "influence over the group's decisions," 45 of the 48 ranked him first. Two things bear emphasis in this regard: subjects had to individually write in the numbers of group members next to rank, hence demanding recall; and their polarity of response cut across all six treatments, despite significant differences among these in the actual *acceptance of influence*. That the confederate therefore made an impact is clear; but that it had selective consequences depending upon the timing of his nonconformity is equally clear.

In detail, then, the findings are in keeping with the predictions made from the model. The operational variable for measuring acceptance of influence was confined to the task itself, but nontask elements are touched as well. In that respect, the findings corroborate the subtle development of differential impressions as a function of even limited interpersonal behavior.

Some unquantified but clearly suggestive data are worth mentioning in this regard. Where, for example, the confederate began nonconforming *after* the first zone, his behavior was accepted with minimal challenge; by the third zone, his suggestion that majority rule was faulty yielded a rubber stamping of his choice. Again, if he had already accrued credit, his pattern of interrupting people out of turn not only went unhindered but was taken up by some others. Quite different effects were elicited if the confederate exhibited nonconformity from *the outset*, notably such comments of censure as "That's not the way we agreed to do it, five."

The findings are especially indicative of the stochastic element of social interaction and its consequence for changing perception. Especially interesting is the fact that these effects are produced even in a relatively brief span of time.

SUMMARY

A study was conducted to test the relationship between competence on a group task and conformity or nonconformity to procedural norms in determining a person's ability to influence other group members. Data were gathered from 12 groups engaged in a problem solving task under controlled conditions. Each was made up of five members one of whom was a confederate who evidenced a high degree of competence during the 15 trials. His nonconformity to the procedural norms agreed upon by the group was introduced at various times, early, middle, or late, in the sequence of trials. Influence was measured by the number of trials (per segment of the entire sequence) in which the confederate's recommended solution was accepted as the group's choice. As a broad effect, it was found that a significant increase in his influence occurred as the trials progressed, presumably as a function of the successive evidences of competence. Past conformity by the confederate was also found to be positively and significantly related to the acceptance of his influence; finally, there was a statistically significant interaction between past and current nonconformity reflected in high influence in the groups in which the confederate had conformed earlier in the sequence of trials but was presently nonconforming. These results were all thoroughly consistent with predictions made from the "idiosyncrasy credit" model of conformity and status.

REFERENCES

BALES, R. F., & SLATER, P. E. Role differentiation in small decision-making groups. In T. Parsons, R. F. Bales, et al. (Eds.), *Family, socialization, and interaction process.* Glencoe, Ill.: Free Press, 1955.

BROWN, J. F. *Psychology and the social order.* New York: McGraw-Hill, 1936.

CARTER, L. F. Recording and evaluating the performance of individuals as members of small groups. *Personnel Psychol.,* 1954, **7,** 477–484.

CHOWDHRY, KAMLA, & NEWCOMB, T. M. The relative abilities of leaders and non-leaders to estimate opinions of their own groups. *J. abnorm. soc. Psychol.,* 1952, **47,** 51–57.

HOLLANDER, E. P. Conformity, status, and idiosyncrasy credit. *Psychol. Rev.,* 1958, **65,** 117–127.

HOLLANDER, E. P. Some points of reinterpretation regarding social conformity. *Soc. Rev.,* 1959, **7,** 159–168.

HOMANS, G. C. *The human group.* New York: Harcourt, Brace, 1950.

MOORE, O. K., & BERKOWITZ, M. I. Problem solving and social interaction. *ONR tech. Rep.,* 1956, No. 1. (Contract Nonr-609(16), Yale University Department of Sociology)

(Received August 17, 1959)

Game Behavior

There has been a great deal of interest in the past few years in laboratory-based studies on bargaining behavior in mixed-motive situations. These studies are designed to explore such behaviors as cooperation, retaliation, exploitation, and competition, as they are affected by various factors in the bargaining situation.

Nonzero-Sum Games

A class of structured laboratory situations used for exploring bargaining behavior are the nonzero-sum games.* These games are usually two-person, two-choice situations which are designed so that either person's pay-off is determined by both persons' behavior. An example is given in the accompanying matrix, where A and B are each provided

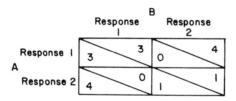

with two alternative responses — response one and response two. The rules of the game situation are quite simple. On any particular trial, each player must decide whether he wants to play response one or two. Each player makes his decision (usually without any knowledge of his partner's choice) and then the experimenter announces the results of the trial. The payoffs for player A are shown in the lower left-hand corner of each quadrant; the payoffs for player B are shown in the upper right-hand corner.

Let us go through the four possible combinations of responses for

*The term "nonzero-sum" refers to the relationship between the two players' payoffs. In nonzero-sum games, what one player wins or loses is independent of his partner's winnings and losses. This is in contrast to zero-sum games in which one player wins what the second player loses (two-handed poker would be a zero-sum game).

the matrix. If both players choose response one, each player receives three payoff units (each unit may represent 1 cent, points in a competitive game, etc). This outcome may be referred to as mutual cooperation, and response one as the cooperative response. If player A makes response one, and player B makes response two, A receives nothing while B receives 4. One may say, then, that B has yielded to the temptation of trying to exploit A's cooperative response. The same situation would be present if A took advantage of B's cooperative response, which would result in the pair's ending up in quadrant three (i.e., A_2B_1). If both players make response two, each receives only one payoff unit.

Responses are defined then in terms of the effects they have upon both the player himself and his partner. Response one may be called the "cooperative" and "trusting" response. Response one is cooperative because it does not penalize the partner, or conversely it makes larger rewards available to the partner than response two does. Response one is also a trusting response because the person is taking some degree of risk that his cooperative response will be exploited rather than reciprocated and that he will receive no reward at all. The person is, in effect, trusting his partner not to make a number two response.

Response two may be defined as a "nontrusting" or "exploitative" response. If one person plays response one, the second player may take advantage of his trust and exploit him by playing response two. On the other hand, the response may be a nontrusting response. If one player believes that his partner will most probably play response two, then the safest response is also response two because it minimizes the loss (the worst that one can do with response two is one payoff unit, whereas with response one he may receive zero payoff).

The matrix shown above is symmetrical and is designed so that unilateral noncooperation yields a larger payoff for the noncooperative person than does his payoff under mutual cooperation. Mutual cooperation, in turn, yields a larger payoff than mutual noncooperation. It should be apparent that in the short run type two responses may result in a larger payoff if the partner is initially cooperative. In the long run, however, exploitative behavior will most likely not be tolerated with the result that both players will end up with very small rewards unless they cooperate. This matrix is referred to as the "Prisoner's Dilemma" game — the dilemma refers to (a) the short-term advantage of defection (playing number two when the partner cooperates) and the long-term disadvantage of such behavior because of the increased likelihood of mutual noncooperation, and (b) the decision necessary on any single trial as to whether one player may trust the other not to play number two.

Game Structural Factors Affecting Interpersonal Bargaining

There are a tremendous number of variables which may be studied by using game situations such as the one described above. First of all one may study factors peculiar to the structure of the situation, which may affect cooperative behavior, such as the degree of power one subject has relative to his partner, the amount of risk involved in making a cooperative response, the amount lost when both subjects make noncooperative responses, and the amount gained by exploitation. The variables may be systematically studied by making systematic changes in the Prisoner's Dilemma matrix. If one were interested in the effects of differences in power of one player relative to the second player upon the number of cooperative responses made, the matrix might be varied as in the accompanying matrices.

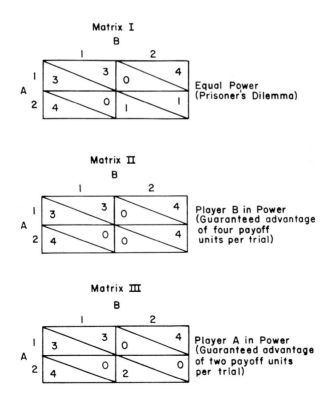

EXPERIMENT 7

As shown by the matrices, slight changes in the payoffs in quadrant four can result in rather drastic changes in the power relationship between the two players. In Matrix I, both players have equal power. If the worst comes to worst, either player may guarantee that his partner cannot *beat* him. That is, by playing response two, either player may be assured that at worst both he and his partner will receive one payoff unit, neither player winning more than the other. At best, with a number two response, the player may receive four units while his partner receives zero if the partner should play number one.

In Matrix II, all the power has been put in the hands of B. Player B may, by playing response two, guarantee that he will win four on every trial and his partner will receive nothing. That is, if player B plays response two, player B receives four points regardless of which response player A makes. Player A is helpless in that he cannot prevent his receiving zero should player B play number two. As a matter of fact, it is somewhat disadvantageous for player B to play the cooperative response since he receives four points for response two and, at best, three for response one.

In Matrix III, player A is in power in that he can guarantee that he will beat player B on every trial if he plays response two throughout. Player A does not have the same degree of power as player B has in Matrix II. One can see why this is so since player B in Matrix III can offer something to A if A cooperates. Namely, although A can be sure of at least a two-point gain on every trial, player B can, in effect, guarantee A a gain of three on every trial if there is mutual cooperation. So, in short, one would say player B in Matrix II has absolute power, whereas player A in Matrix III has partial power.

There is one other peculiarity of Matrix III which should be mentioned. Examination of the matrix reveals that even though A may receive more by playing response one (i.e., if B and A cooperate A will receive three points per trial) A will beat B by a much larger score difference if A stays with response two. For example, if A and B play the game 100 times, 100% cooperation will yield 300 points for both A and B or a difference of zero. If A plays two for 100 trials the very worst he can do is to win 200 points to B's zero points, or a difference of 200.

A cooperative (trusting) response almost always involves some risk that the partner will not reciprocate the trust. The risk involved in making a cooperative response may be varied for player A by increasing the payoff disparity in quadrant two, as given in the accompanying matrices.

212

PAUL G. SWINGLE

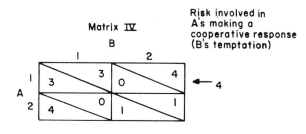

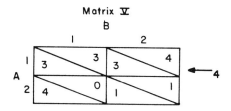

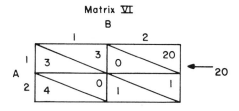

It will be noted that A's risk is equivalent to B's temptation. That is, the risk A is taking in making a number one response increases directly with the gain player B will receive if he yields to the temptation of exploiting A by making a number two response.

Risk must be defined further in terms of a player's relative loss. That is, player A's loss if B does not reciprocate his cooperative response is obviously greater in Matrix IV than it is in Matrix V. In Matrix IV B gains four while A receives nothing, while in Matrix V, B gains an advantage of one point but A does not lose any points. In short, A's relative risk is greater in Matrix IV than in Matrix V.

To calculate A's relative risk (RR) one must consider first what B gains if he successfully exploits A and second that amount which A loses if his cooperative response is not reciprocated. The simple formula shown below may be used to obtain the RR for either player:

Relative risk (for player A):
$$RR_A = (a - b) + (d - c)$$
where a = player B's payoff for mutual cooperation
b = player B's payoff if he can successfully exploit A
c = player A's payoff for mutual cooperation
d = player A's payoff if his cooperative response is exploited by B

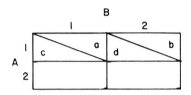

For example, in Matrix IV, A's relative risk is
$$RR_A = (3 - 4) + (0 - 3)$$
$$RR_A = -4$$
In Matrix V:
$$RR_A = (3 - 4) + (3 - 3)$$
$$RR_A = -1$$
This formula indicates that A's relative risk is considerably greater in Matrix IV than in Matrix V, even though B's absolute gain is equal in the two situations. If the formula does not yield a negative value for RR, then no relative risk exists.

A few examples should suffice for illustrating the number of different variables which may be systematically varied, by using matrices, to simulate any number of possible social relationships between two bargainers.

1. High temptation for player A, high power for player B (illustrated in the accompanying matrix).

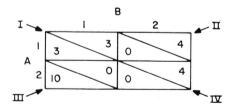

a. Cooperative payoff equals 3 each, neither player with an advantage (I).

b. Player A's risk in making a cooperative response equals minus 4. B's temptation (exploitative advantage), therefore, equals plus 4 (II).

c. Player A's relative risk in making a cooperative response equals minus 4 (I and II).

d. Player B's risk in making a cooperative response equals minus 10 units. A's exploitative advantage (temptation) equals plus 10 units (III).

e. Player B's relative risk in making a cooperative response equals minus 10 (I and III).

f. Risk involved in A's making a number two response equals minus 4 (IV).

g. Risk involved in B's making a number two response equals plus 4 (no risk involved) (IV).

h. Mutual noncooperative payoff equals four units for B and zero units for A (IV).

i. Guaranteed advantage equals plus 4 for B and minus 4 for A (II and IV).

2. Equal power situation, large exploitative payoff, very large risk involved when making a number two (exploitative) response (see accompanying matrix). The game of "Chicken":

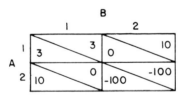

a. Mutual cooperation payoff equals 3 units each.

b. Risk involved for either player to respond cooperatively equals minus ten units.

c. Temptation (exploitative advantage) equals plus ten units for each player.

d. Relative risk for either player to respond cooperatively equals minus 10.

e. Risk involved in making an exploitative response equals minus 100 units for each player.

f. Guaranteed minimum advantage equals zero for both players.

Effects of "Other's" Strategy upon Mixed-Motive Behavior

In the above section, the various ways of manipulating the relationship between the two players by altering the structure of the game matrix were discussed. These manipulations provide one with techniques for exploring the effects of structural factors of a mixed-motive situation upon bargaining.

Another important factor to be considered is the effect of one player's strategy upon another player's behavior. For example, one might expect that a player may be encouraged to respond cooperatively if his partner almost always made the cooperative response and to tend to be uncooperative if the partner almost always made the number two (noncooperative) response.

There are many questions about the effects of one player's behavior upon the second player which have yet to be explored. Does an abrupt change in strategy, such as from unconditionally cooperative (100% number one responses) to 25% cooperative, for example, result in abrupt changes in the second player's game behavior? Or a more general question: Can exploitative behavior be increased by manipulating the strategy to which a player is exposed?

The procedure for manipulating strategy is quite simple. Two subjects are situated so that they cannot see one another although they are aware of each other's presence. Each subject is given a matrix such as those shown above and each is told, independently, that he is player A. That is, both players are led to believe that they are player A and therefore each player believes that his partner is player B. During the game-playing session, the experimenter provides the results of each trial, following a predetermined strategy, to each player so that they are exposed to a strategy decided upon beforehand by the experimenter. For example, if on trial X the experimenter wanted both subjects to believe that their partners had made noncooperative responses, even though both had actually made cooperative responses, the experimenter would simply tell each subject that they ended up in a quadrant number two (responses A_1B_2). Thus, in effect, the subjects are both playing as subject A, against the experimenter who takes the part of B; but the subjects believe they are playing against their partner.

The experiment for this session will involve the use of both the "free play" technique and the "preprogramed play" technique. Subjects will be involved in either a free play Prisoner's Dilemma game, a preprogramed Prisoner's Dilemma situation, or a free play, high risk situation.

INSTRUCTIONS

Experimental Team Size: One to three.
Subjects: Arrange for exactly two naive subjects per team. Sub-

jects should be obtained as in Experiment 2. All subjects should be of the same sex.

Apparatus: Two chairs; pencils; five 3 × 5 in. file cards; two matrices made from cardboard or stiff paper about 8 in. square.

Experimental Situation: Two subjects are seated in view of the experimenter but not in view of each other. (One subject on each side of a wall with the experimenter standing in the area of the doorway will suffice.) The subjects are told that they are playing a game for imaginary money but that they are to pretend that it is real and act accordingly. On each of 100 trials, both subjects make one of two responses and communicate their choice to the experimenter without informing the partner of the choice. After both subjects have made their choices, the experimenter gives the results of the trial to the subjects who record their own winnings or losses.

Condition A — free play Prisoner's Dilemma. We are interested, in this condition, in the amount of cooperative responding which takes place in an equal power, mixed-motive situation when the subjects are actually playing against each other.

Condition B — free play, very high risk, high temptation situation. In this condition we are interested in the effect the very great risk attached to a noncooperative response has upon cooperative responding.

Condition C — Prisoner's Dilemma situation, preprogramed unconditionally cooperative (100% number one response) partner. We are interested, in this condition, in the effects of an unconditionally cooperative partner upon a subject's cooperative responding.

Preparation

1. Form teams of about two students each so that the number of teams is an even multiple of three (i.e., 3, 6, 9, 12, etc.).

2. Assign each team one condition, A, B, or C, so that an equal number of each condition will be run.

3. Find areas to conduct the study which will allow separation of the subjects from each other but not from the experimenter and also provide for limited disturbance.

4. Make up two identical matrices, one for each subject, following the model shown in Fig. 7.1 for your team's condition.

5. Make up two 3 × 5 in. response cards for each subject (four for each pair) by printing a large number 1 on one card and a large number 2 on the other card.

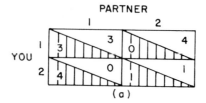

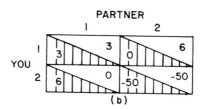

FIG. 7.1. Nonzero-sum matrices: (a) matrix for conditions A and C, and (b) matrix for condition B. The matrix panels should be made of stiff paper or cardboard. Use red ink for the subject's points (shown in shaded areas) and black ink for the partner's points.

6. Prepare one 3 × 5 in. result card, for the experimenter, by printing the number 1 on one side and the number 2 on the other side.

7. Prepare two tally sheets for each pair, one per subject. A sheet of lined paper with the numbers 1 to 100 listed in column form will be sufficient. The subjects will use these sheets to keep track of their own scores.

8. Prepare the experimenter's tally sheet following the model shown in Fig. 7.2.

Condition _____

	Subject			Subject	
Trial	A	B	Trial	A	B
1			51		
2			52		
3			53		
4			54		
5			55		
.			.		
.			.		
.			.		
50			100		

FIG. 7.2. Experimenter's tally sheet. [Under A and B enter the response made (either 1 or 2) on each trial by each subject.]

Procedure

1. Arrange the chairs for the subjects as specified previously. Place one matrix, one tally sheet, one pencil, and two response cards (one with the number 1 printed on it and one with the number 2 on it) at each place.

2. Bring the subjects in, one at a time, seat them at their places, and then read the following instructions:

General Instructions

"The study you are involved in is concerned with small group behavior. You are going to be involved in a situation which is similar to many real-life situations in that what you gain or lose will be determined both by your behavior and the behavior of your partner. You have in front of you a matrix, two cards, and a tally sheet. What we want you to do is to pretend that you are in a bargaining situation in which each of you has two alternative choices. Your choices are marked one and two at the left of the matrix and your partner's choices are numbered one and two at the top of the matrix. Your task is to choose response one or two when I ask you to; your partner will make a choice at the same time. After you both have made your choice, I will tell you what the result is and you can determine the payoff from the matrix. Your payoffs are shown in red; your partner's are shown in black."

Specific Instructions

Conditions A and C

"If both you and your partner make response one, for example, you both receive three dollars each. If you both choose number two you will each receive one dollar. If one of you makes choice number one and the other makes choice number two, the player choosing number one will receive nothing, the person choosing number two will receive four dollars."

Condition B

"If both you and your partner make response one, for example, you both receive three dollars each. If you both choose number two you will each lose fifty dollars. If one of you makes choice one and the other makes choice two, the player choosing number one will receive nothing, the person choosing number two will receive six dollars."

General Instructions (continued)

"Now, we cannot, of course, actually give you all that money, so the payoffs will have to be imaginary. We want you to pretend that it is real, however, and act as you would if it were real money. When I say 'choose,' each of you will let me know what choice you made by holding up either card one or card two. Do not say anything, since you do not want your partner to know your choice ahead of time—simply hold up the appropriate card so that I may see it. After I receive both choices I will let you know what the results were by holding up this card (experimenter shows the file card with the number 1 on one side and the number 2 on the other). If I show you the number 1 it means that your partner has chosen response one. After I show you your partner's choice, find your payoff by looking at the appropriate quadrant of the matrix and record your points on the tally sheet provided. Any questions?"

3. After finishing the instructions, answer any questions about procedure. Be careful not to encourage cooperative or competitive behavior by your answers to questions.

4. Probe your subjects to determine if they actually do understand the matrix. Ask each subject to tell you what happens if:

    a. "You and your partner choose number one."

    b. "You choose one and your partner chooses number two."

Your subjects should answer correctly by indicating how many dollars he receives and how many his partner would receive. If a subject does not understand, review each of the four combinations again.

5. Keeping a steady, but not rapid, pace, the experimenter asks the subjects to:

    a. "Choose." When the subjects hold up their response cards, the experimenter records each subject's response on his tally sheet. The experimenter then says:

    b. "Results." The experimenter, *out of view of the partner;* proceeds as follows: *Conditions A and B*—shows one subject the partner's response choice by holding up the result card showing either a 1 or 2 to the subject to signify either a number one or number two response by the partner; *Condition C*— shows each subject 1 on the result card on each of the 100 trials to signify that the partner has made a cooperative response.

    c. The experimenter then tells the subjects: "Record your points." After a brief pause the experimenter repeats the above sequence until 100 trials have been completed.

Data Organization and Analysis

1. Summarize the data into ten 10-trial blocks and enter the num-

ber of cooperative responses (number one responses) in a table such as given in the accompanying tabulation which gives the total number of cooperative responses in each 10-trial block.

10 - Trial Block

	1	2	3	4	5	6	7	8	9	10	T
Subject A											
Subject B											

2. Combine the class data for each condition and record the data in a table similar to Table 7.1.

TABLE 7.1

TOTAL NUMBER OF COOPERATIVE RESPONSES IN EACH 10-TRIAL BLOCK

10-Trial Block

Subject	1	2	3	4	5	6	7	8	9	10	T
1											
2											
3											
4											
.											
.											
.											
n											
Total											
Mean											

3. Plot the means for each condition in a single graph of the form shown in Fig. 7.3.

Experimental Report

1. Are the shapes of the curves similar? If not, what does this suggest in terms of the establishment of cooperation in one group more rapidly than in other groups, the tendency to exploit subjects under certain circumstances, etc.?

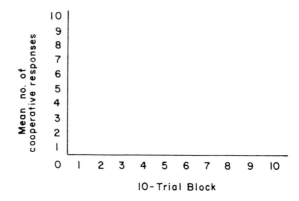

FIG. 7.3. Mean number of cooperative responses in each 10-trial block for each condition.

2. Is there any indication of greater exploitation in condition C (compared with condition A)?

3. What effect does increasing the risk of great loss for a type two response have upon cooperative behavior?

4. Is there any evidence to suggest that one subject in a pair in condition B was a "chicken"? That is, did one subject submit to his opponent's exploitative responses? This may be determined by comparing the number of type two responses made by each subject in a particular pair in condition B. If there is a large difference, this might indicate that one subject had successfully dominated his partner.

Reprinted from Journal of Personality and Social Psychology, 1966, Vol. 3, pp. 206–213,
by permission of the authors and the publisher.

OPPONENT'S PERSONALITY, EXPECTATION OF SOCIAL INTERACTION, AND INTERPERSONAL BARGAINING [1]

DAVID MARLOWE, KENNETH J. GERGEN, AND ANTHONY N. DOOB [2]

In 2 separate experiments Ss participated in a 2-person, non-zero-sum game
with an opponent whose behavior during the game was predominantly cooperative. In Exp. I Ss who anticipated further interaction with their opponent
were less exploitative than those who did not. In Exp. II it was predicted that
Ss would exploit an egotistical opponent to a greater extent when future
interaction was anticipated than when it was not, but that when the opponent
was seen to be self-effacing the reverse would be true. The results supported
the prediction.

The analysis of bargaining behavior within
the context of two-person games has been
the subject of considerable research in recent
years. In contrast to an early concern with
economic and mathematical considerations
(Luce & Raiffa, 1957), recent investigations
have emphasized the interpersonal aspects of
the bargaining situation. These latter studies
view bargaining as a special instance of social
interaction amenable to analysis within the
framework of experimental social psychology.
Deutsch and Krauss (1960), for example,
studied the effects of unilateral and bilateral
threat on the ability of persons to reach agreement in a simulation game; Scodel, Minas,
Ratoosh, and Lipetz (1959) and Minas,
Scodel, Marlowe, and Rawson (1960) examined bargaining behavior in a two-person
game under varying communication conditions, payoff values, and opponent strategies;
Deutsch (1958) related bargaining behavior
to the variables of trust and suspicion; and
Solomon (1960) investigated the influence of
various power relationships on bargaining
strategies. The focus in the majority of these
studies has been on the degree to which a
person will cooperate with or exploit an opponent under varying stimulus conditions. In
general, these investigations seem to indicate
that unless cooperative strategies are fostered
through special experimental instructions or
intersubject communication, persons will
choose to compete with one another and will
play in such a way as to maximize the differ-

ence between their own and their partner's
payoffs.

Given the recent trend toward viewing
economic bargaining as a form of social interaction, it has been only natural to seek personality and attitudinal correlates of bargaining
behavior. Using a two-person game of the
prisoner's-dilemma format, Deutsch (1960)
reported that authoritarians (as measured by
the F Scale) tended to be less trusting of
the other player and to make more uncooperative
choices. Marlowe (1963) found that passive-
dependent persons were disposed to respond
to unconditionally cooperative behavior with
cooperation on their own part. And Lutzker
(1960) reported that internationally minded
as compared to isolationists were more cooperative in a two-person game. Though few
in number, such experimental studies are consistent in indicating that reliable differences
in bargaining behavior are associated with
personality predispositions of the players.

The present investigation sought to continue and broaden the emphasis on the
social aspects of the bargaining situation by
concentrating on two variables which are
basic to most social relationships. When
two persons are engaged in a real-life bargaining transaction, there are at least two types
of information which are focal in determining the course of the relationship. First,
we generally form at the outset of the relationship some impression of the kind of
person with whom we are dealing. These
impressions may determine to a large degree
the type of behavior manifested towards another person (cf. Davis, 1962; Gergen &

[1] This research was supported by National Science
Foundation Grants G-25113 and GS-562.
[2] Now at Stanford University.

Jones, 1963). Second, one's estimate of the longevity of a relationship may also play an important role. For example, Thibaut and Kelley (1959) have discussed the fact that persons are often more revealing to total strangers than to close friends; Gergen and Wishnov (1965) have explored the effects of varying the degree of anticipated interaction on the way in which a person will present himself to another.

The variable of interaction anticipation would seem to have special significance for the area of interpersonal bargaining. The vast majority of bargaining studies have been conducted under conditions in which subjects expected no future confrontation with their opponents. However, in everyday relationships, persons seldom find themselves in the highly transient bargaining arena best characterized, perhaps, by the New York Stock Exchange. More typically, people expect to "live" with their behavior, and expect to defend and discuss it in ongoing relationships. This paper, then, reports on two investigations which sought to relate bargaining behavior in a two-person game to the variables of the perceived personality of the opponent [3] and expectation of future interaction with the opponent.

In the first investigation (Experiment I) the aim was simply to demonstrate that when bargaining with a predominantly cooperative other, persons will play more cooperatively when expecting to be confronted by this other than when no postbargaining interaction is anticipated. Here it was reasoned that the exploitation of another person who is trying to be cooperative is socially undesirable behavior. Thus a face-to-face meeting with an exploited partner would create embarrassment, if not arouse guilt for the subject. Hence, it was felt that subjects would feel a stronger disposition to do the gracious thing and cooperate when they expected to be confronted with their behavior.

Given that the expectation of future inter-

action will induce greater cooperation, Experiment II attempted to show that interaction anticipation would have quite different effects on bargaining behavior depending on the perceived personality characteristics of the opponent. At least one major dimension along which persons often characterize others is that of egotism versus humility. As Gergen and Wishnov (1965) have reasoned, interacting with an egotist can often be threatening, and at the outset tends to reduce one's power in a social relationship. The optimum strategy for restoring power when bargaining with an egotist would seem to be successful competition. It was further felt that this tactic would most likely occur when further interaction was anticipated. There would seem to be less need to restore one's power in a relationship which is seen to be short-lived. It was hypothesized then that when dealing with a partner who describes himself in grandiose terms, the direct effects of anticipated interaction (Experiment I) would not hold. Rather, it was expected that when bargaining with an egotistical other the anticipation of further interaction would lead to *greater* exploitation of the partner.

On the other hand, a person who is seen to be self-effacing and humble seems to elicit quite different reactions. Such a person often evokes feelings of pity and nurturance on the part of others. To exploit such a person would give rise to feelings of guilt. Under public scrutiny, the exploitation of such a person would also be conspicuously undesirable. However, it is also just such a person who invites exploitation. The person who displays only his shortcomings lays himself open to the other's advantage. The variation in anticipated interaction should make an important difference concerning which of these two reactions predominates. Feelings of guilt and the undesirable features of exploitation should be particularly salient when further interaction is expected. On the other hand, when one will not be held responsible for his behavior, or have to face his victim, the invitation to exploitation should be accepted. It was thus felt that when dealing with a self-effacing other, the findings of the initial experiment would be replicated even more dramatically. That is, when further inter-

---

[3] Although the term "opponent" has traditionally been used to refer to the participants in two-person games, in many instances the term is misleading. In this study, as in many others, the notion of a game or competition is never specifically introduced to the subjects by the experimenter.

PAUL G. SWINGLE

action is anticipated, little exploitation should take place; when no further interaction is expected, exploitation should be maximal. The hypothesis for Experiment II can thus be summarized as follows: When interacting with a predominantly cooperative other, with anticipation of further interaction, subjects will exploit this other to a greater degree if he is seen to be egotistical than if he is seen to be self-effacing; when no further interaction is anticipated, the reverse will be true.

EXPERIMENT I

This experiment was designed to study the effects of an anticipated social interaction on bargaining behavior. The specific hypothesis was that subjects who bargain with an expectation of later meeting their opponent will make significantly more cooperative choices than persons who bargain with no expectation of later meeting their opponent.

Method

Subjects. Twenty-three college males, all freshmen at Harvard University, participated in the experiment. Students were chosen at random from the university directory and asked to serve in a study of bargaining and decision making. Virtually all the students contacted agreed to serve. The subjects were informed that they would be paid a minimum of $1.50 for their time, and that they would "have an opportunity to make more money."

Procedure. Subjects participated in the experiment in groups ranging in size from four to six. Upon arriving at the experimental site each subject was seated at a large table. The table was partitioned in such a way that subjects could neither see, signal, nor otherwise communicate with each other. The experiment was described by the experimenter as focusing on the way in which persons make decisions when bargaining with each other under restricted conditions. Subjects were told that each would be working with a partner, ostensibly one of the other subjects at the table. A series of decisions were to be made by each subject and his partner, and as a result of these decisions various amounts of money could be made. During these instructions and those which followed the experimenter never used such words as "win," "lose," "beat," "game," "opponent." In this way it was hoped that the arousal of strictly competitive motives could be avoided.

Subjects were then introduced to what has formally been termed a non-zero-sum game. Such a game can be contrasted with the zero-sum game in which there is no possibility for players to increase their payoffs through cooperation. Subjects were told that they would be faced with a number of decision trials and that on each trial they would be re-

quired to choose between pressing either a black or a red button. Each subject was led to believe that his partner would simultaneously be deciding which of the two buttons to press. On each trial there were thus four possible combinations which could occur for any subject pair. Subjects were then introduced to a payoff matrix which was posted in front of each subject and which displayed the amounts of money each would obtain for each of the four combinations. It was explained to the subjects that if on any trial both partners chose red, each would receive $.01; if both chose black each would receive $.03; if one chose red and the other chose black, the first would receive $.05 and the second would receive nothing. As can be seen, this game is of the standard "prisoner's-dilemma" variety (cf. Rapoport & Orwant, 1962).

After the game had been thoroughly explained, half of the subject groups (confrontation condition) were told:

> In the past we have found that we can learn much more about what went on if we have each pair of subjects meet with me to discuss why they behaved as they did. So, after we have finished here, you will meet with the person you bargained with to discuss why you behaved as you did.

For the remaining subject pairs these instructions were omitted (no-confrontation condition).

The apparatus used to conduct the game was similar to that devised by Crutchfield (1955) to study conformity behavior. With this equipment the subjects' choices register on the experimenter's panel. By throwing various switches the experimenter can inform each subject of the choice which his partner has made, and at the same time also indicate the resultant payoff. The experimenter can, of course, supply the subjects with inaccurate information and announce whatever choices the concerns of the study demand. The present experiment consisted of 30 trials. On 24 of these trials each subject was informed that his partner had chosen "Black" (the cooperative choice). The "partner's" Red choices were randomly distributed over Trials 4–30. Each subject was thus led to believe that his partner was playing a predominantly cooperative game, and was thus faced with a dilemma. He could select Black and thereby maximize joint gain ($.03 each), or he could press Red and exploit his partner's good intentions ($.05 for him and nothing for his partner). Inasmuch as it was the only choice which avoided the maximization of joint gain, the number of trials on which the subject selected Red served as a measure of exploitation.

After the game had been terminated all subjects were supplied with an adjective check list containing 81 adjectives arranged in alphabetical order. Subjects were asked to place a check by those 10 adjectives which they felt best described their partner. After completing the check list subjects in the confrontation condition were informed that they would not have to meet their partner because, "we are short of time and have collected enough data." After paying the subjects what they had earned in the game and for their participation in the experiment, the subjects were allowed to depart.

Results and Discussion

The mean number of Red (exploitative) choices made by the subjects in the no-confrontation conditions was 24.5 ($n = 12$), as compared to a mean of 19.1 in the confrontation condition ($n = 11$). The difference between these means is significant beyond the .05 level ($t = 2.34$).[4] Thus, in line with the prediction, subjects who expected to discuss their behavior after bargaining were significantly less exploitative (or more cooperative).

It was ventured above that the exploitation of a well-intentioned other, combined with the knowledge that one will be confronted by this other, leads to anticipatory guilt or embarrassment and thus the avoidance of exploitation. However, this explanation depends on the supposition that subjects did, indeed, perceive the partner as well-intentioned. Although four out of every five choices which the partner made were cooperative, there is an alternative way in which such choices might have been viewed by the subjects. The persistent selection of Black could have been seen as an attempt on the partner's part to seduce the subject into choosing Black, with the partner then intending to defect to Red. However, a perusal of the adjectives used to describe the partner indicates that this latter way of viewing the partner was very unlikely. The five adjectives most frequently checked as being descriptive of the partner were: persistent, conservative, dependable, naive, and generous. Those most infrequently checked were: treacherous, tolerant, tactful, neat, and greedy.

It would seem, then, that the disposition to act more equitably under conditions of confrontation serves to enhance one's public image. In the no-confrontation condition whatever guilt or embarrassment is aroused is largely personal and not in itself sufficient to inhibit exploitation. This result is reminiscent of the findings in the area of conformity and social influence which indicate that behavioral conformity is enhanced under conditions of

[4] All tests of significance reported are two-tailed.

public surveillance (Argyle, 1957; Mouton, Blake, & Olmstead, 1956).

EXPERIMENT II

Experiment I indicated that under circumstances in which no information is available regarding the person with whom one is bargaining, there is a tendency for subjects to be more exploitative when they anticipate no postbargaining confrontation. One personality dimension which should interact significantly with a variation in interaction anticipation is egotism versus humility. This consideration lent itself to a 2×2 factorial design with the crosscutting dimensions of opponent's personality (egotistical versus humble) and interaction anticipation (confrontation versus no confrontation). The procedure for this experiment was highly similar to that of Experiment I, but may be compared in the following respects:

Subjects. The subjects were 44 Harvard freshmen recruited in the same manner as those used in Experiment I. Care was taken to obtain subjects not living in the same dormitories as those previously used. Eleven subjects were assigned at random to each of the four experimental conditions.

Procedure. Subjects were again seated at the partitioned table and told that the experiment dealt with various aspects of bargaining and decision making. However, in addition, the experimenter indicated that he was interested in some of the social aspects of bargaining and that each subject would be asked to describe himself on a set of forms which would then be given to his partner to examine. In this manner, subjects were told, they would each be able to form some sort of impression of the person with whom they would be bargaining.

All subjects were then provided with a 14-item questionnaire. Nine of these items were in the form of 12-point rating scales anchored at the extremes with such phrases as "clear-thinking"–"fuzzy-minded," and "efficient"–"inefficient," etc. The remaining items were taken from the Janis and Field (1959) self-esteem scale. A representative item was, "In general, how confident do you feel about your abilities?" Subjects answered on a 5-point scale which ranged from "very" to "not at all." Subjects were asked not to place their names on the questionnaires.

After the questionnaires were completed and collected, each subject was provided with either one of two especially prepared questionnaires which ostensibly had been filled out by his partner. These questionnaires were intended to create either the impression that the partner was egotistical or that he was extremely humble or modest. The first nine items on the questionnaire had earlier been given to an independent group of undergraduates. From the ratings made by this group it was possible to establish modal response patterns for the various scales. For the present experiment the questionnaire for the egotistical partner was prepared in such a way that the scale points checked were always closer to the positive end of the scale than the modal responses by 2 scale points. On the other hand, the self-ratings for the "humble partner" always differed from the modal responses by 2 scale points toward the negative end of the scale. On the self-esteem measure the egotistical partner always endorsed the most extreme positive position, while the humble partner always endorsed the most negative position on each of the five items.

After the subjects had been given an opportunity to read the ratings made by their supposed partners, they were given a six-item questionnaire on which they were to rate their impression of their partner. These ratings were not to be seen by the partner. Half of the subject groups were then given the same instructions that subjects in the confrontation condition had been given in Experiment I. The remaining subject groups received no such instructions.

The game used in this experiment was identical to that used in the initial experiment, and the subjects again found their partner to be almost persistently cooperative. After the game was completed, subjects were given the same six-item questionnaire filled out just prior to the game and asked to consider again their impressions of their partner. The session was terminated in the same manner as the initial experiment.

Results

Before examining the results regarding subjects' bargaining behavior, it is appropriate to ask whether the attempt to manipulate the subjects' perception of the partner's personality was effective. The first impression ratings, made by the subjects immediately after being exposed to self-ratings supposedly made by their partner, provide a direct check on the effectiveness of this manipulation. These impression ratings were made on a number of 12-point scales. Two of these scales ("self-centered versus humble" and "modest versus conceited") referred specifically to the intended personality induction. Combining the ratings made on these two scales, the mean ratings of subjects facing the egotistical partner were compared by a t test with the mean ratings of those expecting to interact with a humble partner ($n = 22$ for both groups). With a range of possible scores from 2 to 24, the former group obtained a mean of 22.05, whereas the mean for the latter group was only 6.36. The difference between these means is highly significant ($t = 19.7$, $p < .00001$). Quite clearly, the manipulation of perceived personality was effective.

Turning to the major results, it will be recalled that an interaction between perceived personality and expectancy of interaction was predicted. More specifically, it was hypothesized that when expecting a postexperimental confrontation, subjects would exploit the egotistical partner more than the humble partner, but that when no further interaction was anticipated the reverse would be true. The dependent variable in Experiment II (as in Experiment I) was the number of exploitative (Red) choices made by subjects over the 30 trials. Figure 1 presents the mean number of Red choices made in the four conditions, while Table 1 contains the results of an analysis of variance performed on this data. As can be seen in Table 1, there were no significant main effects due to either the perceived personality or the confrontation variables. As anticipated, however, there is a significant personality confrontation interaction ($p < .05$). Consulting Figure 1, it can be seen that the configuration of the means lends full support to the major hypothesis. Subjects cooperated more with a humble person they expected to meet than with one they did not expect to meet; when the partner was an egotist, however, there was greater cooperation if they did not expect to interact with him.

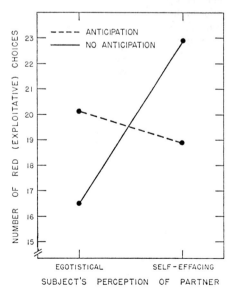

FIG. 1. Mean number of Red (exploitative) choices for subjects in Experiment II.

TABLE 1

ANALYSIS OF VARIANCE OF EXPLOITATIVE
CHOICES IN EXPERIMENT II

Source	df	MS	F
Confrontation (A)	1	1.21	<1
Partner personality (B)	1	73.05	2.12
A × B	1	158.07	4.58*
Error	40	34.48	

* $p < .05$.

An analysis of the pre-post change scores of subjects' perceptions of the partner revealed several additional facts. These six rating scales were arranged so as to form three distinct perceptual clusters: egotism, independence, and likability. An analysis of the prescores on these three dimensions indicated no significant differences between confrontation and no-confrontation subjects within either condition of perceived personality. In other words, as would be hoped, there were no systematic differences in the way the partner was seen at the outset of the bargaining task which resulted from the variation in confrontation. Second, it was also found that in addition to seeing their partner as more egotistical (as discussed above), subjects facing the egotistical partner also saw him as significantly ($p < .05$) less likable prior to the bargaining task. This finding confirms those of Pepitone (1964).

Finally, whereas the perception of the humble partner was found to be virtually unaltered as a result of the bargaining experience, such was not the case with the egotistical partner. As a result of bargaining with the egotistical partner, subjects came to see him as significantly ($p < .025$) less egotistical, less independent ($p < .025$), and more likable ($p < .05$). In short, it seemed that regardless of confrontation, the predominantly cooperative behavior of the partner in this condition was seen as inconsistent with the personality traits ascribed to him initially. The cooperative behavior, in effect, appeared to alter the subjects' perception so that at the termination of the experiment the perceived differences between the egotistical and humble partner was much less marked (though still significant at beyond the .01 level with regard to perceived egotism). One might be led

to speculate that had the game gone on indefinitely, the differences in exploitation due to initial perceived personality might have eventually washed out.

DISCUSSION

The results of Experiment I indicate quite clearly that when no personal information is available concerning the person with whom one is bargaining, and this other plays a predominantly cooperative game, there is a greater tendency to exploit this other when not expecting a later confrontation. The findings from Experiment II, however, modify this picture substantially. When personal information becomes available regarding the other, this information may indeed reverse the role of the confrontation variable. Specifically, when the other person is perceived to be egotistical and self-centered, he is *more* likely to be exploited when future interaction is anticipated than when it is not.

The prediction of this latter finding was based on the assumption that a boastful other tends to force those with whom he interacts into an undesirable low status position. This state of affairs can be described as an imbalance in displayed power, and may be reacted to by attempts to redress the imbalance. In the Gergen and Wishnov (1965) study, for example, subjects faced with an egotist began describing themselves in an extremely positive manner and would not reveal shortcomings. However, it would appear that the need to redress an imbalance in displayed power is less powerful when the interaction is seen to be short-lived. The expectancy of being confronted by an egotist who may have been very exploitative would seem to be an intimidating experience, demanding the defensive reaction of exploitation. In line with this speculation, there was a tendency for female subjects in the Gergen and Wishnov study to magnify their positive features to a greater extent when future interaction with the egotist was anticipated. The male subjects in the present experiment seem to have demonstrated a similar tendency to an even greater extent through their differential exploitation of the egotist as a function of their expectancy of confrontation.

Turning to the subjects' reactions to the humble partner, interpretation of the results raises certain difficulties. It was initially speculated that the self-effacing partner would instigate two opposing tendencies for subjects: the humility of the partner would cause them to feel embarrassed if they engaged in exploitation, and yet this same humility would increase the likelihood that monetary rewards could be obtained through exploitation. It was hypothesized that the variation in confrontation would split these tendencies in such a way that embarrassment would become more salient when interaction was anticipated, and exploitation would become more attractive when there was no possibility of being held responsible for one's actions.

Some check on these speculations can be obtained by comparing the amount of exploitation of the humble partner in Experiment II with the degree to which the partner about whom nothing was known in Experiment I was exploited. In Experiment II all the factors operating to produce the results of Experiment I should be present in addition to those created by the knowledge of the partner's humility. If the above speculations are correct, in Experiment II there should have been more exploitation in the no-confrontation condition and less in the confrontation condition than found in Experiment I. Consulting the results of the two experiments, it is found that these expectations are only partially verified. In the confrontation conditions the results were in the anticipated direction; when the partner was seen as humble the mean number of Red button presses was 18.9, whereas it was 19.1 when there was no personal information available. On the other hand, in the no-confrontation condition when the partner was seen as humble the mean was 22.9; when there was no information available it was 24.5. The indication is that the humble partner tended to elicit fewer exploitative choices regardless of expectancy of confrontation. Although this tendency does not reach statistical significance, it does cast some doubts on the speculation that the humble other invites exploitation when he does not have to be confronted. If anything, the results seem to suggest that there is a generalized pity felt for the humble other, and this feeling manifests itself across conditions. These results have some parallel in the Gergen and Wishnov (1965) finding that subjects would, out of commiseration, reveal more of their negative features to a self-derogating other regardless of whether they expected a long-term relationship or not.

One might raise questions about the relationship of this study, as well as others done in a bargaining context, to more general forms of human behavior. Is the two-person game, in other words, not too rarefied for the results to be translated into useful and cogent principles of social interaction? For those who believe bargaining behavior to be sufficiently intriguing in and of itself, this question may be of little moment. However, one of the major intents of the present study was to highlight the relationship between pure experimental games and more broadly pervasive social factors. In one sense, the experimental game thus becomes a useful vehicle for testing out ideas concerning social interaction. Regarding the present experiment, it is not difficult to think of social situations which have conceptual similarities. One might be led to predict, for example, the reactions of peers in a business organization to each other. In such organizations one is often faced with the choice of competitive exploitation versus cooperation for mutual benefit. The present experiment would suggest at least two important factors, namely, perceived personality and amount of anticipated interaction, which would determine which of these choices would be made.

REFERENCES

Argyle, M. Social pressure in public and private situations. *Journal of Abnormal and Social Psychology,* 1957, **54**, 172–175.

Crutchfield, R. S. Conformity and character. *American Psychologist,* 1955, **10**, 191–198.

Davis, K. E. Impressions of others and interaction context as determinants of social interaction in two person discussion groups. Unpublished doctoral dissertation, Duke University, 1962.

Deutsch, M. Trust and suspicion. *Journal of Conflict Resolution,* 1958, **2**, 267–279.

Deutsch, M. Trust, trustworthiness, and the F Scale. *Journal of Abnormal and Social Psychology,* 1960, **61**, 138–140.

DEUTSCH, M., & KRAUSS, R. M. The effect of threat on interpersonal bargaining. *Journal of Abnormal and Social Psychology*, 1960, **61**, 181–189.

GERGEN, K. J., & JONES, E. E. Mental illness, predictability, and affective consequences as stimulus factors in person perception. *Journal of Abnormal and Social Psychology*, 1963, **67**, 95–104.

GERGEN, K. J., & WISHNOV, BARBARA. Others' self-evaluations and interaction anticipation as determinants of self-presentation. *Journal of Personality and Social Psychology*, 1965, **2**, 348–358.

JANIS, I. L., & FIELD, P. B. Sex differences and personality factors related to persuasibility. In C. I. Hovland & I. L. Janis (Eds.), *Personality and persuasibility*. New Haven: Yale Univer. Press, 1959. Pp. 55–68.

LUCE, R. D., & RAIFFA, H. *Games and decisions.* New York: Wiley, 1957.

LUTZKER, D. R. Internationalism as a predictor of cooperative behavior. *Journal of Conflict Resolution*, 1960, **4**, 426–430.

MARLOWE, D. Psychological needs and cooperation vs. competition in a two-person game. *Psychological Reports*, 1963, **13**, 364.

MINAS, J. S., SCODEL, A., MARLOWE, D., & RAWSON, H. Some descriptive aspects of two-person, non-zero-sum games. Part II. *Journal of Conflict Resolution*, 1960, **4**, 193–197.

MOUTON, JANE S., BLAKE, R. R., & OLMSTEAD, J. A. The relationship between frequency of yielding and disclosure of personal identity. *Journal of Personality*, 1956, **24**, 339–347.

PEPITONE, A. *Attraction and hostility.* New York: Atherton Press, 1964.

RAPOPORT, A., & ORWANT, C. Experimental games· A review. *Behavioral Science*, 1962, **7**, 1–37.

SCODEL, A., MINAS, J. S., RATOOSH, P., & LIPETZ, M. Some descriptive aspects of two-person non-zero-sum games. *Journal of Conflict Resolution*, 1959, **3**, 114–119.

SOLOMON, L. The influence of some types of power relationships and game strategies on the development of interpersonal trust. *Journal of Abnormal and Social Psychology*, 1960, **61**, 223–230.

THIBAUT, J. W., & KELLEY, H. H. *The social psychology of groups.* New York: Wiley, 1959.

(Received September 11, 1964)

PAUL G. SWINGLE

Reprinted from Journal of Conflict Resolution, 1965, Vol. 9, pp. 491–508, by permission
of the authors and the publisher.

―――――――   ―――――――

Gaming

―――――――   ―――――――

War Hawks and Peace Doves: alternate resolutions of experimental conflicts

MARC PILISUK, PAUL POTTER, ANATOL RAPOPORT, and J. ALAN WINTER[1]

The two-person, two-choice Prisoner's Dilemma game offers the players an opportunity to demonstrate either trust, by choosing the cooperative (C) response, or suspicion, by choosing the defection (D) response (Deutsch, 1958). In the conventional experimental situation each of the players has an opportunity to make only the completely cooperative response or the completely defecting response. Cooperative responses when made by both players provide rewards to both. Defecting responses, if they are mutual, are detrimental to both players. The incentive to defect, however, derives from the nature of payoffs following asym-

[1] Research relating to this project was made possible by assistance from the following sources: National Science Foundation, grants G 99 and GS 586; National Institutes of Health, M-423801-02-03-04-05; and Sigma Xi, the Scientific Research Society of America. Marc Pilisuk is now with the Department of Psychology and the Krannert Graduate School, Purdue University; Paul Potter is now with the Economic Research and Action Projects of the Students for a Democratic Society; J. Alan Winter is now with the Department of Sociology, Rutgers University.

metrical choices by the pair members. When one player defects (chooses D) unilaterally while the second player chooses C, the defector is most highly rewarded and to the detriment of the cooperator. When the game is played without communication, rationality (in the strict sense of game theory) provides no solution consistent with the collective interests of the players.

The following example of a payoff matrix for a Prisoner's Dilemma game helps to demonstrate the nature of the dilemma:

		Player A's Choices	
		C	D
Player B's	C	20, 20	−20, 40
Choices	D	40, −20	0, 0

In repeated trials of a game of this kind, a pair of players generally establishes a stable relationship. This relationship is characterized either by a lengthy succession of mutually beneficial outcomes (CC) or by a succession of mutually punishing or non-rewarding outcomes (DD). There are, of course, trials in which only one player tries to cooperate while his partner defects and gains at his expense. But the frequency of such asymmetrical behavior declines after a series of trials and pairs generally fall into either the cooperative pattern or the non-cooperative, from which they depart only rarely (Rapoport, 1965; Pilisuk and Rapoport, 1963). The significance of this lock-in phenomenon lies in the degree to which the game presents a microsimulation of interpersonal behavior. Two individuals are obliged to make a series of behaviors which affect their partner's well-being as well as their own. Eventually, large numbers of these pairs develop a stable interaction pattern which defines them as a social unit.

What characteristics distinguish a cooperating pair of "Peace Doves" from a competing pair of "War Hawks"? Are their personalities different? Are the Doves in a pair more like each other than the members of Hawk pairs? Does the game environment, aside from such obvious experimental manipulation as changing the payoff matrix, affect the relative frequencies of Dove-like or Hawk-like outcomes? And, perhaps of greatest importance to the psychologist, is there a pattern of early play, a system of gestures and responses in the game itself, which so teaches the lesson of cooperation that it is productive of Doves rather than of Hawks?

The game designed to answer these questions is more complex than the two-choice game described previously. The new form permits each player a range of moves in every trial of the game so that his choice is no longer constricted to total cooperation or total defection but may vary from 0 to 20 units of cooperation, as may his partner's choice. The resultant 21 by 21 matrix of possible outcomes is so fixed as to contain the same basic paradox as the 2 by 2 game. Like the 2 by 2 game, the newer design produces its quota of Dove pairs, Hawk

pairs, and some intermediary ("Mugwump") pairs.

The difference is that the newer game more closely approximates many actual situations where the choice is not whether to cooperate or not but rather what degree of cooperation to choose. Also, a versatile set of arms-race-simulating conditions, e.g., missile conversion, inspection, etc., are easily fitted to the game (Pilisuk and Rapoport, 1964). And most important, the added choice flexibility permits a more refined study of gestures and responses which may lead players to suspicion or to trust.

Method

A total of 128 male college students (64 pairs) participated as subjects in this study. The experimental room contained booths permitting up to three pairs of subjects to participate simultaneously while completely eliminating visual and verbal contact between pair members. Subjects who knew one another prior to the experimental session were not paired. Recruitment was from volunteers for paid psychological experiments.

Subjects first completed questionnaires used to assess self-acceptance and monetary risk performance. The characteristics of the game were then described to them and play began. Upon completion of games a brief strategy questionnaire was used to obtain subjective descriptions of strategies employed. After the experimental session was completed, subjects were asked to take home and complete the questionnaires which were used to assess tolerance for ambiguity, internationalism, and social risk preference. Upon receipt of completed take-home questionnaires, subjects were paid for their participation in the experiment, in amounts corresponding to their actual achievements in the game.[2]

When play began, the player sat facing an 8″ × 10″ playing board divided into 20 squares. A two-faced poker chip, white on one side, blue on the other, was on each square. All twenty chips were placed white side up at the start. Each player was also given a full matrix of outcomes showing the payoff to each player for every possible combination of choices by himself and by the other player. (A representation of this matrix, reduced to 5 × 5, is presented in Figure 1.) A play consisted of turning any number of discs (from 0 to 20) from white to blue.

The payoffs may be understood as reward-

ing each player one unit (2 monetary mills) for each blue side he exposes. If both players expose an identical number of blue tokens their payoffs are completely determined by this number. In the event of a disparity between the players in the number of blue chips exposed, the player showing *fewer* blue chips is given an additional payoff equal to twice the size of the disparity. For the player showing the larger number of blue tokens an amount equal to twice the disparity is subtracted from his total payoff. If players A and B expose Bl_a and Bl_b blue chips respectively and receive payoffs P_a and P_b respectively, then (1) $P_a = 2Bl_b - Bl_a$ and (2) $P_b = 2Bl_a - Bl_b$.

In other words, conversion to blue chips is rewarding when mutual but punishing to the degree that it is unilateral. Conversely, retention of white chips is nonrewarding if mutual, but rewarding to the extent that it is unilateral. Specifically: (1) if both play-

---

[2] The tolerance for ambiguity measure is a six-point Likert-type scale containing the eighteen items relating to preferences for regularity or change, clarity or ambiguity, balance or asymmetry, etc. Nine items were selected from a pool of F scale correlate items which had been classified by their authors as measures of tolerance for ambiguity (Webster *et al.*, 1955). The remaining nine items were taken from a measure of tolerance for ambiguity reported in a study by O'Connor (1952). The F scale has been shown to predict noncooperation in simple non-zero-sum games. The authors suspected the "cognitive style" aspect of authoritarianism to be more relevant to game performance than the affective or attitudinal components and selected tolerance for ambiguity for measurement.

The self-acceptance measure was included in the battery to test the notion that acceptance of oneself might be instrumental to the development of trust for a partner. People who are less self-accepting tend also to be less accepting of others (Berger, 1952) and, perhaps, less willing to trust the other player in a non-zero-sum game. Fifty items were selected randomly, one-half of all those used in the Q-sort technique reported in Rogers and Dymond (1954). Actual discrepancies between self-image and ideal image were used.

The internationalism scale contained items from other attitude scales (Levinson, 1957;

Samson and Smith, 1957) combined and modified to produce a set of questions which the authors felt might be appropriate for the population at hand. (Copies of the scale are available on request.) Because internationalism was shown to be related to non-zero-sum game behavior (Lutzker, 1960), we anticipated an even greater effect upon game behavior in games loaded with the semantic referents of the arms race.

Since monetary rewards were used in the game we felt that the individual's propensity to take risks might affect his play. Two measures were used to assess an individual's propensity to take risks. The first, a gambling task involving real monetary rewards, was followed by a task of social risk preference.

The monetary risk preference measure consists of a set of choices among actual monetary gambles which subjects make. (Copies are available.) The measure of social risk-taking was reported by Kogan and Wallach (1961). It investigates the chances which people would be willing to take in a series of life-like social situations.

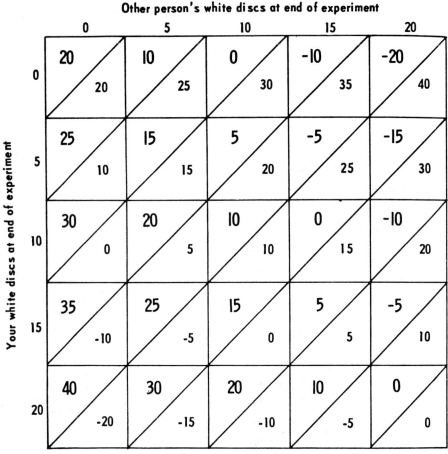

Other person's white discs at end of experiment

FIG. 1. Reduced form of payoff matrix shown to players. The actual matrix used showed all values from 0 to 20. The first figure in each box represents one's own payoff; the second figure, the payoff for the other player.

ers convert fully from white to blue chips, both win 20 units; (2) if neither player converts any tokens to their blue side, neither receives any units; (3) complete unilateral conversion to blue matched against an opposing player's complete retention of white results in a loss of 20 units to the cooperator and a gain of 40 units to the defector; and (4) payoffs between these extremes are determined by both the number of blue chips one exposes and the difference between that number and the number exposed by the other player. The extreme outcomes are identical to those shown in the illustrative two-choice payoff matrix given earlier. Some intermediate outcomes appear in Figure 1.

The game was played in two experimental settings, the *abstract* and the *simulated*. Sixty-four players, one-half the total, played only abstract games. The other half played

PAUL G. SWINGLE

simulated games exclusively. The abstract game has already been described. In it the tokens on the game board are merely tokens, i.e., poker chips which were blue on one side and white on the other. Instructions avoided such evaluative words as "cooperation or competition," "winning or losing," "contest," "opponent," and even "game." While these words were also omitted in the simulated condition, a new set of evaluative symbols was used. The simulated game was introduced with the terminology of an arms-race–disarmament dilemma. A token with its white side showing was referred to as a weapon and contained a schematic picture of a missile upon it. Blue-side-up tokens were called economic units and contained schematic pictures of factories. A game board was a country. The simulated condition was intended to heighten the game's similarity to the arms race without expressing preference for either armament or disarmament.

Payoffs were identical in abstract and simulated conditions. After each play of the 55 plays of the game, a player was informed of his partner's choice by receipt of a note from the experimenter. From this he could refer to his matrix and keep informed of his payoffs.

The second experimental variation involved the manner in which players made their decision as to how far to cooperate or disarm, i.e., how many tokens to turn from white to blue. In the *short game* which has already been described, each player makes a single move converting from zero to twenty of his tokens. The single moves by the two players determine the payoffs to each and terminate that trial or play of the game.

The *long game* consisted of twenty separate moves. On a given move, white chips could be converted to blue, or blue chips

could be converted back to white, provided only that a player might never turn more than two chips on any given move. No feedback was given prior to the twentieth (last) move. Since the intermediate moves of each player had no effect upon payoffs and were not made known to the other participant, the long game appears identical with the short. In fact, the long and short games are *logically* isomorphic. However, they may differ *psychologically*. Forcing players to enact their final decision in gradual steps could alter the decision.

All subjects played 40 short and 15 long games. Half of the subjects began with 40 short games and then played 15 long games. The other half reversed this order. A block design of the experimental variation is shown here:

	Abstract	Simulated
Long First	A_1	S_1
Short First	A_2	S_2

Results[3]

A. SELECTION OF CRITERION PAIRS

The data deal with characteristics of three types of pairs. The pairs were classified into discrete categories in accordance with the performance of both players during the last five games in an experimental session containing 55 games. The pair labels are Dove (cooperators), Hawk (noncooperators), and Mugwump (intermediate). A pair was labeled Dove if (1) both players turned 15 or more of their tokens from white to blue during *each* one of the last

---

[3] Results contained here deal exclusively with the differentiation between criterion groups designated by performance during the last five plays of the game. The effects of experimental conditions on such gross indices of behavior as the average number of tokens turned over in all trials are discussed in Pilisuk and Rapoport (1963).

five games and (2) neither player turned over fewer than 17 tokens per trial, on an average, over these same trials. The Hawk criteria are completely symmetrical. A Hawk pair was so designated where (1) neither player turned more than 5 tokens to their blue side during the last five trials and (2) neither player turned over an average of three tokens or more per trial during these same games. The third and intermediate group, Mugwumps, contains all the remaining pairs which failed to meet the conditions for classification as either Dove or Hawk.

The grouping provides 26 pairs of Doves, 17 pairs of Hawks, and 21 Mugwump pairs. These criterion groups were used for the remainder of the analysis. The groupings, while arbitrary, provide for stringent differentiation between the cooperators (Doves) and the noncooperators (Hawks). (The probability that two players, making random choices, will fall into one of these two groups is less than 10^{-5}.) Some Mugwump pairs, however, were apparently moving toward greater cooperation during the final five trials and might have met the Dove criterion had the experiment continued beyond 55 trials. Some Mugwumps, on the other hand, were showing essentially non-cooperative behavior but not quite to the Hawk criterion. Even among the more homogeneous Dove and Hawk groups, pair histories display some interesting differences as well as similarities. For example, by applying the five-trial block criterion to trials earlier than the last five it is possible to split the Dove pairs into early and later cooperators. And it is possible to identify, among both Hawks and Doves, some few pairs who met the criterion and then lost it. By the end of an hour and a half of game play, however, the Doves were locked into the pattern of mutual cooperation, the Hawks were locked into a conflict of dis-

trust, and the Mugwumps had achieved neither of these stable patterns.

B. THE INFLUENCE OF PERSONALITY VARIABLES

Five personality variables were assessed. They were: (1) self-acceptance; (2) monetary risk preference; (3) tolerance for ambiguity; (4) internationalism; and (5) social risk preference. A brief rationale for the selection of these variables has been given in footnote 2.

We asked two questions about the differences in the personalities of the Doves, Hawks, and Mugwumps. First, we asked: Do the individual Doves, Hawks, and Mugwumps differ on the dimensions of personality we thought relevant to game behavior? That is, is the average Dove (or Hawk or Mugwump) different from members of the other two groups? Second, we asked: Do pair members among Dove, Hawk, or Mugwump pairs differ in the extent to which they are similar to their partners? The import of the second question may be seen in two variants of it. Do members of a pair of Doves resemble one another more closely or less closely than members of a typical Hawk or Mugwump pair? And does the instability of the Mugwumps' resolution reflect a greater personality disparity between partners than might be found among either Doves or Hawks?

Mean scores on each of the five individual difference measures are contrasted for Doves, Hawks, and Mugwumps in Table 1.

Examination of the differences between means on each variable presents a consistent and negative picture. The F values are not statistically significant. The variables selected here do not predict well to criterion group performance. With the possible exception of tolerance for ambiguity, which may favor the potential for achievement of

TABLE 1

PERSONALITY DIFFERENCES AMONG DOVES, HAWKS, AND MUGWUMPS

Personality Measures	Means			$F_2/127$	p
	Doves	Hawks	Mugwumps		
Self-acceptance[a]	1.885	1.545	2.007	0.03	NS
Tolerance for Ambiguity[b]	−10.038	−3.618	−3.929	0.003	NS
Internationalism	21.558	25.235	24.262	0.01	NS
Monetary Risk Preference	45.154	47.029	45.905	0.003	NS
Social Risk Preference	45.250	45.353	43.619	0.003	NS

[a] Low scores indicate greater self-acceptance.
[b] Low scores indicate greater tolerance for ambiguity.

the Dove group criterion, there is little even to suggest that personality characteristics might be exerting a noticeable influence. This may appear in some contrast to the work of Deutsch (1960b) and Lutzker (1960) in the simpler two-choice games, but it must be recalled that they used total cooperation by an individual over all trials of a game.[4] Here, in addition to using a more complex game, the prediction is to the *terminal* behavior of the *pair* of players.[5] One negative finding which calls for special note is that internationalism scores did *not* predict significantly to criterion groups, even for those experimental groups playing under the simulated arms-race–disarmament condition. One highly internationalistic subject, an active advocate of disarmament and other liberal causes, displayed game be-

havior which was filled with unpredictable treachery and rearmament, at his opponent's expense. His comments on this performance were that while he felt he ought to move toward disarmament he also felt, at the same time, the challenge of the game. The opportunity he perceived to make a killing was too great.

In one sense, it is not surprising that individual difference variables predict poorly to game outcomes. The very fact that Prisoner's Dilemma games so frequently result in "lock-ins" of either cooperation or noncooperation attests to the fact that randomly matched personalities do come to resemble one another in performance.

Such results suggest that individual personality has little effect on game behavior but do not rule out the possibility that personality characteristics of the pair, the match of traits between partners, may be effective. After all, the fact that diverse players come to resemble one another in game behavior does not explain why the resemblance is in cooperative (Dove-type) behavior in some cases and in much more competitive (Hawk-type) behavior in others. Similarity scores for a pair were obtained, using all personality measures in combination. Each measure was divided into thirds of high, medium, and low scores. When members of a pair both fell into the same third a score of 2 was entered, adjacent

---

[4] Actually the experimental situations are not strictly comparable. Deutsch predicted to the Prisoner's Dilemma game played once. Lutzker's payoff matrix presents the subject with an essentially different problem—the game of "chicken" rather than the Prisoner's Dilemma game. The two games are related, but in "chicken" unilateral cooperation is more rewarding than mutual defection and the motives for noncooperation are thus altered. The matrix shown on p. 491 above would be a "chicken" matrix if (0, 0) were changed to, say, (-25, -25).

[5] Prediction from personality measures to gross levels of cooperation was only slightly more promising. No correlation as large as ± 0.4 was found.

TABLE 2

PERSONALITY SIMILARITY OF DOVES, HAWKS, AND MUGWUMPS[a]

| | SIMILARITY | | |
	Low 5 or less	High 6 or more	N
Doves	50% (13)	50% (13)	26
Hawks	41 (7)	59 (10)	17
Mugwumps	43 (9)	57 (12)	21
	45 (29)	55 (35)	64

[a] Entries are percentages over rows. Numbers in parenthesis are frequencies.

TABLE 3

COMPARISON OF DOVE PAIRS HIGH OR LOW ON TOLERANCE FOR AMBIGUITY WITH COMBINED HAWK AND MUGWUMP PAIRS

| | PAIR RATING ON TOLERANCE FOR AMBIGUITY | | |
	Hi–Hi or Hi–Med	Lo–Lo or Lo–Med	N
Doves	68.5% (13)	31.5% (6)	(19)
Hawks and Mugwumps	30.8 (8)	69.2 (18)	(26)
	46.6 (21)	53.4 (24)	(45)

χ^2: 16.00 $p < 0.01$

NOTE: Actual frequencies are given in parenthesis. N for this table is 45,[*] i.e., 19 Dove pairs and 26 Hawk and Mugwump pairs. Pairs receiving Hi–Lo or Med–Med ratings are excluded from this analysis.

thirds were scored 1, and extreme thirds were scored 0. Summed over five variables this produced a possible range of similarity scores from 10 (very similar) to 0 (very dissimilar). Table 2 compares the more similar pairs (scores of 6 or more) with the less similar pairs (scores of 5 or less).

The data, again, show nothing of statistical significance and hardly anything in trends worthy of further examination. Refinement of similarity indices using actual numerical discrepancies and correcting for small intercorrelations among the separate measures would obviously contribute little to understanding why some pairs become Doves, others Hawks, and others Mugwumps.

One single personality variable seemed to offer better differentiation of criterion groups than did the five-test battery. Pair members who were *both* high on tolerance for ambiguity were more likely to become Doves than were pairs lower on this variable ($p < 0.01$). Pair scores in tolerance for ambiguity are shown related to criterion groups in Table 3.

C. THE INFLUENCE OF THE EXPERIMENTAL SETTING

There were four experimental groups, as shown in the block design (see above, p. 235). Two groups, A_1 and A_2, played only abstract games. Groups S_1 and S_2 played only the simulated arms-race games. Groups A_1 and S_1 each started with fifteen long games followed by forty short games, whereas in groups A_2 and S_2 the forty short games came first. The number of pairs of Doves (cooperators), Hawks (defectors), and Mugwumps (in-betweens) in each of the four conditions is given in Table 4.

The findings in Table 4 can be summarized, but certain interactions between the effects of the two experimental conditions are difficult to interpret. A comparison of the conditions A_1 and S_1 (long first) with the A_2 and S_2 (short first) conditions in both the abstract and simulated forms would tend to indicate that playing the long game first produces more Doves relative to the proportion of Hawks and Mugwumps. This long-short difference tends, however, to be muted in the simulated (S_1 and S_2) conditions. Hence, simulation makes the likelihood of becoming Doves or Mugwumps more nearly equal in the long-first and short-first conditions. However, the likelihood of becoming Hawks, while favored by the short-first conditions, shows this effect most markedly under simulated conditions.

TABLE 4

THE EFFECT OF EXPERIMENTAL VARIATIONS ON FORMATION OF CRITERION GROUPS

	Doves		Hawks		Mugwumps		
Abstract—Long First (A₁)	68.8%	(11)	25.0%	(4)	6.2%	(1)	16
Abstract—Short First (A₂)	12.5	(2)	31.2	(5)	56.2	(9)	16
Simulated—Long First (S₁)	50.0	(8)	12.5	(2)	37.5	(6)	16
Simulated—Short First (S₂)	31.2	(5)	37.5	(6)	31.2	(5)	16
	40.6	(26)	26.5	(17)	32.8	(21)	64

χ^2 (total) 15.22; $p < 0.06$ (df: 2); χ^2 (interaction) 5.77; $p < 0.05$ (df: 2).

Arms-race labels, then, seem to be of secondary import and seem not to exert independent effects upon criterion groups. The labels do, however, show some effects in interaction with the other experimental condition.

The apparent conduciveness of long-first conditions A_1 and S_1 to the production of cooperating Doves may be seen in Table 5, which contrasts all long-first games with all short-first games.

This comparison shows, rather clearly, that partners who started by playing the slower long games and then switched to the rapid short ones were quite likely to turn into cooperating Doves. Conversely, those who began with the rapid short games were more likely to turn into either the undistinguished Mugwumps or the uncooperative Hawks. Whether this distinction is a function of boredom and/or need for activity is not known. Certainly, in starting from a fully armed position, twenty separate opportunities to do something—in this case, to disarm—may be more difficult to resist than a single opportunity. Full control of this "mechanical" feature would require a reversal of the game with the initial level being the disarmed state. At this point, another hunch is that a cognitive reappraisal process quite apart from boredom is operating to induce cooperation (see discussion below).

When all players of abstract games are compared with all players in the arms-race-simulating games, the insignificance of simulation stands out clearly (see Table 6). Abstract games produce the same number of Doves, of Hawks, and of Mugwumps as do simulated games. In terms of final outcome for the pair, arms-race labels apparently make no difference.

One might argue that the absence of effects of the arms-race label should be expected, because the label does not affect the strategic structure of the game. However, the long and the short versions of the game are also strategically equivalent. Yet pronounced differences are observed in the two versions. Why? The authors suspect that something in the protracted nature of the long game permits more time for cognitive reappraisal of alternatives. Some yet unpublished results suggest that when the "player" is actually a team of three persons, a period of communication within the team (but not between teams) increases cooperation (Martin, 1964). Perhaps time favors such reappraisal by giving the individual player more chance to discuss alternatives with himself. Once begun, the rewards of the cooperative path tend to be reinforcing and self-perpetuating even if a switch is made to the short game.

D. EARLY DIFFERENCES IN PLAY

Criterion groups were distinguished, orig-

TABLE 5

THE EFFECT OF LENGTH OF INITIAL 15 GAMES ON FORMATION OF CRITERION GROUPS

	Doves	Hawks	Mugwumps	
Long First (A_1 & S_1)	59.4% (19)	18.8% (6)	21.9% (7)	32
Short First (A_2 & S_2)	21.9 (7)	34.4 (11)	43.7 (14)	32
	31.2 (26)	26.5 (17)	32.8 (21)	64

χ^2: 9.34; $p < 0.01$ (df: 2).

inally, by their performance on the last five of 55 consecutive games. Early experience in each of these criterion groups is defined by pair behavior during the first five games, in particular, but also by pair behavior in games six through ten.

Three measures of early game behavior were used: (1) *cooperativeness*, measured by the number of tokens turned from white to blue—the greater the number, the more cooperative; (2) *cooperative gesture*, defined as a play of the game in which a player converts 10 or more tokens, one-half or more of his total, from white to blue (in any given trial there may be a cooperative gesture by both, by one, or by neither player); (3) *discrepant outcome*, defined as a game in which one player converts five or more tokens from white to blue in excess of the number turned by his partner. The significance of discrepant outcomes, as a measure, is that they indicate an experience in which one player has gained at the other's expense. It means that one player on that trial was, unilaterally, cooperating more than his adversary. Over a period of five trials it is possible for both players to have both experiences—being at the short end and at the long end of the discrepant outcome. It is also possible that only one player experiences the short end; or discrepant outcomes may have been totally absent.

D-1. Some indicators of cooperativeness in early play. First let us consider each token turned from white to blue, from missile to factory, during any block of five trials of the game, to be a cumulative index of the cooperation achieved by that pair: i.e., the greater the number turned, the more the cooperation. Then, separating the Doves, Hawks, and Mugwumps according to their eventual performance as before, we find some very early differentiation between groups. During the first five trials the average Dove converted 8.5 tokens per game, the average Hawk 4.8 tokens, and the average Mugwump 4.2. (The Hawk–Mugwump difference is not statistically significant.) Fuller data are shown in Table 7.

The amount of cooperation for each of the three criterion groups may be calculated for every block of five nonoverlapping trials, as shown in Figure 2.

The Dove group clearly retains its dis-

TABLE 6

THE EFFECT OF ABSTRACTNESS ON FORMATION OF CRITERION GROUPS

	Doves	Hawks	Mugwumps	
Abstract (A_1 & A_2)	40.6% (13)	28.1% (9)	31.2% (10)	32
Simulated (S_1 & S_2)	40.6 (13)	25.0 (8)	34.4 (11)	32
	31.2 (26)	26.5 (17)	32.8 (21)	64

χ^2: 0.11; NS (df: 2).

TABLE 7

COOPERATIVENESS IN EARLY GAMES

Games	Doves	Hawks	Mug-wumps	$F_2/637$	p
1–5	8.5	4.8	4.2	26.66	<0.05
6–10	9.3	3.3	5.1	35.76	<0.05

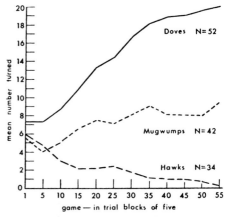

FIG. 2. Comparison of time courses of co-operative moves between three criterion groups distinguished by pair performances on the last five trials.

tinctiveness from the others. The Hawk group establishes itself below the Mugwumps on the seventh trial and remains there through all remaining trials. In sum, then, our findings show that Doves start higher on the cooperativeness index and ascend rapidly. Hawks start lower and decline, while Mugwumps start lower and ascend slowly.

The very fact that lock-ins (of Dove-like cooperation or Hawk-like defection) do occur suggests a degree to which partners come to play like each other. But how alike were partners during the first five games? Some insight into this question is given by calculating the performance of Dove members from each Dove pair who cooperated less than their partners. Average cooperation for the more niggardly Doves was 6.6 tokens per games (first five games). This still exceeds the average Hawk player's 4.8 tokens and even exceeds the average of the more cooperative member of each Hawk pair, which was 5.6 tokens.

The finding suggests that the relatively high level of early cooperation by those who later proved themselves to be Doves was not the result of a single player extending himself unilaterally. However, other findings reopen the question. If we examine the case in which one *and only one* player converted more than 50 percent of his tokens from white to blue (disarmament), we find that 10 out of 26 Dove pairs met this criterion over the first five games. Meanwhile, only two out of 17 Hawk pairs and two out of 21 Mugwump pairs showed one and only

one member cooperating more than halfway.

Again, if we examine the instances in which a disparity of 25 or more tokens (an average of five tokens or more per game) occurred over the first five games, the same pattern emerges. Seven out of 26 Dove pairs showed this disparity. However, only two out of 17 Hawk pairs and three out of 21 Mugwump pairs showed this disparity. Obviously this does not resolve the case for or against the usefulness of early unilateral efforts in predicting ultimate criterion groups. But it does suggest the need for a finer analysis of game-by-game play, and such an analysis follows.

D-2. Early cooperative gestures as predictors of terminal pair performances. The data on cooperative gestures, converting 10 or more of one's white or weapon tokens to blue, are given in Figures 3 through 5.

Certain patterns emerge. First, if a pair had even a single early experience of mutual cooperation, i.e., both making cooperative gestures on the same trial, that pair was likely to become a Dove pair.

Second, we observe that instances of

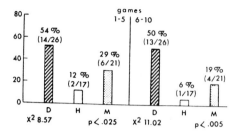

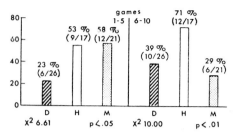

Fig. 3. Percentage of pairs showing at least one mutual cooperative gesture. D: Doves; H: Hawks; M: Mugwumps.

Fig. 5. Percentage of pairs showing (four or more) mutual noncooperative gestures. Use of four or more as an index reflects an approximate median split.

simultaneous gestures of cooperation were relatively infrequent during early play. The occurrence of unilateral gestures was more frequent among each of the three criterion groups.

Third, few of the Mugwump pairs were making cooperative gestures during the first five trials. The situation changed in the second five trials. Here numerous Mugwump pairs showed such gestures. But— as may be seen in Table 8—the gestures were not made simultaneously and, in fact, they tended to be made by only one player during the entire block of trials. By contrast, individual Hawks extended unilateral gestures of cooperation more often in the very first five trials. But, faced with non-reciprocation, these gestures became much less frequent in the second block of five trials. In sharp contrast, *both members* of

Dove pairs tended to extend gestures during early play. In fact, by the second block of five trials those Dove pairs which were not demonstrating cooperative gestures by both members were likely to be demonstrating few unilateral gestures either. Some Dove pairs apparently showed mutual willingness to cooperate from the start. The other Dove pairs were apparently more like the Hawks than like the Mugwumps in their early play. This can be seen also in Table 8, which shows that both Dove and Hawk groups increased their frequency of mutually non-cooperative, armed gestures from the first to the second block of five trials, while Mugwumps reduced their frequency of mutual defection.

D-3. Early discrepant outcomes as predictors of terminal pair performance. A discrepant outcome, as noted earlier, means that one player has suffered and the other has benefited during a trial. What does such an experience do to the pair's future? Discrepant outcomes occurred in almost all pairs. Figure 6 compares the instances in which such outcomes were repeated (occurred at least twice within a block of five trials).

During the first five trials, significantly more Doves than Hawks or Mugwumps experienced two or more discrepant outcomes. However, by the second block of five

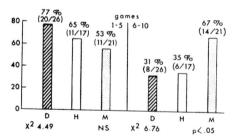

Fig. 4. Percentage of pairs showing at least one unilateral cooperative gesture.

TABLE 8

EFFECT OF RECIPROCATION OF COOPERATIVE GESTURES ON FORMATION OF CRITERION GROUPS

	PRODUCTION OF COOPERATIVE GESTURES		
	Simultaneous and mutual	Unilateral	None	
Games 1–5			
Doves	66% (17)	23% (6)	12% (3)	26
Hawks	12 (2)	65 (11)	24 (4)	17
Mugwumps	29 (6)	29 (6)	43 (9)	21
	32.5 (25)	32.5 (23)	25 (16)	64
Games 6–10			
Doves	54% (14)	8% (2)	34% (10)	26
Hawks	12 (2)	12 (2)	77 (13)	17
Mugwumps	29 (6)	43 (9)	29 (6)	21
	35 (22)	20 (13)	45 (29)	64

NOTE: Figures given are for the occurrence of a single incident. None = mutual non-cooperative or armed gesture.

trials the Dove pairs were performing most congruently, showing fewest discrepant outcomes. Only the Mugwumps increased their frequency of discrepant outcomes during trials six through ten. This finding lends support to a conjecture introduced earlier— that even before the lock-in occurs, Dove and Hawk pairs tend to be moving toward greater symmetry (or sensitivity) in play than is true for the Mugwumps.

Figure 6 does not indicate whether the repeated occurrences of discrepant outcomes always favored the same player or whether both players had the experience of being

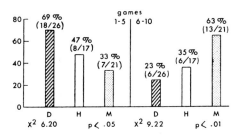

FIG. 6. Percentage of pairs showing repeated (two or more) discrepant outcomes.

both victor and vanquished. Table 9 contrasts relative frequencies with which the discrepant experiences were reciprocal, unidirectional, or entirely absent for the three criterion groups.

During the first five games, only the Dove pairs showed a high frequency of cases in which both players experienced the discrepancy from both directions. By the second block of five trials, the Doves and the Hawks showed the greatest number of pairs with no discrepant outcomes at all. The Mugwump pairs were still showing discrepancies during those trials. The data suggest that early experience of the good (and bad) effects of incongruent performance is an indication of future Dove-like cooperation—*if* each player has had a taste of the medicine of being caught disarmed and an opportunity of seeing the other player cooperate more than himself.

Discussion and Conclusions

The terminal states of Dove, Hawk, and Mugwump may be viewed as products of

TABLE 9

RECIPROCATION OF DISCREPANT OUTCOMES AND THE FORMATION OF CRITERION GROUPS

| | PRODUCTION OF DISCREPANT OUTCOMES | | | |
	Reciprocal	Unidirectional	None	
	Games 1–5			
Doves	42% (11)	50% (13)	8% (2)	26
Hawks	6 (1)	71 (12)	23 (4)	17
Mugwumps	14 (3)	53 (11)	33 (7)	21
	24 (15)	56 (36)	20 (13)	64
χ^2: 11.69; $p < 0.025$				
	Games 6–10			
Doves	62% (16)	31% (8)	8% (2)	26
Hawks	12 (2)	71 (12)	17 (3)	17
Mugwumps	43 (9)	38 (8)	19 (4)	21
	42 (27)	44 (28)	14 (9)	64
χ^2: 6.87; $p < 0.10$				

the forces that bring individuals into social units which are either cohesive and facilitative, or divisive and despairing, or uncertain and unstable. Evidence from this experiment suggests that the locus of these forces lies primarily in the circumstances of the interaction rather than in such characteristics as personality traits brought to the situation. In addition, the early trials of interaction, like the early years, may have enduring effects upon later behavior.

From analysis of early interaction it seems clear that the interaction pattern which induces mutual cooperation is a two-party affair. For lasting cooperation, parties to a conflict situation do have to make overtures, for that is—in the last analysis—all they can do. But what also seems necessary is that cooperative gestures of the other are met with similar responses on one's own part at early stages in the conflict process.

Gestures of cooperation, whether or not they are defined as we have done here, are clearly both causes and effects of game performance. Our examination of the result of natural game conditions indicates that a unilateral initiative toward cooperation, if not quickly reciprocated (i.e., if it remains unilateral), does not lead to the development of a cooperative pair. On the other hand someone must initiate cooperative play, and it is relatively rare, in the absence of overt communication, that both players do this simultaneously. The findings on cooperative gestures (Table 8) and discrepant outcomes (Table 9) suggest that both unilateral and reciprocal elements are important in game performance. Their relative importance, however, would seem to be most readily determinable in a more structured experimental situation with stooges or a false feedback procedure.

At some point in the sequential moves and countermoves of a conflict situation it seems likely that a person takes cognizance of the intent which the other player is trying to communicate (or perhaps communicating without trying) through his moves. One subject, for example, offered the following comment after the experiment: "At first I thought he [the other player] was stupid letting me win like that. But after a while I saw that he was trying to get me to turn over more factories so we could both win." Obviously, there was a cost involved here in the signaling of intent. The authors are currently working on a modification of the game which permits signals of intention, in the form of inspections, without cost to either player.

The realization that behavior can be used to communicate one's hopes and expectations and threats to the other player raises the contest from what may be viewed initially as a game against nature, a game in which the other's moves are only partly predictable and wholly out of reach of one's influence. A second realization, however, seems even more critical for enduring cooperation in a pair. It is the experience that both oneself and the other party are really part of the same system, unified by a common fate, and no longer independent decision-makers. Viewed from this perspective, the game does have a rational or strategic resolution which is easily found: cooperate fully on every trial. We have numerous instances of such comments as: "I could see from the start that turning them all over was the only thing for *us* to do." This perception of "we" or "us" is clearest if we look at some comments of Dove pairs whose cooperation came late and who played more like Hawks at the beginning. "I could see at this point that *we were both* in a rut and weren't going anyplace." The data we have showing more frequent early instances of mutual cooperative gestures by Dove pairs or more frequent reversing of roles in the case of discrepant outcomes suggest the very conditions which might teach the lesson of interdependence and common destiny.

Why a pair of potential antagonists seems better able to learn this during an early run of protracted decision games (long games) than during an equivalent run of short games is not entirely clear. At this point, our best guess seems to be that slowing the pace of the decision process, before the pattern of play has settled, enhances the opportunity for players to recast their concept of the conflict situation. Such cognitive recasting could then produce the realization that (1) communication through behavior is occurring, or (2) the two parties are really part of the same system, or both. From among five individual difference measures, only mutual tolerance for ambiguity seemed relevant to arriving at mutual cooperation. The ability to reframe old perceptions is a part of tolerance for ambiguity. The finding would seem consistent with the conclusion that a cognitive recasting which occurs during the moves and countermoves of an interpersonal conflict is necessary for the self-organization of the two parties into a single cohesive unit.

The most remarkable thing about the Hawks as a group is that they hardly ever tried to cooperate. Following a few unilateral and unreciprocated gestures at the very beginning, the frequency of cooperative gestures (either unilateral or reciprocal) becomes so low that one might conclude that one reason why Hawks never learned to cooperate is because they never experimented with or explored the communication channels that the game was structured to provide. One cannot say of them, as a group, that they are more deceitful or treacherous or aggressively competitive players. On the basis of game performance, what stands out is their conservatism, caution, and reluctance to try a new approach. This observation is also supported by the fact that the one personality indicator that did predict to game outcomes was tolerance for ambiguity. Players who were less tolerant of ambiguity seemed unwilling to explore the various potentials in the game situation.

In contrast, the Doves as a group were experimenting with cooperation from the start. Some tried and succeeded early, others failed but tried again later and were successful. Some of them use, and some of them report, interesting strategies of rewards and punishments intended to lure the other player toward mutual trust. The description of such strategies and the search for their determinants and their consequences make an intriguing problem for future research. The Mugwump pairs probably represent several entities. Some may have contained a member who never changed his initial perception that success in the game depended solely upon outsmarting one's partner. Others may have rejected the formation of a predictable social unit because of fascination with gamesmanship—much like the Don Juans who enjoy the hunt but cannot stay with the marriage. One might argue that all individuals faced with sustained interaction do eventually develop stable and reciprocal behavior patterns—but our experiments were continued through only 55 trials.

We have stressed in our conclusions the theme that reciprocal behaviors at an early stage of the interaction process are of major importance in the development of later trust, and that personality indicators seem less relevant. Two alternative theories are brought to the fore by this. The first says that circumstances of play alone determine the resolution of conflict. By chance, this theory would state, certain moves made by one party meet moves made by the other, and the distribution of these random pairings provides the starting point for stochastic

processes (probabilities of performance contingent on the prior happenings) which lead to the final outcomes.

The alternate theory is not that the player's cooperation is a product of some inherent propensity, a personal proclivity which he carries about either to cooperate or not. The extremely high correlation of cooperation rates found between randomly matched pair members seems adquate for rejection of such a theory. But the alternative to the random-start, stochastic-interaction theory is the view that players do bring to the game setting certain proclivities, not to act in a certain way, but rather to *react* in certain ways to the contingent circumstances presented by the other player's behavior. To test this latter theory one will have to think of personality traits as contingent reaction propensities; measure these propensities; and study their effects upon experimentally arranged contingencies of opponent's behavior. This is an important task for future research. What our present reaearch has done is to help crystallize these alternative theories regarding the ways in which interaction synthesizes individuals into social units.

REFERENCES

ATKINSON, J. W., and A. C. RAPHELSON. "Individual Differences in Motivation and Behavior in Particular Situations," *Journal of Personality*, 24 (1956), 349–63.

BERGER, E. M. "The Relation between Expressed Acceptance of Self and Expressed Acceptance of Others," *Journal of Abnormal and Social Psychology*, 47 (1952), 778–83.

BIXENSTINE, V. E., N. CHAMBERS, H. POTASH, and D. V. WILSON. "Effects of Asymmetry in Payoff on Behavior," *Journal of Abnormal and Social Psychology*, 67 (1963), 308–13.

BIXENSTINE, V. E., H. M. POTASH, and D. V. WILSON. "Effects of Cooperative Choice by Other Player on Choices in a Prisoner's Dilemma Game." Manuscript. Nebraska Psychiatric Institute, 1961.

DAVIS, R. H., P. B. CARPENTER, and C. W.

MISSLER. *A Game for Studying the Problems of Arms Control.* Santa Monica, Calif.: Systems Development Corporation, AP-779, 1962.

DEUTSCH, M. "Trust and Suspicion," *Journal of Conflict Resolution,* 2, 4 (Dec. 1958), 265–79.

———. "The Effect of Motivational Orientation upon Threat and Suspicion," *Human Relations,* 13 (1960a), 123–39.

———. "Trust, Trustworthiness, and the F Scale," *Journal of Abnormal and Social Psychology,* 61 (1960b), 138–40.

EDWARDS, W., and P. SLOVIC. "Information Seeking to Reduce the Risk of Decisions." Paper presented at Midwestern Psychological Association, Chicago, May 1962.

FLOOD, M. M. "Some Experimental Games," *Management Science,* 5 (1958), 5–26.

GUETZKOW, H. "A Use of Simulation in the Study of Inter-Nation Relations," *Behavioral Science,* 3 (1957), 183–91.

KOGAN, N., and M. A. WALLACH. "The Effect of Anxiety on Relations Between Subjective Age and Caution in an Older Sample." In P. H. HOCH and J. ZUBIN (eds.), *Psychopathology of Aging.* New York: Grune and Stratton, 1961.

LEVINSON, D. J. "Authoritarian Personality and Foreign Policy," *Journal of Conflict Resolution,* 1, 1 (Mar. 1957), 37–57.

LOOMIS, J. L. "Communication, the Development of Trust and Cooperative Behavior," *Human Relations,* 12 (1959), 305–15.

LUCE, R. D., and H. RAIFFA. *Games and Decisions.* New York: Wiley, 1957.

LUTZKER, D. "Internationalism as a Predictor of Cooperative Game Behavior," *Journal of Conflict Resolution,* 4, 4 (Dec. 1960), 426–35.

MARLOWE, D. "Psychological Needs and Performance in a Two-Person Non-Zero-Sum Game." Paper read at Eastern Psychological Association, Atlantic City, April 1962.

MARTIN, NILES W., JR. "Some Effects of Communication of Group Behavior in Prisoner's Dilemma." Unpublished Ph.D. thesis, Case Institute of Technology, 1964.

MCCLINTOCK, C. G., A. A. HARRISON, S. STRAND, and P. GALLO. "Internationalism, Isolationism, Strategy of the Other Player and Two Person Game Behavior," *Journal of*

Abnormal and Social Psychology, 67 (1963), 631–36.

MINAS, J. S., A. SCODEL, D. MARLOWE, and H. RAWSON. "Some Descriptive Aspects of Two-Person, Non-Zero-Sum Games," *Journal of Conflict Resolution,* 4, 2 (June 1960), 193–97.

O'CONNOR, PATRICIA. "Intolerance for Ambiguity and Abstract Reasoning Ability," *Journal of Abnormal and Social Psychology,* 47 (1952), Supplement.

OSGOOD, CHARLES E. "Suggestions for Winning the Real War with Communism," *Journal of Conflict Resolution,* 3, 4 (Dec. 1959), 295–325.

PILISUK, M., and A. RAPOPORT. "A Non-Zero-Sum Game Model of Some Disarmament Problems." Paper given at Peace Research Conference, University of Chicago, November 1963.

———, ——— "Stepwise Disarmament and Sudden Destruction in a Two-Person Game," *Journal of Conflict Resolution,* 8, 1 (Mar. 1964), 36–49.

QUANT, RICHARD E. "On the Use of Game Models in Theories of International Relations." In K. KNORR and S. VERBA (eds.), *The International System.* Princeton, N.J.: Princeton University Press, 1961, 9–76.

RAPOPORT, A. *Fights, Games, and Debates.* Ann Arbor, Mich.: University of Michigan Press, 1960.

———. "The Use and Misuse of Game Theory," *Scientific American,* 6 (1962), 108–18.

———. "Tacit Communication in Experiments in Conflict and Cooperation," *International Psychiatry Clinics,* 1 (1964a), 225–44.

———. *Strategy and Conscience.* New York: Harper, 1964b.

———. *Prisoner's Dilemma.* Ann Arbor, Mich.: University of Michigan Press, 1965.

——— and C. ORWANT. "Experimental Games: A Review," *Behavioral Science,* 7, (1962), 1–37.

ROGERS, C., and ROSALIND DYMOND. *Psychotherapy and Personality Change.* Chicago: University of Chicago Press, 1954.

SAATY, T. L. "A Model for the Control of Arms," *Operations Research,* 12, 4 (July–Aug. 1964).

SAMPSON, P. L., and H. P. SMITH. "A Scale to Measure World-Mindedness Attitudes,"

Journal of Social Psychology, 45 (1957), 99–106.

SCHELLING, THOMAS C. "Experimental Games and Bargaining Theory." In K. KNORR and S. VERBA (eds.), *The International System*. Princeton, N.J.: Princeton University Press, 1961, 47–68.

———. *The Strategy of Conflict*. Cambridge, Mass.: Harvard University Press, 1960.

SCODEL, A. "Induced Collaboration in Some Non-Zero-Sum Games," *Journal of Conflict Resolution*, 6, 4 (Dec. 1962), 335–40.

———, J. S. MINAS, P. RATOOSH, and M. LIPETZ. "Some Descriptive Aspects of Two-Person, Non-Zero-Sum Games," *Journal of Conflict Resolution*, 3, 2 (June 1959), 114–19.

SOLOMON, L. "The Influence of Some Types of Power Relationships and Game Strategies on the Development of Interpersonal Trust," *Journal of Abnormal and Social Psychology*, 61 (1960), 223–30.

THIBAUT, J. W., and H. H. KELLEY. *The Social Psychology of Groups*. New York: Wiley, 1959.

WEBSTER, H., N. SANFORD, and M. FREEDMAN. "A New Instrument for Studying Authoritarianism," *Journal of Psychology*, 40 (1955), 73–84.

Appendix: Writing the Experimental Report

After each experiment is finished the experimenter will be required to turn in a report of the findings. The report should follow the standard format for experimental articles, which consists of the following sections:

1. Problem

This section introduces the reader to the problem being explored. It should contain sufficient background information obtained from the experimental and theoretical literature to indicate what the problem is, what specific questions the experiment is supposed to answer, and why the questions are important.

2. Method

The method section provides the reader with complete information as to how the experiment was done, the equipment used, and a description of the subject population.

The information should be detailed enough to permit the reader to replicate the experiment in every detail. The section is usually divided into several subsections as follows:

Subjects: The experimenter must present sufficient detail to strictly specify the nature of the population used and the means by which the experimental sample was selected. Thus the age, sex, educational background, experimental naiveté, and selection criteria must be presented. For example, if an experiment was concerned with the effects of anxiety upon reaction time, the subjects subsection might be: "One-hundred experimentally naive male freshman college students enrolled in the introductory psychology course at Hardknocks College completed the Jones and Smith anxiety scale. The 10 highest scorers (mean score 92) and 10 lowest scorers (mean score 21) were assigned to the high anxiety and low anxiety experimental groups, respectively."

Experimental Situation: This subsection may be labeled and used as the experimenter sees fit. It may be used to describe the experimental situation such as testing condition and time and place of a

APPENDIX

field survey. It may also be used to describe specialized apparatus used in the experiment. In complex experiments where many different experimental conditions or manipulations are involved, this section might be used to present a brief overall view of the entire experimental situation to which the writer may refer when procedural differences are discussed in other parts of the report.

Procedure: The procedure section includes all information relative to the experimental treatment and manipulation of subjects as well as the method of recording the data. A good practice to follow is that of constructing a flow chart for each experimental condition, which would include everything that happens to the subjects from the time they are first solicited for the experiment until after the experiment is complete. This flow chart is not part of the experimental report, but the reader should be made aware of everything on the chart which may have affected the subjects' behavior. Experimental errors are, of course, very important and are reported in this section.

3. Results

In the results section the experimenter must present his data in quantitative form with the precision and clarity necessary to provide the reader with the foundation for the theoretical arguments to follow. The experimenter has stated a problem and questions about the problem in the introduction and is, in the results section, presenting the evidence to support his answers to those questions. It is on this evidence that the experimenter's arguments stand.

A good procedure to follow in writing the results is to first decide how to pictorially or tabularly present the data. Once this is decided, the experimenter simply presents these graphs or tables and calls the reader's attention to the critical or unusual aspects of the data. The writer should always remember, however, that the purpose of this section is to present data to answer the experimental questions or to point out findings of interest (i.e., findings that were unexpected or unusual).

Although statistical tests are not required for the experiments in this book, the statistically knowledgeable student may wish to test the significance of the differences between the various groups which are being reported in the results section.

4. Discussion

The discussion section provides the reader with the theoretical importance of the experiment, the relationship of the experimenter's results to other results reported in the literature, and the implications of the findings for future research. The experimenter should also present the limitations of his findings and any alternative explanations for the results, in the discussion section. The writer must be certain that his data firmly support the conclusions and inferences offered in this section.

5. Abstract

The abstract is placed first in the report but is written last. A good abstract is very difficult to write. It should give the essential details of the experiment, including the problem, the subjects, the procedure, the important results, and the major conclusions. All of this should be in 120 words or less.

6. References

Every reference cited in the text is included in the bibliography. Related books or publications read but not cited do not belong in this section.

7. Footnotes

Avoid footnotes. Anything important may usually be presented in the text of the report. When a footnote is absolutely necessary (e.g., a personal communication from another investigator, an experimental irregularity which should be on record, or an unconventional statistical technique) it should be referred to by a number in the text and listed by number on a separate page.

8. General Rules for Good Report Writing

The object of the report is to communicate the relevant theoretical, procedural, and empirical information about the experiment to a sophisticated reader as efficiently and clearly as possible. Its purpose should be information transmission not amusement, but the presentation should be well written so that the reader's interest is maintained.

Ideas, data, techniques, etc., obtained from other publications or personal communications should be acknowledged by references in the text to the publication as listed in the reference section or, in the case of a personal communication, to a footnote.

The experimental reports are usually written in the third person, past tense.

The student should refer to the articles included in this book for examples of style and format.

Author Index

A

Adorno, T. W., 39, 43
Argyle, M., 226, 229
Arkoff, A., 163–167, 169–171, 173, 174, 176–180, 185, 186
Aronson, E., 78, 79, 92
Arrowood, A. J., 163–176, 178–180, 182, 183, 185, 186
Asch, S. E., 37, 40, 43, 115, 118
Atkinson, J. W., 246

B

Bales, R. F., 186, 204, 208
Barron, F., 39, 40, 43
Barton, A. H., 93
Berger, A., 126
Berger, E. M., 233, 246
Berkowitz, M. I., 206, 208
Berry, P. C., 140, 147
Bixenstine, V. E., 246
Blake, R. R., 44–49, 226, 230
Block, C. H., 140, 147
Block, J., 40, 43
Bond, J. R., 178, 186
Borgatta, E. F., 186
Brehm, J. W., 78, 92, 94–104
Bronfenbrenner, U., 76, 92
Brown, J., 117, 118
Brown, J. F., 204, 208
Brunswik, E., 111, 114, 118, 174, 176
Bush, R. B., 93
Buss, A. H., 7, 23

C

Campbell, J., 140–147
Caplow, T., 163, 165, 175–178, 185, 186
Carlsmith, J. M., 94, 95, 104
Carota, N., 119–126
Carpenter, P. B., 246
Carter, L. F., 204, 208
Cartwright, D., 92
Chambers, N., 246
Chapanis, A., 89, 90, 92
Chapanis, N. P., 89, 90, 92

Child, I., 89, 92
Chowdhry, K., 204, 208
Cohen, A. R., 78, 79, 90, 92, 94–104
Crowell, D. C., 177–186
Crowne, D. P., 120, 125, 126
Crutchfield, R. S., 36–43, 225, 229

D

Damaser, E. C., 116, 118
Davis, K. E., 223, 229
Davis, R. H., 246
Deutsch, M., 223, 229–231, 237, 247
Dien, D., 177–186
Doob, A. N., 223–230
Dunnette, M. D., 140–147
Dymond, R., 233, 247

E

Edwards, A. L., 85, 92
Edwards, W., 247
Estes, W., 93

F

Festinger, L., 65, 77, 78, 89, 92–95, 104
Field, P. B., 226, 230
Fleming, W. H., 94, 104
Flood, M. M., 247
Fode, K. L., 119, 120, 126
Frank, J. D., 113, 118
Freedman, M., 248
Frenkel-Brunswik, E., 43
Friedman, C. J., 120, 126

G

Gallo, P., 247
Gergen, K. J., 223–230
Gough, H. G., 39, 43
Greenbaum, C. W., 91, 93
Greenfield, P. M., 119–126
Guetzkow, H., 247

H

Hain, J. D., 44–49
Hare, E. P., 186

Subject Index

A

Achievement motivation, 85
Ambiguity tolerance, 40, 232, 233
Anxiety, 40
Arms race, 232, 235, 238, 239
Attitude change, 65–104
Authority, 5–23, 31, 43, 50–63, 113, 141, 187, 204, 228

B

Bias, 66, 67, 70, 105–126, 199, *see also* Demand characteristics, Experimenter expectancy
Brainstorming, 127–147

C

California Psychological Inventory, 39
Chicken, 215–222, 237
Coalition formation, 149–186
    theories of, 150, 151, 164
Cognitive dissonance, 65, 104
Communication, 175, 223, 244, 245, *see also* Conversation
Competence, 204–208, *see also* Expert
Competition, *see* Interpersonal Bargaining
Concept Mastery Test, 39
Conditioned social behavior, 187–208
Conflict, 16, 17, 37
    resolution of, in interpersonal bargaining 231–248
Conformity, 29–63, 187, 204–208, 226, *see also* Obedience, Social forces
Content analysis, 71
Conventionality, 29, 40, *see also* Conformity
Conversation, 196–203, *see also* Communication
Cooperation, *see* Interpersonal Bargaining
Correlational studies, 79
Cover story, 24, *see also* Ethical treatment of subjects, Deception, False feedback
Cues, 11, 113, 114

D

Deception, 27, 37, 41, 113, 114, *see also* Ethical treatment of subjects, Cover story, False feedback
Delayed auditory feedback, 80–92
Demand characteristics, 111–118, *see also* Bias, Experimenter expectancy
Dependent variable, 2, 3, 24

E

Ecological validity, 111, 119, 174, *see also* Experimental setting, Field experimentation, Laboratory experimentation
Effort, 76–93
Emotional response, 16
Ethical treatment of subjects, 5, 6, 27, 33, 34, 42, *see also* Deception, Cover story, False feedback
Expected frequency, 197
Experimental confederate, 7, 24–26, 37, 197, 205, 244
Experimental design and control, 3, 26, 66, 82, 96, 105, 106, 111, 112, 114, 116, 117, 121, 141, 188, *see also* Transparent experiment
Experimental setting, 17–19, 26, 27, 111, 114, 238, 239, *see also* Ecological validity, Field experimentation, Laboratory experimentation
Experimental social psychology, 1–27
Experimenter expectancy, 119–126, *see also* Bias, Demand characteristics
Expert, 60, 61, 187–195, *see also* Competence
Extraneous variable, 4

F

F Scale, 39, 223, 233
False feedback, 9, 25, 37, 38, 41, 244, *see also* Cover story, Deception, Ethical treatment of subjects